Seize the Day

Published by Brolga Publishing Pty Ltd
ABN 46 063 962 443
PO Box 12544
A'Beckett St
Melbourne, VIC, 8006
Australia

email: markzocchi@brolgapublishing.com.au

All rights reserved. No part of this publication may be reproduced, stored in a retrieval system or transmitted in any form or by any means electronic, mechanical, photocopying, recording or otherwise without prior permission from the publisher.

Copyright © 2015 A.M. (Jack) Harris.
National Library of Australia Cataloguing-in-Publication entry
    Harris, A. M. (Alfred Martin) author.
    Seize the day 9781922175717 (paperback)
    Subjects: Men-Australia-Biography.
    Soldiers-Australia-Biography.
    Spies-Australia-Biography.
    Intelligence service-Australia.
    Dewey Number: 920.710994

Printed in Australia
Cover design & typesetting by Wanissa Somsuphangsri

BE PUBLISHED

Publish through a successful publisher. National distribution, Macmillan & International distribution to the United Kingdom, North America. Sales Representation to South East Asia
Email: markzocchi@brolgapublishing.com.au

Seize the Day

A. M. (Jack) Harris.

In memory of my sister Bonnie,
and my former platoon commander David Butler,
who both asked me to re-write this story.

Novels by the same author.
The Tall Man.
Grains of Sand.
The Buronga Boys.
Adam and Lily.
Adam Kelly's Cup.

Autobiography.
Only One River To Cross.

Forward

This is the story of a very special Australian. Jack Harris' life has been one of remarkable achievement, largely unknown until now. He has come a long way from Buronga as an athlete, professional boxer, merchant seaman, linguist, warrior, spy, successful author, businessman, scholar and entrepreneur. A long list, yet each endeavour represents an achievement from which he learned and used in the next stage of his life. You will be struck immediately by the vitality of the man, his determination to be involved in all that is going on and by his desire to extend himself. Yet it is uncanny in the way he is always drawn to the action. Where does the line between instinct and reasoning begin?

Indeed, you may read some of his exploits with scepticism, even disbelief. For example, you really have to wonder why, after being so badly wounded in Korea in 1950, he would want to return? Once there, with a crippled left hand, how did he ever get involved in line crossing? In hastening to verify the truth of his story, I have to say that Jack, in his understated way, makes some incredible episodes in his life seem commonplace. So much of the real danger he faced was when he was totally isolated from his own soldiers. There was no one to observe and later report, no one whom he could have drawn on for vicarious support. There are few people surviving who have attempted what he achieved and can talk of similar experiences.

While he would call himself a soldier and, with reticence, admit he had travelled in company with warriors there is no way he would ever acknowledge that as a line crosser he had taken his soldiering to a level known to very few. Quick, highly intelligent and absolutely pragmatic, his decision making was invariably instantaneous. Above all, he has always been a very positive person. Doubt and fear have never been part of his vocabulary. That is not to say he was in any way foolhardy he was far too bright for that, rather we should say those two critical, and at times most difficult factors would have been speedily appraised. In any case, he would hold them as words never to be spoken for they are infectious in themselves and are indicative of personal frailty. So it is that much in the narrative is somewhat matter-of-fact and the reader has to remind himself or herself from time to time of where all this is going on.

For sheer excitement, if that is the word, one has only to look at his period behind the enemy lines with his Korean companions to marvel at his audacity. When you reflect on the risks and the dire consequences of a lone Caucasian, dressed in Chinese uniform, carrying Chinese weapons and papers, in a totally Asian and hostile world, the hairs on the back of your neck begin to rise. To have made such a trip ten times, to a depth of fourteen miles through and beyond the enemy lines, and to remain each time for many days, trusting only the people you are with, leaves one totally in awe. The tensions must have been very heavy. At any time, an accidental encounter with say, a lost enemy soldier could have blown everything.

It was a remarkable feat of arms and courage of the very highest order. The whole of Jack's life follows this inspirational path and reminds us all of the need for determination in our lives and of the premier Australian quality, absolute refusal to be deterred by an setback.

Major General D. M. Butler. AO. DSO.
Portsea. April 2012.

Preamble

To some readers I hope that it does not appear that I have an enduring preoccupation with myself because in the words to follow I am only trying to review my life in full. To begin, I sailed to Australia's war in Korea from Japan in mid-1950 and, thinking now about that service, I find that many recollections, some buried deep in my memory bank, have flooded back with the utmost clarity, the more so after chatting with old comrades. Afterwards, though, I am sometimes haunted with remorse about what I should have done, but really could not. War is unreasonable, even though in my time getting over the wire in the approved British tradition was applauded, comradeship was honoured, we thought we knew why were fighting in Korea, and that our military success was laudable.

By the time of the Apple Orchard Battle of 22 October 1950, I had come to understand that in battle the infantry soldier has very little knowledge or understanding about what is happening beyond the ten men in his section. Those men are of prime concern and so it was that the men I walked with at the opening of the Orchard Battle had no fear of being shot or wounded, but there was apprehension about what was ahead of us, who might be waiting at the top of the hill, and in the unknown. My first ordered objective was the clearing of mines or men from a culvert to our front so as to allow the Sherman tanks to proceed with safety. Getting there, in a heart-breaking moment the young soldier with me nervously fired his rifle, almost shot me in the head, and badly wounded another soldier who had stepped down to examine the culvert on the far side. It was a mess to begin with, but at the end of the battle some three hours later we had come through, and had grown in stature. We had been to the crest, we had looked down, our enemy were in mass flight and the young soldiers, including myself, were now seasoned warriors.

On 30 October 1950 I was wounded at Chongju, a town not far from the Yalu River and the Chinese border. My commanding officer was killed the same day. I was returned to Australia for medical treatment, then attended a one-year course in Chinese; some time later I was back in Korea in charge of what was called a Special Agent detachment. On 2 July 1953 I swam across the flooded Samichon River with three South Korean agents. On the far bank of the river I divided my party into two groups. Then with an agent named Pak I proceeded along the river but we were ambushed and Pak was killed. I can still see six red dots, the bullets from a machine gun, hitting Pak and killing him instantly and I am often concerned that I never managed to get hold of Pak's body, get him into the Samichon, and have him carried down to our own lines. It would have been impossible of course, but one can dream things incompatible with fact.

I should here note that the routes we explored when moving through North Korea, and places like Kunwari and Namsong-Dong are fictitious. As I have cautioned in an earlier work, the so-called 'dark forces' are still in control in that part of Korea today, so many years after the conclusion of the war there and any person, or relatives of that person, who may have assisted the allies during that war would still be subject to retribution.

Additional to this, many of the names I mentioned when writing about Buronga have been altered from the original to avoid and hurt, or discomfort. Buronga I have also discovered, is a lovely place with a happy community, not a sandy patch of hill covered with bag shanties all served with the one corrugated track of my childhood memories.

I conclude here by stating that I spent eight of the best years of my life in the army. What followed after my discharge was fashioned by that experience, and the friendships I knew as a soldier. For all that I am eternally grateful.

> A. M. (Jack) Harris.

The author at age 20, when he joined the army at Mildura in May 1946

Chapter One

The Korea I returned to at the end of winter in 1953, appeared different to the place I had left, after being wounded in action at the beginning of another winter, in 1950. Then the land had been noisy with the pandemonium of our victorious army racing northwards in pursuit of a shattered North Korean Army following the success of General Macarthur's Inchon landing which had cut Korea in half just above Seoul, the capital of the south. Now, the snow which had been so bitter and heavy in 1950 was melting away from the rugged Korean hills. The rivers were ice-green torrents and the trees were shooting out new buds to search for the sun. In the valleys and on the mountain slopes azalea flowers could be seen and many birds were singing. The land was alive with beauty, a place of peace and harmony.

After three years of bitter war a strange peace had settled over the wide valley holding the Samichon River for the armies facing each other across the Thirty-Eighth Parallel had reached a stalemate. The time of massive offences, of the movement of vast numbers of men and fleets of heavy tanks, had passed. Great armies no longer hurled each other back and forth across the narrow strip of land that was Korea. Instead they had settled down to a war of ambush, of wait-and-see, and the land, torn by conflict and stained by the blood of men of a score of nations, and the soldiers of North and South Korea, brooded with a curious acquiescence on the outcome.

Korea is a land of many rivers. Some are big and brawling, some quiet backwaters, many heavy with the yellow clay of the hills, others swift and green, a few so shallow, clear and cold above gravelly sand-bars that a man might walk across them without wetting his knees. Among them is the Samichon with its source high in the mountains of the north. In places it flows placidly, the water inching along over a sand-and rock encrusted bottom but when the convolutions of the land dip and sway erratically, the quiet stream becomes a white-crested torrent ripping and scouring its ancient bed. It winds a searching course between broken drifts of forest with bold sweeps and curves to where, somewhere close to the 38th Parallel, it slows and widens. In deep pools and shelving banks it runs through a flat plain under the shadow of the mountains; here from time unrecorded fertile paddy fields have lain a patchwork over the undulating ground on either side and supported the hard-working populations of small, scattered villages snug in their groves of old, green trees.

In the spring of 1953 after a winding stream of circumstance, I was attached to the headquarters of the Commonwealth Division to command the divisional agent detachment whose task was to infiltrate behind the enemy lines and gather intelligence. The officer in charge of the detachment was a Major Hurgaard, a sensible man who had briefed me well, so that I now knew the bowl of land and the hills about it, which looked barren and uninhabitable, was not. It was peopled, and if not by toiling farmers as it had been for centuries, then by hard men who spent their days in holes and tunnels and their nights in dangerous patrolling, for at this time whoever dominated the valley dictated also the pattern and conduct of a war which had blasted it through three bitter and unrewarding years of conflict. From what I could discern, the uncultivated paddy fields still retained their ancient symmetry but I knew they were crossed and recrossed by clinging strands of barbed wire, deadly webs spun over the holes and approaches of the men who lived in them. The valley floor was also set with land mines and an uneasy hush hung over it all, yet in the night, and sometimes during the day, it pulsed and stirred with the sounds of gunfire and the rumble of tanks. But usually the war fought in this place was the silent battle of night contact, of horror and sudden confusion, of cowardice and bravery, and seldom was there anything but the night to watch and pass judgment.

In the dusk four of us were huddled close, just outside the communication trench of a forward company. A tank on the reverse slope of a hill behind us, with only the muzzle of its gun visible, intermittently fired its cannon directly across the valley. The big gun smashed heavily, its tracer floating lazily along the trajectory of the shell; a red ball which blazed fiercely lessened gradually to a spark and was suddenly snuffed out. The tank, which was firing on fixed lines, also banged regular bursts of its heavy machine-gun, every few shots being interspersed with tracer. These too arched across the valley and died in the distance. Another tank, in support from a knoll on the right flank, took up the fire task when the first grew silent. Several mortars were firing, the spluttering whistle of their shells murmuring through the air. After dark the cacophony of war never really ceased.

With every whistle and smash of the shells each of us on the exposed ground near the trench instinctively hunched our bodies into a tight ball, then relaxed cautiously to watch the fight of the missiles. A slight mist was just then creeping sluggishly across the valley; the soldiers' last light was at hand. At a word from me, the tallest in that group, the others stood erect and followed me down a designated and mine-cleared small track and through a disordered pattern of barbed wire entanglements. In a small pit at the base of the hill we had just descended, we squatted down. One man in our group began to whisper to another, but he ceased at a caution from me as I pointed back up the hill as I could hear the sound of approaching men.

We waited and in the dim light we could see an armed party of soldiers moving towards our position. I stood up and softly called a password. The lead man of the approaching file stopped momentarily, answered, then advanced again. An English soldier serving with the Durham Light Infantry, he came up close to me and peered into my face.

"Huh. It's you, Sergeant," he said. "They told me you might still be down here. Rather you than me, I reckon!"

"Yeah." I responded as I squinted back into the gloom. "But I'm not going out this time. But we will be heading down to the river in a few moments. What are you blokes ambush or standing patrol?"

"Standing patrol. We're just going beyond the mine-gap."

"Good. Two of us will be returning later. We expect to be here at first light but if things go wrong we may have to beat it back. You be careful, will you?"

"Sure. We've been well briefed. We know pretty well what you're doing."

"Good." Quietly cursing my nervousness, for I knew the soldier was correct, I turned to my three companions. "Let's go."

The four of us went forward and out through the mine gap, going into the deepening mist. Once beyond the gap we took up single file, about three feet apart. Keeping to the edges of the fields we made rapid progress directly across the valley. The shells and machine gun bullets continued to plough the night over our heads as our footsteps rustled and whispered among the brittle grass along the way. After about twenty minutes I halted and the others dispersed until one, a thick-set man moved forward from the rear, his face glistening wetly in the pale gloom.

"We'll wait here for a while, Lim," I told him.

Lim nodded his shaggy head before turning back for a

whispered consultation with the other members of the patrol. We were motionless, except for the slightest movement of our hands as we brushed away the hordes of mosquitoes buzzing and circling about our heads. But for the sounds of shells thudding into the presumed enemy positions, and the incessant whirr of insects, quiet possessed the still, hot air. The deepening night slowly covered all of us waiting in its soft embrace and when I stood erect and gazed back in the direction of our friendly lines I felt partly ashamed as I allowed my thoughts to dwell on the security I knew lay there, in the comparative safety of my small headquarters, and in contrast with my present situation. It was something that some small part of my mind did of its own volition, when the main forces of my thoughts were engaged on a problem such as the one now facing me; it was something, some nagging shred of an old memory which made me prefer the warmth of the cave to the monster-peopled dark, and was now trying to enforce its preference on me. But of a sudden I focused all my thoughts on the present. I swung my head sharply about and stared hard at a large hill which loomed to my immediate front. I then gestured with my hands and the others got to their feet. We gathered together momentarily, not speaking, but each feeling the comfort of the others' nearness, then once more we pressed forward.

Our advance was much more cautious now; we stopped frequently to listen intently to the noises of the darkness. Once, as large rushes loomed in the night, we went on hands and knees and pressed slowly through the dry, crackling undergrowth. Swarms of insects arose from our path, and once, with shocking suddenness, a pheasant flew up from a position directly under my hand, its wings whirring madly. The four of us halted and crouched down. I reckoned I could hear the heartbeats of all of us thumping like small drums.

"You bastard!" I whispered, while wiping an uncertain hand across my damp face.

I uncoiled myself, the cloth of my trousers whispering against my flanks, and the others stood with me. Our advance was continued and soon we came to an open sand patch that glistened whitely in the night. Here I expelled my breath in a gusty exclamation. The white sand indicated the first boundary of our patrol: the bank of the Samichon River. We moved forward over pebble-strewn sand until a large tree brandishing leafless limbs stood before us. Once under its gaunt limbs our patrol gathered closely together, seeking human companionship and nearness in the hope that it might afford protection and safety when we were so surrounded by danger.

"Pak!" I spoke softly, almost a whisper, and a small figure detached itself from near the tree. "You all right, son?"

"Yes, sir."

"You must get through, you understand?" I knew the others were listening. "Our friend should have some good news for us this time."

"Yes sir. I do understand."

I reached out, pressed Pak's shoulder, and then called softly, "Chet." Another figure, more thickset than the first, came up to me. "Chet, you do what Pak tells you and there will be no trouble." Chet had pressed close to me for I understood that my voice could hardly be heard above the monotonous drone of the many insects. "Come. We'll cross over now."

Chet grinned at me, his teeth a white flash in the blacking on his face. I looked closely at him for a moment, then I too smiled and soundlessly began to unravel a piece of nylon rope from about my waist. I worked swiftly, adjusting the rope then handing one end to Lim before stepping down the bank and into the river. I shivered as I stepped into the cold water and a sudden panic skittered through me as my feet slipped from under me. It dispersed in a moment, melting from my nerves as my common sense, bred from a number of previous missions and their remembered shocks and problems, took its place. I went forward but the tug of the current swept my footing away and I had to breast-stroke clumsily forward, my body being carried downstream by the force of the water I was battling against. Then, without warning, my hands met a big, rough boulder and I knew I had reached the river's centre point. I lay there, tensed and waiting as the water swamped about me while the rope, much of its length buffeted by the water, tugged at my waist. Everything appeared to be still on the bank ahead of me which I had to move to. I could not see much and I could hear nothing but the sound of the water about me. Beyond the boulder which I was clinging to the water moved slowly, a silent strip of darkness with none of the noisy verve of the stream which I had just battled to cross. But in a way it was more menacing in its quietness, as the quiet man can be more deadly, or a hidden snake, or the sensed presence of an intruder. Also, its farther side lipped the enemy's shore, knew the touch of his feet, was fouled by his excrement. It was defiled territory and as I slid forward I felt my lips draw back in a grimace of distaste.

The bottom beyond the boulder was sandy, the water shallow, and I went easily across it, the white ruffles foaming around my tensed knees. I stopped for a few moments, stripped a waterproof cover from my Chinese Burp gun and eased the safety-catch forward. I moved, the drag of the water lessening as it edged down around my calves, then my ankles until suddenly it was gone. When I stepped onto the bank the gravel beneath my feet crunched softly but to my anxious ears the sound filled the night with dissonance. I cursed softly in an agony of apprehension and annoyance. But nothing moved and I was where I was supposed to be, in enemy territory. The valley I had crossed to get to the Samichon River was no-man's land, and while there was always the danger of meeting an enemy patrol, one never knew when or where. Here, it was different. On this strip of land men sat cunningly concealed, never betrayed by movement, or noise and they closely watched their front to see that none passed by. If any attempted they could die.

I stood there on that shelving bank, my body tensed, watching and listening for any danger; but no challenges came to me, no sound other than that of the flowing river. I was facing the opposite bank, waiting, my mind racing in many directions, frantically seeking some reason why I might refuse the last small act which would commit Pak and Chet to the mission before them. But even as my mind hunted about, my hands mechanically gave a sudden jerk to the rope to let my companions know that, for the time being at least, all was well. Now they too could use the rope attached to the tree and, steadied by Lim, cross the river.

When Pak and Chet were beside me on the bank, panting with the exertion of their crossing, only their dark-painted faces partly visible in the night, I watched as they sat and squeezed water out of their socks and replaced them, tied up their shoes, checked their weapons and stood before me. I shook hands with both of them and they went off, all without uttering a word. Lim had done his work with the rope, feeling the weight, gauging the passage of each of us as we crossed. Now he waited until he felt vibration on the rope again as I crossed back to him, and stood, dripping wet before him. Then he coiled the rope in and we turned silently on our way back along the outgoing route. After a while we stopped and squatted down close together.

"All right, sir?"

"Yep. They are good lads, Lim. They'll make it back."

We both fell silent. The undertone of night with its threat of danger and its promise of concealment encompassed both of us. I felt good. Things were off to a promising start.

Chapter Two

At first light we moved carefully in past the standing patrol of the forward company as the poor visibility of the valley was improving. I called a greeting to a number of shivering British soldiers and they spread their arms wide, welcoming us in return. After all, they had spent long hours peering into the darkness which often seemed hostile to them as they listened for any sound that might indicate the approach of their enemy, anxious to take a prisoner, or perhaps to explore the defences of the outer perimeter in preparation for an attack. All night through they had gripped their weapons and waited, hoping that any enemy would not choose to come at them, firing in the dark. They had waited, thinking of home, of love, of the need for a smoke, and perhaps, sometimes, of death. They would always be ready for the first warning when they would shoot and, in a weaving, terrified run, get back through the minefield to warn their comrades and, primarily, preserve their own lives.

But the enemy had not violated their night, and now in the welcome light of dawn they stood and sat, sucking hungrily on their cigarettes, chaffing one another as Lim and I walked up to them. They laughed at themselves and at the two mud-spattered men, me and Lim, in a strange happiness that another fresh day was dawning. In the satisfaction which refused to acknowledge a fear of another night, they would not now consider the crawling dread of the next outpost position, which would begin again in a few short hours.

The corporal in charge spoke to us in a laconic fashion, as some men do when they joke about serious matters.

"Had a good time, Sergeant? Looks like it!"

I did not immediately answer but grinned in companionship.

"Wonderful. The water was great. Those buggers worry you at all last night?"

"Nuh. Haven't been in touch with him for about three weeks now. Bloody good thing too! Came right up to this spot!" He pointed a little way into the valley. "Killed two of our blokes; snatched another, they did! Cunning bastards!"

"True."

"But I'm thinking he'll be coming again soon." The comment came from one of the soldiers sitting on the ground near the corporal. He spoke in a thick Scottish burr and winked broadly at me as he spoke.

"You know exactly when that will be, Scotty?" I asked.

"When he hears that me, James McFee, is going on leave to Tokyo, and will not be mounting patrol for three weeks," The Scot spoke complacently, ignoring the storm of derision his words had unleashed.

"Huh! Would you get that?" The corporal spread his hands upwards in mock resignation. "No self-respecting Chink would ever try to take you prisoner, McFee, you Scotch rooster. You would not be worth the trouble: besides, they got no Scotch-Chinese interpreters."

"You may have a point there," I commented with a grin. I did it in the hope of prolonging this moment of warmth and comradeship and humour, to let the bawdy familiarity of soldier-talk smooth away the remembered anxieties of the night just passed. "Who interprets for you in Tokyo, Scotty?"

"Say no more!" the Scot remarked, his burr thicker than ever. "Y're all jealous that I'm goin' to Tokyo with ten pounds sterling in me pocket!"

"Ten pounds!" one of the soldiers ejaculated. "Christ, that

wouldn't even get you an old bag outside the gates at Ebisu!"

"I'm not intending to pay for anything but me beer," the Scot remarked witheringly. "You must understand that creatures of fleshly delights fall easily to the charms of McFee!"

"For Christsakes!" the corporal swore. "Jock, you'd be the biggest bullduster ever!"

"Not me," McFee responded darkly. "And I can assure you it will not be dust that I'll be wasting on some of the superior Geisha gurrls I know in Tokyo!"

I joined in the laughter which followed McFee's reply, and as I looked about at the laughing men surrounding me, I wondered for a moment at the duplication of this same sort of scene in many defensive positions set all along the parallel in this bright dawn; of all the other soldiers, secretly fearing, as these men did, what another night might bring, but finding relief from their concern in merriment. Almost as my mind conceived the image of our allied armies dug in all along the 38th Parallel the Australians and the Canadians and Turks, the Americans and all the others nations involved it was replaced by the thought of the Chinese and the North Koreans facing them across the small waist of Korea. A lot of men were bogged down in this war and all, I knew, had only one wish and that was to see tomorrow. I knew that the Chinese and North Koreans would be standing-to now, in their defensive positions and I could not but wonder if they too were laughing and joking about the same things as their enemies: about women and home and love, about killing and getting killed, even though in the bright sunshine of the new day, that seemed improbable. But I was recalled to the present moment by the voice of the corporal.

"What was that?" I asked him.

"I said," the corporal repeated. "Our commanding officer has organised a cup of coffee for you at the O-pip, if you felt like it. Knowing our CO I think you'd better feel like it. Okay?"

"Good! That sounds wonderful." Turning to Lim who had been following the quick, slangy conversation with a half-comprehending grin, I added to it by saying, "Come on, Lim, let's blow."

As we walked away I called over my shoulder to McFee. "Have a good time in Tokyo, Scotty! Don't do anything I wouldn't do!"

"I might be doin' a few things you couldn't do, Sergeant!" Mcfee promised bleakly and he was swamped again by the ready derision of his companions.

Lim and I stepped warily through the marked gap of the minefield, then around a slippery curved path which led to a sand-bagged forward observation post. One of the sock-hatted soldiers watching us from there ducked his head down into the post and yelled for his platoon commander. A young-looking lieutenant pushed his head out of the door of the bunker and stared at us.

"I have orders from above to prepare a hot coffee for you. With something strong in it. I presume you are interested?"

"Presumption correct. Got enough for two of us, twice?"

"Sure. Come'n get it."

Lim and I went quickly down a communication trench, ducked our heads and entered a big, rough-hewn bunker. The smell of earth and dampness pervaded the place but I knew that this bunker, like the hundreds scattered over the hills, was home for a soldier. A poor place and a transitory one where comforts were few and which a shell could turn into a shambles.

The young officer groped about into an empty old shell case and brought out three battered enamel mugs marked and chipped by the rough use of many hands. He slipped his fingers through the handles and with a dextrous movement placed them bottom down on four large shell cases which was the dugout table. He looked up at me and smiled. "The rum's over there," he pointed. "Help yourself."

I reached behind me and into a suppurating cleft cut in the wall. The rum bottle I found was muddy but I handled it with due deference, placing it carefully on the improvised table, and soon the comforting aroma of hot coffee and rum blossomed on the damp air of the dugout. Lim stood back from the table, sipping at his drink with a gusty appreciation while the lieutenant and I discussed our patrol.

"It must have gone well," he remarked. "But you sure are a mess! Can I get you some dry gear?"

"No. I'm roger. I was a bit damp before but I've dried out well. Except for my feet which are still damp but I'll soon be home. I know I look somewhat dishevelled, as they say, but I'll get my gear cleaned up."

"Yes. I suppose so. I was told you wear a Chinese uniform but I found it hard to believe, until now when I see what you're wearing. But if you were ever captured, wouldn't you be executed?"

"No doubt. But I travel in enemy country and I have no option but to try and hoodwink the people back there, where I move about."

"A silly question I suppose, but are you ever scared? I know I'd be petrified. I'm National Service, you see." He sounded apologetic about it.

"I went for the heavy-duty rosary beads out there tonight myself," I remarked. "All over a bloody pheasant!"

"A pheasant? How come?"

"We were crawling across a paddy field and the blasted thing shot up like a singed bat out of hell right under my hand. You know how the wings whirr? I thought it was a landmine or some such. I reckoned I was going to give birth!"

I laughed at my own story but inwardly marvelled that I could feel so happy, so buoyant as I always did, after a successful start to one of our missions. I would feel good for several days to follow and then the old gnawing fear would start again. What time, next time, what bloody time, would it not be simply a bird but a real bomb, or an enemy patrol which would give me a gut full of lead for my stupidity? Bugger it all! My thoughts were dispersed as the young officer coughed, and looked at me inquiringly after having said something.

I had missed a question once more. "Sorry. What was that?"

"I said that I've heard you have been out for several days yourself. Just you and these Korean chaps you control?" He nodded towards Lim. "It must be lonely work nerve-wracking as well."

"I have excellent men." I nodded directly at Lim, and continued. "But we are small fish and it's a mighty big ocean out there, with too much water to net. Practically and looking at a map I suppose it does seem hopeless, but the odds are all with a small party pushing through the enemy lines. Which completes my sermon for today. We must be on our way. Thanks for the coffee and that additive."

We laughed and I made a request. "I know you'll be very careful for a few days, sir. Those two men who went out tonight will be back in ten days. You'll watch out for them?"

"Of course. They're in good hands."

"I know. I just wanted to thank you."

We left the dugout to make our way along a trench which sloped up until in a thin tear it wound its way through the earth and emerged on the reverse side of the hill. Dug in farther down that same slope was a company command post. I asked Lim to wait outside while I entered and reported briefly, and as a courtesy to the major in command, that my mission was well on the way, we had crossed the river and that I appreciated his help. I came out, signalled to Lim and together we hurried up to our camouflaged jeep and drove off into the early morning sunshine which was lending a sort of enchantment to the harsh contours of the hills. The day was softened but the impact of war was indelibly imprinted on the land for the enemy occupied positions about five thousand yards to the north, and as many of our lines were well within range of their big mortars. The road on which we travelled had high nets erected as protection, for if small puffs of dust raised by passing vehicles became discernible to the enemy's forward observers, the area quickly became a target for a deadly rain of mortar fragments.

But now all was quiet. Tanks, mortars, machine-guns, cannon and soldiers, all were still. Many of the men who had survived the night had probably not yet taken hold of this new day in which they would fight, cut, destroy and be destroyed. But the business of war was, for the moment, at a standstill.

Our jeep was stopped at the bridge spanning the deep, fast-flowing Imjin River where our identity passes were checked. The drive continued until I swerved the vehicle off the main highway and onto a small track. Along this rutted lane way I was halted at a barrier by Korean youngster dressed in the uniform of South Korea's National Police. He saluted smartly when he saw I was driving, then, with a big grin, he pressed on the weighted end of the barrier, raising it. I moved the jeep onto the top of a rise and drew it to a sliding halt in front of a group of old Korean homes, formerly a farming homestead. Doors and windows all about swung outwards and soon the courtyard was filled with a mob of yelling Koreans; this was the headquarters of my agent detachment, with its recruits and trained agents, some awaiting missions, some undergoing instruction.

I knew them all. Getting out from the jeep I spoke to some, talked with others, shook hands with two who had just returned from instruction in Seoul. Before going into my hut I sat on the front step, lit a cigarette and let my thoughts go in shadow and sunlight with the smoke, while allowing my eyes to follow the contours of the land about my place. It was a hard country creeping inward to envelop the paddy fields once won by the toil of the uprooted Korean farmers who had been forced by war to quit their villages. The fields tumbled down in an abandoned fashion from the hills, and with them, water which had been channelled to grow wheat and rice was spilling aimlessly over a narrow channel.

At the bottom of one of the abandoned paddy fields one of the agents, doubtless to pass the time away and probably to recall a life from which he had been rudely divorced by the coming of war, had erected a miniature water wheel. The water fell gently on to it and turned a spindle to which the builder had attached two small hammers. Under the impulse of the water the spindle clicked around to move the hammers and they rose and fell, beating with an easy rhythm as they did so on two tiny brass bells. The ring of the bells was crystal clear and peaceful, filling the valley with quiet, and beauty and peace.

But I knew that there was no quiet, no beauty and certainly no peace or comfort for Pak and Chet over the Northern mountains to my front where lay a thin haze. How were they doing? I wondered. They were somewhere behind that haze, while I lay in peaceful security, smoking. But why not? I asked myself. This whole stupid bloody business, this war, was drawing to a close. Both sides were sick of this conflict. I had been in it from the beginning in 1950, and I would like to get out of it, all in one piece, damaged though I was, by my first wounding.

But right now, another mission was under way and this was the worst time for me, the waiting. I would wonder perhaps if the men on this or any other mission would be able to penetrate all the way through the enemy lines undetected. But if caught and questioned would they reveal this place, my headquarters, and also tell of the route we were using to get to our safe houses? Were some of my agents working for the enemy and taking to them valuable front-line information about the forward elements they were passing through? I could never be completely sure, even though I could communicate with them in Japanese, something their conquerors had imposed during their fifty-odd years of Korean occupation. Because I could never be completely sure of all of them and could only fully trust Lim and Pak, I only went out with those two men on top assignments. It was a tough job, rugged and demanding of the body, cruel and exacting on the nerves. I accepted that the reward for some was revenge, and

Pak and Chet in their village headquarters near the Imjin River

that those who hated most bitterly might be most fully trusted. The reward for others was the fulfilment of an ideal, but that in extreme danger or capture the coward mind might elect to live against the dictates of an idealistic heart.

I believed I knew them all, the hater, the patriot, the idealist, and the mercenary, the lover of money; and most of all, I knew that the mercenary must be treated with the utmost caution, since if a man can gain from both sides, he is doubly happy. I knew them all, as well as a man might ever get to know another; in darkness and in light, in danger and in safety, with blood on their hands and hate in their hearts, but I could only trust two of them fully. And because my body was flesh, and my mind was tired with yearning, I knew I might not even fully trust myself. It was the price I paid for dealing in deceit.

★

Sitting there, thinking about my present life and the circumstances which had placed me in this spot, I involuntarily flexed my left hand which had been badly shattered and was bereft of all the knuckle bones, the metacarpus, was still in place but it had led to my medical re-classification out of infantry service. Of course there are battle risks for an infantryman, and I remembered how my commanding officer Lieutenant Colonel Green had come to me when I was stretched out, badly wounded, and he had placed his hand on my shoulder, to say he was sorry to be losing me. He had returned to his part in the battle and later that day, he was mortally wounded. But here I was now, an intelligence operator, often sent to cross a dangerous river and patrol the land far beyond in more danger than any I had encountered as a fighting soldier.

Chapter Three

I was born in Mildura in 1925. I never knew my father but I was told many years after our one and only meeting that, when my mother was pregnant with me, he had visited a brothel and picked up what was then referred to as the pox. My mother had left him and with my sister Bonnie, she moved in with her parents, Martin and Mary Roach. I was born in their small home in Mildura. I did come face to face with my father one memorable day, however, when I was leaving school and walking down the road with some school friends. I noticed a beautiful old draught horse, the sort used for pulling heavy loads of what was quaintly called night-soil but which I knew was shit, plodding down the road towards us. When it got close, a big man striding alongside the horse halted it, rudely picking me up dumped me on the broad back of the animal. To my astonishment he declared, "I'm your dad, son!"

I sat hunched up and ashamed on the huge horse, said not a word, and when the man, someone I could never refer to as my dad, had dragged me angrily from the horse and dumped me on the footpath, I knew I would have to give a bloody nose to the biggest boy in the group of school mates, all giggling and whispering that Harris was the son of the local shit-carter. I got the bloody nose, however, but it did lead to my grandmother getting Rocky Daniels, an old ex-champion fighter and the local milk carter, to teach me how to box. Many years later I was to fight, and successfully, in the West Melbourne Stadium.

I never knew the circumstance but my grandparents,

apparently without any money, set up home on the Buronga Ridge, located across the Murray River, in 1932 when I was eight years old. I loved the area, the name Buronga was Aboriginal and I believed it meant 'many stars reflecting in the water'. Centuries before, the Aborigines had roamed all along the water way, hemmed in all along its banks with huge eucalyptus trees which were ancient long before the white man ever saw them. On some, scars can be seen where the natives had cut bark from which they fashioned their canoes, made by removing a long oval of tough covering and then binding and shaping the ends together to make a bow and a stern. The craft were unstable and crude but they suited the lifestyle of the earliest people, for they were easy to carry and simple to replace. Many canoes must have been built over the centuries when black men squatted over long strips of bark, a piece of flint in their hands, while their women worked in the shade, watching them, as their piccaninnies splashed and yelled in the shallows. Then, the river and its many billabongs teemed with fish and shrimps, along with platypus and millions of water birds.

That is all gone now, but the river is broad and tranquil, with the sky often an imperial blue. The river in many parts is a turbulent stretch of water, fed from the far off Snowy Mountains but with lock gates at Mildura, the river slows and widens, providing the entire region and the irrigation fields with water sufficient to grow anything planted. The land is so lush that it goes a long way to redeem the harsh, shanty outline of the shacks on the ridge at Buronga, lying above the river like the rippled spine of a sleeping lizard. The ridge is at the far end of a desert and its only street is a wavering ribbon of sand drawn between the glistening boles of tall trees. But it is a good place if your needs are simple. Fish from the river, land and water to grow vegetables, plenty of shade to keep your chickens and ducks at peace and productive. There are lots of rabbits near and about while the large town of Mildura is just across the Murray Bridge for shopping and, according to my grandparents, an abundance of good cheap wine, both white and red, can be had from many of the surrounding vineyards.

My grandfather had been a blacksmith and after emigrating from Ireland in 1925, he had first set up at Menindee. Driven out because of lack of work he now set up again at Buronga. I never knew what he had been doing while he lived in Mildura but now with the re-built forge he soon had enough work to keep his family fed. There were plenty of draught horses used on the many vineyards all about and he was a skilled tradesman, gentle with animals, and he prospered, in a relative sense.

The others coming after the Roach family to Buronga slapped up their shanties, following the standard method of building: rough-shaped bush posts for uprights, hessian sides, later calcimined white, scrounged or stolen corrugated sheeting for the roof. And if it could be had, metal guttering that led to water tanks set beside the shacks where most women kept small gardens of hardy shrubs like oleander or fuchsia. Many also trailed climbing geraniums to blossom like hard-won trophies against the white of their bag walls.

I began working with Martin as soon as I was strong enough to wield a hammer properly. We were great friends and sometimes when the day's work was done the old man would hug me close to his heart, then pretend to wrestle with me, and hold me near to his whiskered chin. Before I grew too big to be carried, he would take me up on his shoulders and carry me all the way back to our shack, the thick flannel stuff of his shirt smelling wonderfully to me of sweat and smoke and the sweet dung of the horses. I also came to know some of Martin's history; it did not come to me all at once but sometimes from talking with him at the forge, at other times chatting with Mary after our evening prayers, and often listening to our neighbours talk when Martin held his court at the board table in the kitchen where his own home-brewed beer was served. It was actually brewed in Mary's huge clothes washing cauldron and it was very potent, the full bottles often exploding, much to Martin's chagrin, before it could be consumed. But what was drunk made people very excited and given to making long, red-faced speeches.

I came to understand that Martin had fought in what became the hopeless Easter Uprising of 1916, when a provisional Republican government was proclaimed. Only about one thousand men were available to fight against British rule in Ireland, and Martin was one of the ill-equipped Irishman who went against thousands of British soldiers. The Irish troops occupied the General Post Office and parts of Dublin; savage street fighting went on for several days and until the Republicans were forced to surrender. When Martin yielded he had been shot in the shoulder and had taken a bayonet thrust in the thigh, and a rifle butt in the face had broken his nose. The defeated Irishmen had tried to huddle together, seeking warmth, but the British soldiers jabbed viciously at them with their bayonets, keeping them apart. If a man fell he was brutally kicked and sometimes run through with steel; but after a short time the British troops were relieved by Australian soldiers who had served on the Western Front. Many were of Irish ancestry, some whose forebears had been deported to Australia for life simply because they had sworn a secret oath as members of Trade Unions, and soon overcoats materialised to cover many of them, and particularly the wounded and hurt.

Hot mugs of tea were also provided and the instant kindness

of the Australians, so at variance with the brutality of the British soldiers, caused many of the Irishmen who had borne that British maltreatment in black silence to break down and weep. One good point of the whole mess Martin was often to declare, was that he was able to convince Mary that the family, including Eileen who was to become my mother, should emigrate to Australia. He had never forgotten the kindness of the soldiers who had saved his life, and he thought their country would be a fine place to settle, away from the troubles of Ireland, which had split into two self-governing areas, Northern and Southern Ireland. And so they moved on.

As time passed the sensitive relationship between Martin and me never faltered in the strength of its friendship, but the pact I knew with Mary was much more complex, for it was a thing of the soul, something set in the heavens she often spoke about. She was a willowy woman who carried a quiet but unquestioned authority in her bearing. Like Martin, she was a Catholic but broad-minded and clear- thinking, and not a devotee, as I was later to understand, of that part of the church which remained under Roman obedience after the Reformation. She believed in heaven and hell, in angels and devils, but she was practical about life and the manner in which it should be lived. Life and the happiness that sometimes went along with it, as she explained to me, was like fluid in a cup. There was a problem, though, in that there was not enough happiness to go around to satisfy everyone and to keep all cups full. As this was the case, I must understand that the time would come when my cup would not hold much happiness but I must believe, knowing that if I persevered, then our God, who had the power and control over nature and human fortunes, would fill my cup to the full once again. Of an evening she would kneel with me and Bonnie and we would say our prayers together, where over our beds hung a crayon drawing of

Christ exhibiting his heart in red and gold and blue, the colours, she often told us, of love and pride and suffering.

With the passing of the years other families came to be scattered all about the saffron hump of land above the river, and all close to our place which had become the hub of many people's tattered wheel. Being that sort of woman who had accumulated the sort of wisdom which books and learning do not impart Mary became, almost naturally, spokeswoman and arbiter for the ridge dwellers. Her authority was undisputed, and so she was able to fend off the authorities when they came looking for drunks, vagrants or petty criminals. She was able also to manipulate and pacify local council members when they turned up demanding payment of the crown rent on the land. Bonnie and I were often at Mary's side, patient listeners to her well-constructed pleas for mercy, observers to her diplomacy. Given her experience as a nurse in Ireland, Mary was also medic to the ridge dwellers, administering to the sick, most of whom could not afford medicine let alone the luxury of a doctor, and calling on a lifetime of experience she gave succour and hope to many of the ill and lost in spirit. With Mary on the ridge it became home for a community, not simply a resting place for derelicts.

As the depression years lingered on, more and more shacks came to sprawl about our place and in the wind-patterned hollows beyond. The new comers were different to the earlier settlers, many being accountants, factory workers, along with drovers, sheep men and farmers. Elderly swagmen were frequent passers-by with corks to ward off the flies swinging from the broad bush hats and all their possessions wrapped in a bag or a blanket called their swag draped across their shoulders. A blackened billycan dangled from a hip and many were accompanied by an old cattle dog, normally a kelpie, often simply called Bluey. The swaggies were men of a low status, somewhere I heard it declared between the indigenous Aborigine and the immigrant Irish. Derided by many as thieves or vagabonds, most somehow understood if they called into the shack of Martin and Mary requesting hot water to make tea in their billycans and some hot tucker, hopefully beef stew for which they offered to cut wood or clean up about the place, Mary would provide whatever was needed. They invariably fed their dog from a spare bowl carried for that purpose, and would later head for the river bank to set up a camp, but Sergeant Murphy of the Mildura police would appear almost on cue and herd them on.

Murphy seldom exercised his authority on the ridge, though, and he never allowed his constables to go anywhere near the place unless he accompanied them. He knew well enough that whenever the ridge dwellers got enough cash for any work they might find in the vineyards or for labouring on the roads, they would drink and brawl, even run crazy. He knew that on Saturday nights in particular, the ridge would often be littered with male and female debris of fearsome fights and monumental drinking bouts. But having so much respect for Mary's ability to sort things out with wisdom and tact, and being Irish himself, he never interfered with what might happen on the ridge knowing that when the Sunday morning sun aroused them, the fighters would generally shake hands and make up. They would probably have another beer, possibly having forgotten what it was they had fought about.

Bonnie, older and wiser, was a second mother to me, among other things helping me with my school work as my attendance was patchy, for I often helped Shoofty Vetch when he went out getting in his cross lines for fish that he would sell at Wentworth, paying me for helping him. I also worked in the Clemenza vineyards during the picking season and I was able sometimes to buy Mary a nice present as a form of repayment for her love and guidance. As well I helped Rocky Daniels on his milk run with Clarrie Simpson. I had a few friends about the place but my best mate was Clarrie, whose mother was what they called the common-law wife of a burly man known simply as Plug. Minnie, according to Mary, was the 'latest mum' of Clarrie, and that after his natural mother had left him, her violent husband never again bothered to seek the seal of church or state on any of the temporary liaisons he later contracted. He was a wild drunken larrikin given to beating Minnie and Clarrie when he was in a drunken rage. Clarrie would often share a cigarette he had stolen from Plug breaking one in half, lighting his portion and passing the burning match and my half over to me. Together in complete harmony we would inhale with what we took to be a natural talent. We never discussed the violent Plug or his bullying and besides, we were having problems in my own home, for my mother Eileen, when she visited Buronga from Melbourne where she was working as a housekeeper, had taken to drinking heavily. She often sat at the kitchen table drinking wine and quarrelling with Mary and Martin. Once, when I found a part empty methylated spirits bottle secreted under her bed and woke to her ask if she was drinking it, she instantly got up and pushed me so violently in the chest that I crashed all the way back into the kitchen stove. I sat in the dirt crying, until Bonnie came and took me outside.

When I asked Bonnie why our mother was drinking so much, even the spirit which was mainly used for mixing paint, she told me that Eileen deeply loved our father and she could never understand why he had cheated on her. Because she could not accept what he had done to her, she found escape in drinking. I then queried why our father had picked me up and dumped me on that horse carting shit, Bonnie reckoned that it was his desperate attempt to shame me and stop me from becoming what he was, and how something terrible he had done to our mother, had badly changed all of our lives.

Clarrie was several years my senior and I had started working on Rocky's milk run with him, when I was twelve plus a few months. The year was 1938. We accompanied Rocky on the ridge at Buronga in a horse-drawn cart, delivering milk and cream to those who could afford it. Rocky loved to sing as he drove about the place, warbling ditties which for people living about the place were as much a part of his character as his ragged appearance. They were the kind not usually heard outside the Returned Soldiers get-togethers or rugby after-match beer-ups, but nobody living on or about the ridge ever took offence to them. Clarrie and I loved to sing with him while feeling very grown-up and worldly-wise.

We had to quit the milk run when the grape picking season commenced. We worked on a property owned by an Italian named Enzio Clemenza. He was an Italian who had emigrated from France, not Italy, after the first war, a fact which kept him from being interned then as an enemy alien. Some people wondered what might happen to him if there was another war, for it was known that Mussolini had recently invaded Abyssinia and now he was watching Hitler's war preparation. It seemed that the Italian leader might join him in some conflict against all of us, which could affect Clemenza. On his arrival in Buronga, he had taken up land along the river and there he had grubbed out a place for his vines, grafting onto the small stems that came from America the centuries-old love of vineyards, all inherited from his native Italy.

The land Clemenza first worked was so poor that some of the locals said he would never make it as a grower. But he did, partly because he was sustained in his work by his wife, Rosa.

Even now, after so many years in Australia, and married to one of one of the richest men in the district, she still wore her hair in the plain, severe style of her homeland. She also wore un-ornamented black clothing and drab shoes and stockings, hostages of her days of struggle when she and her husband never stopped working and planting. The way Rosa had often stood so close to her husband, with a black shawl over her head and black peasant stockings to match her ankle-length boots, was ridiculed by some. Only her husband had understood that Rosa's stern Catholic God had burned into her soul a fear that what He in this good land had given might, in less generous mood, so easily take away in flood or drought.

The pickers came in their droves, and by their nature as well as their numbers disrupted the peaceful, easy-going rhythm of Mildura and the many small country towns about. They were not all bad people, of course. Many were hard working decent folk who followed seasonal work from North Queensland to Tasmania, from cane cutting to apple picking and grape harvesting. Clarrie and I picked with Bonnie and, working as a threesome, we had good yields; but it was hard, hot work and on Saturday we were happy to get away and attend the dance held in the Mildura Town Hall.

We paused just inside the door, absorbing the colourful scene, and it was obvious that nobody, stranger or otherwise, could possibly have lost their way to the Town Hall that evening, for the place glowed with lights, was surrounded with horse-drawn vehicles, and throbbing to the sound a large crowd makes. Sharp at eight o'clock Elsie Dunning small, sober-faced and very determined looking, struck the first chords on the piano set on the high stage and the proceedings were under way. She and her group kept up a monumental beat that should have brought down the lilies and cherubs of the heavy white moulding, while clouds of bright streamers and great balloons shook and swayed above the dancers, the balloons released among general pandemonium during the last dance of the evening.

Clarrie had the first dance with Bonnie but he was then shouldered aside by other young men who wanted to take her in their arms. I could understand why, as I thought she looked tall and lovely, encased in a blue dress she had bought for the evening from her first payment from the grape picking. I did not dance much, nor did Clarrie, as his partner Bonnie was much sought after by older men. But when the musicians had played their last encore we left the place and strolled down Deakin Avenue heading for home, Clarrie with Bonnie and me, all happy together. The air about was warm and musty with a hint of ripe grape aroma from the vineyards all about. Generally though, the place was sleeping, but somewhere a car honked or a motor-bike muttered, while behind us we could hear the tinny sound of a piano as some die-hard reveller tried to manufacture yet another tune on the high stage in the Town Hall. Peaceful though it all was, I knew there was also the danger of war in that surrounding air.

Clarrie and I had learned a lot about the possibility of war from my uncle Luke who believed in Churchill and his fears about Hitler and the Japanese forces. Uncle Luke did not quit Ireland with his parents but he turned up in Buronga several years later, flat broke, and asked if he could move in with his mother. He did not make the request to Martin for it seemed that the old man did not want him about the place. Luke did not move into the shack either, but built himself a bough shed out back. It was a single room, roughly square, with a roof of corrugated iron and walls of matted salt bush, constructed after a local building technique which ensured reasonable privacy, and maximum cool in summer. Its only fault was that it did not keep out the drifting red sand which sifted through it with every breeze.

Having nothing much to do once his accommodation was settled, Luke took over part of Mary's responsibility as doctor for the ridge where the many quarrels from the growing population often led to cuts and sometimes even to muscle injury and broken bones. Luke once confided to me that he could scarcely remember when or where the rough practice had begun, but he had acquired a skill of sorts and an interest in minor surgery during what he euphemistically called 'The Troubles' in Ireland, which I now understood he viewed differently from his father. Mary had also once mentioned that Luke was a Protestant, one thing which naturally distanced him from Martin with his Catholic belief. But Luke also worked as a barber and this may have laid yet another foundation, given the necessity to staunch cuts, a familiarity with razors and scissors, a known knack in paring corns, lancing whitlows, and even tearing out carbuncles.

As a growing boy and later in my early teens, I came to understand that a great part of Luke's concern for other people stemmed from his natural willingness to help and lend a hand to those in trouble, a trait I tried to copy. I also attempted to adopt and understand what Luke's crude but practical measures did more for a raving drunk, or a thrown rider, or a terrified bush kid or mother, or a wandering sick Aboriginal, rather than any high-priced doctor's care. To me, he was a big, smiling generous-hearted man who was always good to me, and over the years I came to love him. Sometimes when Luke had too much to drink, he would hold me close to his large stomach and weep. I knew it had something to do with the difference between him and Martin, but I never queried him on the matter but let him keep his secret in some corner of his untrammelled mind. It was a good mind, for he had studied under the Jesuits in Ireland but following some disagreement he had abandoned the priesthood, and turned to another, which Martin referred to as a so-called religion.

By ridge standards Luke was an intellectual, which was why he had become an accepted authority on the looming war. It was his opinion which made Eileen decide she would move me and Bonnie to Moonee Ponds, then an outer suburb of Melbourne, to live with our paternal grandparents. Eileen had some vague notion that if I got my Merit Certificate followed by some technical training, it would be sufficient for me to get a job with a large engineering company, which would be a reserved occupation and keep me from being called up for military service, should that war Uncle Luke talked about happen.

Some time later, happen it did, and Luke with Mary, helped arrange the party that saw Clarrie off to the conflict. The occasion was celebrated at our home and many people contributed to the occasion, the most generous being Clemanza. He arranged for barbeque pits to be dug and the place was heavy with the aroma of a whole pig and a large sheep being roasted over glowing coals of Murray River wattle, where four of Clemenza's workers acted as cooks. They basted and turned, basted and turned, all the time being fortified by the strong red wine which Clemenza kept sending to them in a steady flow. Two of Clemenza's horses which had dragged the barbeque equipment from his vineyards stood tethered nearby, and as if trained to give atmosphere to the occasion, they snorted while tossing high their magnificent heads and surveying the guests as they arrived.

I stood nearby watching the way Clemenza worked and the manner with which Mary welcomed each guest, for it was obvious the people she had invited were the guests of her home, as well as her heart, and she made everyone fully welcome. It was indeed a happy day for her because my mother Eileen had appeared to say farewell to Clarrie. She was accompanied by a laughing man she called Jock. He described himself as a man from Scotland now with a dairy farm in Gippsland. It was manifest that my mother was happy with him and she did not touch a drink of alcohol that night; she confided to me and Bonnie that her troubles were all in the past and we gladly believed her, hoping she would be happy at last. Everyone was at ease and comfortable that night, in that place and on the land about them which had produced much of the fare. The meat and vegetables, the fruit and the wine, and thinking about it, I glanced about me, noticing how the light was changing as the evening deepened. The glow of the fires lit the faces of the people about, and occasionally the rolling eyes of the horses watching them. I felt very much at peace and contented with life. Looking closely at Clarrie I could see that he had grown to be the tallest person at his party. His height made him stoop slightly, but not from any weakness, and while he moved slowly, he did so without hesitation. I knew that Martin could take a lot of credit for Clarrie's blooming into young manhood, for one night when his father had been raving at Minnie and Clarrie, Martin had stormed into their shack and ordered them to settle the matter outside with Queensbury rules. Martin later told me he had watched Clarrie boxing with me and he knew Clarrie could handle himself, especially against a raving drunk. So it proved to be, and when Clarrie had knocked his opponent bleeding badly to the ground, Minnie had finished him off with a couple of well aimed blows at his head with a broom handle. From that moment forward Clarrie was boss of the particular shack, and he was able to openly express his love for Minnie, which she could respond to.

By this time many of the guests had done clustering about the glowing barbeque pits, shielding their faces and arms while sawing off the portions they fancied. Mary had lit several candles and kerosene lamps inside and most had begun to wander in to sing and dance. I wandered outside again to get another wine for Mary and I noticed how the calcimined walls, which looked so drab and grey in the sunlight, had been softened magically by the flickering lights inside. There was such a beautiful and underwater clearness to everything that it caught at my heart, making me sorrowful about Clarrie's departure from Buronga the following morning. But I knew that if the war lasted I might also get away, but I doubted it for it was expected that Hitler would be beaten, or that he would seek peace. I was too young yet, anyhow, to join any army.

Just then the clear tenor voice of Rocky interrupted my thoughts and I peered through the wire-screened front door to see the ageing milkman giving voice to yet another ditty. This time it was the one that had to do with the sexual life of the camel which at the height of the mating season attempts to deflower the sphinx. Clarrie was then motioned forward to give his rendition of Sir John Moore's funeral and how they buried him gently at dead of night, the sods with the bayonets turning. I stepped back inside as my mother organised a dance which was managed, even in the confined space, to the sound of Shoofty Vetch scraping on his fiddle; the old fisherman was a good player and Luke joined him, pumping away at his accordion, Rocky nearby doing his best on a mouth accordion. But the dancing was interrupted when someone took a wild swing at someone else and the people were so jammed in together that the laughing, slightly inebriated Minnie took one of the badly aimed blows. She had been jumping about with her back to the combatants, a full glass in one hand, when a punch took her over the left ear. She was sent flying, along with her beer. She hit the dirt floor screaming and the contestants were instantly shoved aside by an angry Clarrie before he went to his mother and with considerable strength lifted her clear off the ground, stood her upright and planted a big kiss on her mouth. Minnie blushed with a mix of pride and tenderness, patted her disordered hair, accepted another beer and glanced about her as the place went on pulsing with sound and movement.

But finally the ridge settled down one way or another for the night. It was an evening of desert stars and trees with the river below ghostly along in the moonlight. I was lying in my bed, thinking about my tomorrows, and those of Clarrie too. I knew most of the ridge dwellers would be sleeping, but the eternal things, the stars, the trees, the river, kept their eternal watch. I heard an owl hoot somewhere and like an echo, its call was answered. Those bird calls did not disturb the night's silence but deepened it as I leaned over, snuffed out a candle on the dirt floor and I waited for sleep as all about me the ridge slumbered on towards whatever tomorrow might bring.

It had been decided that Clarrie and I would walk into Mildura that following day. The last man he spoke to was Martin who had been unable to attend his farewell party because he'd had pleurisy which had progressed to pneumonia. Looking down at him, I saw that Clarrie could not restrain his tears for he must have known he would never see this old man again. I wanted to weep also as I recalled how this now, frail grandfather had once carried me all the way from his forge, cuddling me in his arms, and tickling the back of my neck with his whispery chin. I could remember it all taking place, but it seemed now to have happened to an other small boy who might have been a child I had only heard about, and this now sick old man might never have been the one who had carried me on his strong shoulders so long ago. But I loved him and my heart ached to see him in this condition.

Martin managed to control the awful rasping sound in his

chest as he muttered, "Clarrie, do something for me, will ya, son? Just slip ya hand under me pillow. Got somethin' there for ya."

Clarrie dropped to his knees, felt under the pillow and pulled out a small, folded piece of cloth.

"That's it!" Martin gasped loudly. "That's it! Let me show ya!"

Slowly he then unfolded a dark brown tie with a green emblem in its centre. He held it in his hands for a moment in a manner strangely reverent and his head was bent as though he was once again the altar boy of his youth, ready to place the stole about a priest's shoulders.

"See that there shamrock?" he whispered, as if afraid to speak too loudly and spoil his exhibition of that national emblem of Ireland. "It's on me army tie, you know! Given to me in 1916, it was. The Easter Uprising young Jack here can tell you all about it, he will remember. The English soldiers who cut us to pieces would have taken it, but the Aussie Diggers guarding us told them I could keep it. I reckon it's been me lucky omen, you know? Got me this far, anyhow. But I want to give it to you, son, right now in the hope that it will keep you safe and well. Bring you back home, a hero too, if I know you?"

Exhausted, he laid back, his chest rising and falling in tune to the rales of his ragged breathing.

Clarrie stood up, folded the precious tie and stowed it into his shirt pocket. Looking at Mary, standing with hands folded at the head of the bed, he stooped to kiss Martin on the forehead. "I love you, grandad," he whispered, through his tears. "I'll come back. Just you wait for me."

Later striding with Clarrie through the brisk morning I noticed how he sometimes put his hand to his pocket, feeling for the necktie. I was comforted to hope that somehow that little bundle of cloth from Martin's past would bring Clarrie back to Buronga.

Chapter Four

Under Mary's care, Martin clung to life but he died the day he was told that Clarrie had been killed in his first action in New Guinea. Martin was buried in the Mildura cemetery after a brief service in the main Catholic church. I did not realise that my mother had such a beautiful clear and full-powered soprano voice until she sang at the grave-site. I thought proudly, '*That's my mum!*' and afterwards when we held a wake at the shack on Buronga Ridge most of the neighbours made sure that the old man went out in style with Eileen singing again, accompanied by Shoofty on that violin of his, Luke on the fiddle, Rocky belting a drum and sometimes pumping his accordion with great gusto. The drinking and feasting never seemed to stop, with Enzio Clemenza contributing most of the viands, including many choice dishes and the wine, which he had held back in cared-for storage for just such an occasion.

I had no alternative afterwards, but to leave Buronga. I loved my mother and wanted to go along with her wishes, just to make sure that she never again turned to the destructive solace of heavy drinking. In Moonee Ponds I would be much nearer to her and Jock's dairy farm in Gippsland which, while some way from Moonee Ponds, was many hours nearer than Buronga was from Melbourne.

I discovered paternal grandmother was a capricious and contradictory woman, carping and critical, who found fault with everyone and everything. Small and thin, she wore a tight bun of hair on the back of her head. She was a vegetarian and mostly served boiled cabbage, potato and carrots. Her husband was also thin; he was bald-headed, and so afraid of his wife that he was obsequious to her and everyone else. When I was introduced to my uncle Bernie, a big man built like my father Bonnie and I wondered how these grandparents had ever got together for what I had once heard Martin call the pleasures of the flesh. Marriage and living together, from what I had mostly observed when living on the ridge, was generally nothing but painful servitude for many women. But here, a kind and helpless man was dominated by an appalling female. When I met Bernie that son, I was told I was to help him on his milk run, just as I had with Rocky Daniels at Buronga. I was to give the five shillings a week that I was to receive, directly to that new grandmother of mine. I found the work hard, the hours long, but the running along with six crated bottles in one hand and a pail of milk in the other strengthened my body while the milk and cream supplemented my vegetarian meals. Bonnie was working in a nearby general store and she was able to bring me sandwiches and cake, which I enjoyed sitting up in bed in a darkened room, hidden from prying eyes.

That part of my life passed slowly and unpleasantly but I managed to get my Merit Certificate, much to Eileen's pleasure. The only thing that gave me any sense of happiness from my schooling was that I had nice teachers who never strapped me when I fell asleep at lessons, exhausted from those early-morning milk runs. They seemed to understand that I was up at four to go on the milk run and go from that work direct to school. Those same teachers encouraged to get me out on the playing field at lunch time for a game of cricket and I became proficient at the game. But I was also reckless. One day, chasing a ball, I went under a boundary fence but ducked up too quickly and cut my head badly. I was cleaned up and bandaged but when I was taken home, the place was empty. So my teacher kindly took me to his home where his wife tucked me into a comfortable bed. For the first time since I had left Buronga I was encased in happiness, a feeling heightened by music I could hear being played on a machine. I later asked the lady looking after me the name of the music and she said it was 'Finlandia' by a man whose name I could not remember, but who years later I was able to track down and begin my love of classical music. That crack on my head was an incident that led to a pleasant discovery. Later on in life accidents that happened to me all led to better circumstances. Having finished my secondary school, Eileen enrolled me in a technical college where I studied hard for a few months. But Eileen apparently fell out with Jock, she had a furious argument with our paternal grandparents, and Bonnie and I found ourselves being bundled on the overnight train to Mildura. The following day we found ourselves happily back with Martin and Mary at Buronga. There may have been no technical school in Mildura so Eileen took me along for enrolment in the Mildura High School. After an interview I was wary about my future there for I had not studied algebra or science to the level of the Year Eleven students there. I worked hard but understood little, although in the English class I studied diligently and seemed to do well. That was until one day the teacher asked who could recite a sonnet. No one volunteered, but I put up my hand and was told to get on with it. I then launched into that endless verse about Mad Carew which I remembered well. I accompanied my words with all the movements and gestures I believed were necessary to the drama. *'He returned before the dawn /His shirt and trousers torn/ A gash across his temple dripping red/'.*

    I grabbed at my shirt, pulled at my trousers, wiped all that blood from my temple, pounded on *'When the ball was at its height/ On that still and tropic night/ The colonel's daughter hurried to his bed/ The door was opened wide, the silver moonlight shining through/ An ugly knife lay buried in the heart of Mad Carew/* '

Plunging an imaginary knife deep into my chest I looked up, breathlessly awaiting to be applauded but the teacher looked very hard at me and asked if I did not know that a sonnet contained only fourteen lines. His remark was followed by derisive laughter that swamped over me in a humiliating flood and I sat heavily in my chair, knowing my school days would be over and in failure at the end of the year.

The following year I was employed for a few months as a house painter but when I told Mary that the man I worked for, a professional painter, was drinking a lot of the spirit we used to thin the oil-based paint, she took me from that work. I never mentioned that my mother had once been drinking that same spirit! A few weeks after, I was back in Moonee Ponds living this time with Eileen and Bonnie. Some time later Eileen got me apprenticed to an engineering company working out of North Melbourne involved in supplying the armed forces with certain requirements, hence my military call-up deferment. I liked the work, the metallic hum of the factory and the schooling at the technical college, and I became a competent fitter and turner. Whenever I could get away I hurried back to Buronga, looking for love and that splendid Murray River.

Some time later Bonnie married Harold, the son of the shop man Bonnie worked for. He was a cheery person with a nice smile and a nature to match. Older than Bonnie, he became a surrogate father to me, helping me with problems at my work, with growing up and matters of the heart, and telling me about books I should read, for he was a scholarly person. I also had a girl friend named Doris. Harold advised me on such matters as safe sex not that he practised it as Bonnie was happily pregnant. So I was contented at home and at work and in love.

I was also progressing slowly through the preliminary rounds of boxing at the West Melbourne Stadium, getting a pound a round for each contest, which was nice money along with the small amount I received as an apprentice. Three years slipped by and I lost two important bouts in the boxing ring and so it was unlikely that I would promoted to the main events, and big money. At the same time Bonnie had the misfortune to lose her first child, a son called Brian, and I let go my lingering belief in that God my grandmother had cherished. When the Catholic priest, a fat, well-fed man with a flowery tongue, told Bonnie and Harold that God needed their child and he had been called to heaven to serve as one of his angels, I abandoned God. I had long had doubts about woman being created from a rib ripped out of Adam anyhow, and about that Ark with Noah who had fed and watered two of everything on board for forty days and nights of pouring rain. But Harold and Bonnie accepted the priest's words and grew even closer together in their sorrow, but I was shut out of that embrace. Seeking comfort I tried to believe that some heavenly entity existed controlling events and our environment, for how else could there be a river like the Murray with its blue water and majestic silver trees?

Although I had received good marks at the technical college and a report noting that I was now entitled to a statuary increase in salary, my employer rudely refused my request for any more money. Troubled and depressed by that and other matters, I outlined some of my problems with Harold. He listened carefully and advised me to 'cut, and get out', as he put it. I thought he was offering good advice for, although I had gone along with my mother's wish over the apprentice deal, I had wanted, like Clarrie, to get away to the war. But believing that my name might be indexed in the files of the fighting services, I decided to join the Merchant Navy, a civilian outfit receiving glowing reports for its service to the war effort.

I hurried back to Buronga. As I had earlier suggested following Clarrie's death, Minnie had moved in with Mary, for I believed that Clarrie's father would most probably start beating her again now that Clarrie could no longer protect her from his bullying. I found her to be the same sort of silly, sweet woman with such an amplitude of good cheer that she could disgorge without effort huge peals of jolly laughter. Mary had found her good company and liked having her in the house. Luke had also moved into a spare room and out of his bough shed. I explained to him that the purpose of my visit was to ask for his war-time ration cards so that I could use them and enter the Merchant Navy, but under his name. He instantly agreed and Mary also approved of my scheme to get away.

I entered the Merchant Navy as a trimmer, had a tattoo cut into my right forearm, and went to sea. I found that being a trimmer, a man equipped with a large shovel and wheelbarrow used to push coal from various parts of the deck to the firemen, was a fearsome job, especially in rough seas. But there is comradeship working in a vessel, often in bad weather with the men below decks often sweating, filthy and foul-mouthed, a closeness of workers that is mutually binding and keeps them, as long as they can curse and labour, in its embrace. I believe I would have stayed at sea until I could no longer stand; curiously one day when I could metaphorically no longer stand, I was thrown down a long flight of steel stairs and hurt my shoulder so badly that I returned to Buronga, looking for recovery.

It was now early 1946, I was twenty years of age and the army was advertising for men to join up, and serve in Japan with an occupation force. Believing that my shoulder would pass inspection, I enlisted and sailed for Japan. I joined the 67th Australian Battalion in Kaitaichi, a suburb not far from Hiroshima. Within eight months I was a sergeant in that battalion's intelligence section and I requested leave to attend a nine month's course in the Japanese language to qualify as an interpreter.

I was helped in my study of Japanese by Midori Suimoto, the sister of my language teacher. She was a lovely slim girl and when I was introduced to her she was wearing a classical Japanese gown of gold and silver thread with chrysanthemums and egrets etched into the fabric. Her obi, the wide sash worn by Japanese women was a soft purple shade. Her head, I thought, would nicely fit under my chin. Her face was delicate, her skin smooth and clear, her nose small in the tradition of Japanese beauty. Her eyes were black and brilliant under her well developed brows. She glowed with health and vitality while her body emitted a husky fragrance which tantalised me.

The Suimoto home had miraculously escaped the fire-bombing campaigns; it was a small place with a dull, but spotlessly clean tatami covering the wooden floors and stretching to the paper-coated walls on all sides. Midori showed me over the place. At one point she gestured to a table on delicately carved legs which sat in one corner and on which a bonsai, an artificially dwarfed pine tree, sat in a small bowl. Midori explained that her husband, an officer in a Japanese engineering battalion, had cared for the tree since he was a boy. As a soldier he had been captured when the Russians took Manchuria, and had been sent with hundreds of thousands of other prisoners to labour in the Siberian slave camps. Some of the world leaders had protested to Stalin, demanding that the captured men be sent home but, needing workers in those frozen wastes, he simply refused. Midori did not know if her husband had survived the surrender. She had never heard from him, she told me, as we went to walk outside and to a small hill nearby. It was shrouded in pine, cedar and maple, all so close planted that the Suimoto home peeped out as though through a shield of green. We returned to her garden, a designed landscape, with a stone pool crossed by a slender bridge where tiny bells tinkled in a breeze. Everything was compressed into a miniature world, all complete and enthralling, so different to anything I had ever encountered.

I understood that the invitation to meet Midori and study Japanese had economic reasons behind it. Japan was mostly in ruins with Hiroshima, only a few miles distant, a frightful wasteland. All the major cities had been flattened. Hundreds of thousands of homes and other buildings had been destroyed, over a million Japanese soldiers had died in the war and as many civilians, if not more, had perished at home. Japan had become a nation of people living overwhelmed in a land of devastation, and those who had once believed their emperor to be a god, were now forced to understand that a hundred generation of emperors had not been gods at all, but merely men. That acceptance meant the collapse of their faith, and all they had inwardly cherished. It was an appalling and transforming, as well as a hungry time for many Japanese, and I was able, as Midori's brother had guessed, to buy food from the mess sergeant and give it to them: butter and cheese, hampers of ham and other meats, along with milk and cream and good rice, which was scarce in most markets.

I did not feel I was doing anything wrong. These people were hungry, the food was available, and my language studies were progressing far better than any of the other students. There was something else of course. I was very attached to Midori and when she finally invited me into her bedroom, I found it to be a place with a floor of tatami matting, with dwarf pines set along one wall, all creating a spare, controlled beauty. The bathroom nearby where she took me and ritualistically bathed my body prepared me fully for her sexual abandonment and my sense of completeness when finally, we lay still, our naked bodies locked together. It filled me with a sense of wonder, and I could not but hark back to Doris of my working days, and how she had said she really liked good fucking. But I knew, after making love to Midori, that Doris had been happy if someone just wanted her body, so she simply let the man have his way, as it was quaintly called. With Midori I came to understand that Japanese boys and girls, when in their teens, have sex fully explained by their parents who give them woodblock art works of Japan which are very specific, and the books they are given to read stress patience for the man, an understanding of her body by the woman. Sex to the Japanese is supposed to be a pleasure to both people. Midori and I certainly found a mutual enjoyment, and thinking about it, I knew the Japanese had the right approach to an essential part of married life. It may be apocryphal, but I recall reading that some Europeans dislike the thought of their women screaming at the moment of climax, and they prefer going to a brothel and paying a prostitute to pretend having one.

I was confused about Japan and what I was encountering: here was Midori, sensual and sensible with a sparkling sense of humour, a prudent temperament and delightfully kind. Yet many Japanese soldiers had been sadistic brutes whose cruelty to the people and to China generally, was well documented. In the war with the Allies they had been merciless to prisoners of war. Starving, torturing, working to death and killing without pity. The war crimes trials, then taking place in Tokyo, had produced much sickening evidence of exactly how barbarous Japanese soldiers had been to the people they had vanquished. Stories were also circulating about how 'comfort women' were rounded up in the countries Japan had occupied. Women and very young girls had been taken under guard and sent to live in barracks where Japanese soldiers were stationed. Once in place, the girls and women spent days and months, even years, serving Japanese soldiers in whichever way the soldier desired his sex. Some of these comfort women were said to have obliged as many as eighty men in a single day. One of the main countries for recruitment of these helpless women was Korea. A story coming out told how concerned Korean fathers were about their daughter's virginity. A Korean girl returned home after years of being trapped in this dreadful situation, she told her father, and asked to be allowed back home. The father immediately slapped her face, denied her entry and thereafter ignored her. Many of the girls, though, never returned home because towards the end of the war thousands of them were loaded onto ships which were taken out to sea and scuttled, destroying the evidence of their years of sickening existence.

Japanese soldiers had been brave men with their code of honour making them fight almost to the last men. In some of the islands in the Pacific many hundred of thousands died, refusing to surrender. Some senior officers, including many generals, committed *seppuku,* or ritual suicide, by first drinking a glass of saki, plunging a knife deep into their stomach and having their head severed from the body by a loyal and junior officer.

Japan is a beautiful country and I had often visited the site of the Imperial Palace which had not been bombed during the war because of its historical significance. It had a wide moat around the front where swans glided through water lilies while red and gold fish swum effortlessly beneath them. The huge walls beyond the moat were of fashioned blocks, all different in size but fitted together so cleverly they seemed to curve smoothly upward with effortless grace. There was such a singular beauty about the palace and the moat, with cherry blossom in bloom, and in the far distance the snow-covered crest of Mount Fuji. In a way the tranquillity I knew walking about the palace convinced me that all Japanese men could not be bad, and the women, or one of them at least, were of fine character.

In time Midori and I came to talk about marriage, as it seemed that her husband must be dead. Just then, however, there was a non-fraternisation ban in place, which meant that British and Australian soldiers could not marry Japanese women. The Americans had no such ban and it was hoped that later the British also would abandon their restriction. At that time, if it became known that I was cohabiting with Midori, I could face court martial. But our plans had to be abandoned when Midori was told by the Japanese government that her husband was being returned from Siberia. He was said to be very ill, psychologically scarred, and she was expected to care for him, to nurse him back to health.

On our last night together Midori lay beside me, weeping softly. When we parted we kissed, and for both of us the meeting of our lips meant more than the urgency our bodies had known in love, and more too than her room where we had so often slept close together. The kiss took in more than the exquisite garden outside her home with its bamboo and cypress which seemed to protect the Suimoto home. I felt abandoned, knowing that my cup of happiness my grandmother once talked about had been rudely tipped.

I was returned to my battalion in mid-1950. It had been re-named the Third Battalion, The Royal Australian Regiment 3RAR, just before it was ordered to Korea. Having requesting a reposting from the sedentary intelligence section, I was then a platoon sergeant with 9 Platoon C Company. Our battalion was to fight all the way to Chonju, a town about sixty miles from the Yalu River; it was there that I was wounded and our commanding officer Green was killed. Another accident in my life, which this time led to my return to Australia, a year's study of Chinese, my re-posting back to Korea in early 1953 and now, my waiting for Pak and Chet to return from their mission behind the enemy lines in North Korea.

Chapter Five

The ultimate testing of Pak, as the story came to me from Tony Lavender and Lim, was first set in motion when in the spring of 1951 vast columns of allied armour blasted their way out of the perimeter of Pusan, where they had been confined for months by the North Korean armies. This tremendous operation had been planned at the highest level and executed with precision by swarms of men and vehicles, yet in the curious indirect and impersonal fashion of war, it might have been mounted for no other reason than to accomplish the fate of Pak, living in a remote village of North Korea.

In the first shock of the break-out the Northern Armies fled, thrown into chaotic retreat by incessant mortar and artillery barrages and massive bombardment from sea and sky. The United Nations armour ground inexorably to Seoul, liberated it, pressed on to the enemy capital of Pyongyang, took it easily and moved on again. At the village of Packchon it hurled itself against the defenders and here the towering machinery of the advance paused as the Northerners were fighting grimly to slow the advance and buy time as the village between the two contending armies was rapidly reduced to rubble. After one clamorous day the bridge beyond the village was crossed, the position taken and the war machine pressed on. Behind it, it left the village of Packchon still to be secured.

The patrols, each man's weapon at the ready, probed through the reeking streets. They peered through shattered paper windows and past doors which hung broken. They crept cautiously into the mean places which had been homes to many, examined the hard mud-packed floors, the dry mud-daubed walls, and the few cooking utensils strewn about, some with the last meal clinging to their dented sides. No soldier touched anything, remembering lessons learned earlier: a lifted pot which exploded with a shattering noise; a cupboard door which, when opened, pulled the fuse of a grenade; colourful ornaments which had been booby-trapped and left behind to maim and kill the covetous.

At one home some men in the patrol stopped; they had seen it all before, a score of times. The sergeant entered a room and scarcely looked at the body of an old man, only glanced at a bundle of bloody rags which had been a young girl. They could tell him nothing except that they were dead: the old man shot, the girl raped and killed. He turned to another man waiting at the door and raised his hands, palms up, in a gesture of hopelessness or resignation. He was about to walk out, eager to quit such a small charnel-house, when a sound like a human groan drew his attention to a dark corner of the hut. A tall youth crouched there watching him.

The sergeant paused. He had become a hard man who had been moulded by war to feel callous indifference to the suffering of all but those nearest to him, his fellow-soldiers. Blood seen most every day now was no longer the mysterious stream of life to be guarded and nourished and wondered at. It was like water, except that it was red, it was sticky, and after a while it stank. Life was no longer sacred, terror was the normal currency in war's exchange, and pity for one's fellow men a thing of the past. It had to be that way.

But the youth in the shadowed corner became to him quite suddenly an image of Korea's misery, and another groan from him brought tears to the sergeant's eyes. He strode across the mud floor, his hands at his sides, his lips saying awkwardly, even a little self-consciously, that everything was now safe. The youngster cringed back, defenceless, sharp panic in his black eyes but eventually he allowed himself to be led, stumbling and blinking in the raw, dusty light of the day into the street. He had been shot in both shoulders in a sort of mock execution and he was placed, with other hurt human flotsam, in the back of a truck which had followed slowly behind the patrol, as one of the soldiers put it succinctly in soldier talk, to pick up the scraps.

In the days which followed, Pak was treated, first in an army field station where his wounds were cleaned and he was given penicillin; he was then transferred to a large civilian hospital in Seoul and generally, he was fed and cared for. He grew calmer and as the shock quitted his young and healthy body his mind went over what had happened. He recalled how his father had returned from exile in Sumatra when the Japanese were forced out of Korea in 1945, driven back from the place they had occupied for nearly fifty years and when Japanese was the language forced on his countrymen. Old Pak hoped his land would be free but foreign statesmen decided that Korea would be divided by a parallel in its centre, with the Russians to control the North, the Americans the South.

Old Pak watched as the Russians established a huge, well-equipped North Korean army which in mid-1950 invaded the South with a force of seven divisions, an armoured brigade and several other independent regiments, along with hundreds of aircraft. South Korea, on the other hand, with the Americans apprehensive that the South would invade the North, had denied its force any weapons of substantial offensive capability. The Northern armies crushed the soldiers fighting them, including an American force soft from occupation duties in Japan. Some died savagely and gallantly in their weapon pits. Thousands were captured and most were executed when they were led away their hands shot through the palms and secured with wire. But somehow the Allies held on, confined to Pusan, the last port south. But as they fought, General McArthur launched his brilliant Inchon landing when tough and trained marines cut a path from the coast to beyond Seoul, trapping a huge force of North Koreans in the South. There they were cut to pieces.

The invaders were flung back from what had been the extremity of the Korean Peninsula. River by river, village by shattered village, bitter in defeat and casual in cruelty, the Northerners forced a way back. Vague rumours preceded them, of women being raped and very young men forced into their army, but the people found such tales hard to believe. Even if they were in defeat, these were men, soldiers of the North returning to their homes, not mad dogs out to savage their own. The people soon learned the truth: some it cowed, some it killed, but one, Young Pak, it turned into an agent of mine, the enemy of his own people.

It happened that when the fringe of the Northern withdrawal touched Pak's village, the day came when all men, young and old, had to fight with the High Command in panic, the troops in fright. It was thought that the Chinese forces then gathering in great numbers in Manchuria wanted to enter the battle and the retreating senior officers were desperate to hold their ground until the Chinese made up their minds, and hopefully came to their aid. One afternoon a political officer arrived in the village and sought out the Elder, Pak's father. He entered their thatched place and brusquely informed the Elder that he must personally order everyone to resist the invader. The Elder, who had risen to receive his unwelcome guest, stood with his long, thin hands opening and shutting, half in fear and half in anger. Pak and his sister Soon-za watched him from a bench near the wall. The Elder rejected the proposal, and, motioning to the door, turned his back on the visitor. Young Pak remembered his father most clearly in these last moments. He knew the turned back was not the act of a coward but that his father had merely turned away from a Korea in which he was now a stranger and of which he wanted no part. He was never so likely to die as at that moment and he did.

The political officer incensed by the father's eloquent contempt of the back turned upon him, grasped his shoulder with one hand, and with the other struck brutally with his pistol. The old man's face erupted in a scarlet flow as the weapon rose and fell, rose and fell.

His rage spent, the killer turned to Pak and Soon-za, the young man, stunned by the brutality of what he had witnessed, the girl too shocked to scream, but with her face stark white framed in her hair's blackness. The officer stepped back, cracked a name, and like a whistled cur a soldier appeared in the doorway. Pak, sensing what was going to happen to his desirable but very young sister, bunched his body to spring to her defence. But the officer who had beaten in his father's face said something about Pak being useless as a soldier and shot him first in the right and then in the left shoulder. Flung back and in shock Pak was then, like his father, belted across the head with the pistol. Everything was blacked out.

When he awoke, his body throbbing painfully Pak edged slowly with agonising carefulness to stare closely at the broken head and face of his father. He looked about for Soon-za, then saw the bundle of bloodied rags in the corner. Turning from his father he made his way over the floor towards her but stopped when he saw flies crawling and buzzing over her blank and bloodied eyes. He sat in a corner staring in dazed horror until the soldiers on patrol found him.

When he was finally released from hospital Pak drifted into shattered Seoul, aimless, his mind partly refusing to accept what had happened to his family. For months, as he was later to tell me, he never turned a corner of the mean place where he lived without expecting to meet and embrace his father or his sister. But when reason returned it brought with it a plan for revenge which involved taking up arms against his people, those of the North. He joined the army of the Republic, fought well and ruthlessly but, fighting with venom in his rifle sights and hatred in his heart, he was vulnerable. Wounded honourably this time, it was now that he was interviewed by Lim, out seeking the sort of men he wanted to join Englishman Tony Lavender's agent detachment.

Lavender was a British warrant officer who had been decorated both by the British and the Americans for his successful intelligence work in occupied Europe. Because of his experience he had been ordered to set up an intelligence gathering operation in South Korea. He was told to find agents and locate a suitable place to train them. With Lim as his interpreter he had visited many hospitals, prisoner-of-war camps and South Korean army bases, gathering as he went what he referred to as a curious collection of chaps: some he thought were paranoids and misfits, quite a few were God-knew, what. But he had stressed that he could totally trust Lim, his agent master, men like Pak and Chet, and a couple of others he named. With that he departed, leaving the running of the detachment to me.

Waiting for Pak and Chet to return was a particularly anxious time for me, as Chet was an new and untried agent. He had been selected by me on the recommendation of Lim, who had reported that Chet's village had been destroyed and his family killed when those masses of Chinese soldiers waiting in Manchuria, came to the aid of North Korea. Their progress was ruthless, forcing Chet out of their path and into mine. Now, as

I anxiously awaited the return of these two agents, the training of all the other agents carried on as if there were no problems or concerns: weapon training, map reading instruction, how to observe and report while behind the enemy lines, and how to move without detection in the hours of darkness. They were given long hours of training in the weapons they would carry while on patrol, until the wicked Burp gun hung from the shoulder like a third arm, the grenade snuggled on the belt like a bird at roost, and the knife at the hip would leap almost unbidden to the hand. They carried the enemy Burp gun firstly for its fire-power, and secondly they knew that if the enemy were to hear a weapon of their own make firing within their own lines, they would not take so much notice nor investigate as quickly as they would if they heard an unfamiliar foreign weapon. The grenade they carried, though, was the British Mills, famous for its fragmentation, devastation and power, as opposed to the Chinese grenade which I did not favour. The Mills, I knew, was effective

Lim, the author's number one agent: tough and the most decent of men.

in ambush or to force a way out of a dangerous situation. We trained constantly with the knife because it made no sound in the darkness.

To Lim went the responsibility of training in knife-throwing. A slab of timber approximating the height and width of a standing man was placed at one end of a banked paddy field. While the expectant agents waited, Lim, conscious of the eyes fastened on him, turned and paced deliberate steps from the target. Ten, sometimes twenty yards from it he would pause, hefting the finely balanced knife in his right hand, then place his free hand on his hip, and with a sudden convulsive heave pitch the right arm over. Invariably the knife thudded into the upper portion of the target, whereupon Lim, with a stately importance, strode to retrieve his knife, to go through the performance again and again, first one hand and then the other, from all positions, kneeling and sitting and from a swift turn round to face the board. Knowing how important it was for men to have confidence and trust in a man leading them, I let Lim impress the men watching him, for he was good at what he was teaching. But Lim knew what he was about, and when he tired of the knife he went to the dusty courtyard of our headquarters and on a tatami spread for the purpose, he instructed the men in unarmed combat, the must of the silent killer. Stripped to the waist, a sweat-rag knotted carelessly about his thick throat, he stomped on the hard grey earth, his heavy torso channelled with dust, a wild and stinking creature, vibrant and coarse, gleaming with perspiration. He abused those who held back, and embraced those who pushed him about; he loved the training because it was hard and tough, and because he was its master. The men all caught some of his enthusiasm, and when they had overcome their first tentative fears of being slammed breathless on the hard matting, they joined in and fought vigorously. But only after long hours of training did they learn the secret and terrible grips that broke an arm or a leg, that choked and paralysed and silently killed when silence could be the price of success or failure.

Pak and Chet were still out in enemy territory and despite their hard hours of training many of the agents were manifestly worried, for if things had gone wrong, it augured ill for the next to go out. They did not know, once they had left the security of the friendly lines and our own mine fields, if the enemy might now be waiting just beyond that safety, or on the track out, or just over the Samichon. Fear was a member of any mission, but the thought that the enemy might be forewarned, might be watching at a spot where they knew we would be treading, added to their apprehensions. And if captured, what then? Wearing a Chinese uniform, carrying a Chinese weapon and faked identification papers could only mean torture and a long way to death, which could only come as a mercy. We all waited.

It was the morning of the eleventh day after their departure, a date long overdue that I received a call from Major Hurgaard at Divisional HQ. He informed me that Pak and Chet had returned and they were in good shape, as he put it. They were being sent back to me under safe escort and he told me to make sure they had taken photographs. A cautious officer, Hurgaard insisted that all the agents must take photographs to prove where they had been, as reported. I agreed with Hurgaard's assessment, especially after the discussions about trust I'd had with Tony Lavender prior to his departure from our agent network

It was a dark day with rain-packed clouds sending downpours to the dry earth. Lim and I were just finishing our breakfast when we heard the slipping grind of a vehicle trying to climb the small mountain road which led to our agent detachment headquarters. We stood at the door looking anxiously through a thick veil of rain as a jeep stopped with a shudder at the crest, water hitting it with great force. Ignoring the downpour, Lim and I hurried to the vehicle to hug the sodden forms which struggled from the vehicle. One was Pak; Lim grabbed hold of his small form, emitted a whoop of joy and raised his face to the dark sky. I grabbed Chet, took one of the cold hands of the shivering youngster and threw my free arm about his shoulders. Going quickly inside, yelling and roaring, his big chest heaving, Lim called for tea, for clean, dry clothes, for hot water, but he was so excited that he carried out most of his own demands, while being followed querulously by a man we called Kimchi, after that hot Korean food, who was our cook and house-keeper.

At the sound of the uproar many of the other agents, I had twenty in all under my command, came from the main house which acted as my headquarters, became the centre for a yelling mob. In the safe return of Pak and Chet they saw a reprieve from the capture and death which might have befallen them, and they celebrated their own safety as much as theirs. Lim, having quietened down, let the uproar continue and with arms akimbo, a glad smile on his big, rugged face, watched and condoned.

When the uproar had subsided and the welcome was over, Lim asked Kimchi to prepare a good meal, and the food, heavily spiced with garlic and peppers, was quickly placed before Pak and Chet, now warm and clean. Kimchi was ecstatic to look after them for he was a man bound to his cookhouse and so he both loved and envied the men whom he had to serve. No one spoke while the two men wolfed the first hot meal they had enjoyed in many days. But when Pak, his hunger finally satiated, relaxed with a soft sigh on the cushions set behind him, he said that he and Chet were out longer than had been anticipated because Han, the old man in the house at Kunwari, had given them a lot of information and had taken them into the hills about his village on several occasions. A number of new gun-sites had been located and their positions had been carefully sketched. Pak showed their placement on a map, and I believed the air force could take them out. There were other matters to discuss, with Chet contributing, but Pak, obviously worn out, insisted on finishing his story, although by the time he came to the end of his recital he was blinking and stumbling over his words. Lim and I had to lean forward to hear what he was saying: how he and Chet had left the village, what they had seen on the way back, and where the ambush positions were along the river and by an anti-tank ditch, until in the dead hours of early morning, they had finally crossed the river and the valley to find safety in our own lines. When he was finally done, Pak shuffled the many papers he had carefully kept dry and looked closely at me.

"There is one other matter, sir, which might be of importance."

"Yes?" I looked at Pak with renewed interest while Lim growled in anticipation.

"Han told me to tell you that the Elder at Namsong-Dong has information for you."

"Namsong-Dong?" I was puzzled, for the village named was much further into enemy territory than Kunwari from where the agents had now returned. "How is the Elder to give this information to me?"

"He says it will be necessary to go to his place to get it. New military installations, apparently. Worth gold, according to him. Hopefully to be paid to his brother in America." Pak handed me a piece of paper.

"Is that so? Well, we've been there before, we can go again. I went there with Lim. But, son, I want you and Chet to get out of here now, have a hot shower and a proper sleep. I must say, I am very proud of you both. Major Hurgaard will be too, that I know. Off you go now, and thanks for everything."

As Lim half-led, half-carried the weary men from the room, I stared unseeing at the mud-packed straw wall in front of me, wondering about a patrol to Namsong-Dong. I turned my face to the ceiling and listened to the rain drumming on the thatched roof. Water which would run down the walls, across the yard into the road, would join the swelling stream in the re-entrant, and foam, yellow and gritty, into the river in the bed of the valley, the same rain that was even now swelling the Samichon River, which I was beginning to fear and did not want ever to make my way across again.

Lim returned and I asked tiredly, "What do you make of what Pak has told us? I am worried that Old Kim was in touch with our house at Kunwari."

The Korean raised his shoulders expressively and let them droop until his hands hung slack at the seams of his wide trousers. "Me too, sir. But regarding Namsong-Dong There is only one way to learn," he said evenly. "Someone must go."

"Yeah, someone." I grinned in a mirthless fashion. "But look, I must get over to Div, and see the Major. Will you grab a couple of ground sheets and bring up the buggy?"

Hurgaard's lips swelled around his cigarette as he leaned back in his chair, his loose green shirt clinging across his shoulders. He inhaled deeply, his cheeks hollowing, etching the darkness of his face in sharp relief. He then spoke, his South African accent sounding pleasant to my ears.

"Well, if this old geezer at this place thinks he's got something, we just have to go and find out what it is. But we cannot send any gold to anyone. Too dangerous, you know? Also, we just don't have the funds." His hand strayed across a large-scale map on his knees, given to him earlier by Tom Woods, his intelligence sergeant. "But what he knows could be of interest at this particular time."

"You mean the peace talks, of course. But do you really think the Chinese want to talk at this time?" It was a subject on many lips. It was said that peace had been discussed diplomatically a long time ago, in 1951 in fact, but General MacArthur not having been informed that peace was being considered, declared publicly that his armies had defeated the Chinese, and they should stop fighting and ask for peace. Humiliated and outraged, the Chinese withdrew from the talks. McArthur a five-star general and a famous and brave soldier, six Silver Stars for gallantry and other awards, including a Congressional Medal of Honour was sacked and removed in disgrace from his command by President Truman, but the fighting went on unchecked. Now, however, there were many rumours of impending peace. I wondered if Hurgaard had something substantial to offer. Given his rank and position in the intelligence community, he should have. "What do you really think, sir?" I wanted to know. "Do the Chinese want peace?"

"They must. We believe the Chinese are suffering at home as well as here, in this land of so-called Morning Calm. Chinese deaths and casualties are enormous and they will have to pay for the huge amounts of war equipment they are getting from Russia. Peace would be very acceptable. They want out of this place. Things are not good between China and North Korea, nor with China and Russia either. China now feels that Stalin tricked Mao into entering into war with America. He urged Mao on, hoping he would be beaten so Russia could move in and take over some of China's mineral and oil rich provinces. Stalin blundered, though, as China, despite its losses, is still in there fighting."

"Mind you, America would not mind ending this bloody mess either, sir," I reminded Hurgaard. "It is reckoned that

American losses amount to more than thirty thousand dead. South Korea has two hundred thousand. Combined North Korean and Chinese, from all causes, is put at over one million plus, dead."

"Yes, they are the rough figures I have heard. For the enemy its only a guess. But the objective of war should be victory, total and complete, like we knew with Hitler. But in the case of Korea, I believe that soldiers and politicians alike would like to shake hands and settle for a more modest objective, like peace with enough honour to make it credible. There is also this Little Switch operating, as you know the exchange of sick and infirm prisoners from both sides. Colonel James is involved in it, somehow. He seems to be mixed up in everything, including what you are doing. Why don't you have a chat with him? But back to this business at Namsong-Dong!" He slapped the map on his knees. "I see it is a few miles north of that other safe house of yours. I'll leave you to get on with planning to get your men there. Contact me later?" Hurgaard reached out and pulled one side of the map across the other and patted the edge down so that it lay flat on his table. I knew he was closing our meeting and shutting out the picture of the rugged country my agents, and probably me, would have to cross to get to that place.

Tom Woods was an old friend of mine and when I had finished with Major Hurgaard I went with him to the divisional sergeants' mess. I was first in and stood for a moment, illuminated in the cone of harsh light from a naked bulb which hung just above the entrance. For a brief cold second I felt isolated and remote from the other occupants of the mess. I suppose it had something to do with the secrecy of the discussion with Hurgaard, and a sinking sensation within me about what I would have to plan, and my involvement in it. Almost immediately, however, my thoughts were scattered as yells of recognition came at me from the gloom beyond the light and I felt slaps of welcome as I took the mug of beer the barman shoved into my waiting hand. They came in ones and twos to greet me to talk and insult me and show in the only way they knew that they were glad to see me. They were good men, tough men, and great to drink with, and the war only twelve miles away probably seemed as remote from them as did their homes in sober moments.

Soon Nobby, excitable and flushed as always, banged his beer-mug on the top of the bar, faced the expectant mess, and we knew he was going to give us his rendition of 'Missus O'Malley'. He strode to the centre of the floor, licked one index finger with an exaggerated gesture and smoothed one eyebrow, patted his ragged hair and stood back to wait for silence. When it came, he raised one foot a few inches from the floor, leaned slightly forward and put his hands close together. In one movement he slammed one foot on the floorboards of the tent, clapped his hands and to his own beat, started to bellow his song, accompanying himself with the reverberations of his hands and feet.

It was a ritual, one of the curious ceremonies which creep into the lives of men in army messes everywhere; it is a fragment of continuity, something dependable when they could rely on so little else. When Nobby came to the chorus he gestured for support and the tent rocked with noise as every man present stamped and bellowed whatever few words of the song he happened to know. The floor bucked and the stove jumped on its base. Bottles clanked together on the shelves, beer-mugs were belted up and down on the thick wooden tables and somewhere in the rear I could hear the wild strumming of a ukulele.

Whatever noise they might make, and whatever actions they might perform, were incidental to the fact that they were made in a bond of noise and bawdy humour. The ritual kept at bay for a while whatever lay in wait for them in the future. For me, it held back the thought of that long patrol to Namsong-Dong, for I had now decided that I must lead the patrol into whatever danger might lay in wait among the tangled hills on the other side of the Samichon, that dividing river.

Chapter Six

The following days passed quickly and, now that we had a mission to plan, the agent detachment took on a new sense of purpose. I had decided that Pak and I would be the two to go, leaving Lim and others in reserve in case something prevented us from leaving. Lim had earlier entered my room, sat hunched on the floor in silence and stared at his splayed toes. I waited until he raised his eyes, knowing what the request would be and saddened that he would be refused.

"You should let me go with you," Lim pleaded, and I experienced a sense of shocked thrill to see the naked devotion in his eyes.

"Can't, Lim." I told him speaking more gently than I had intended. "You are needed here, you know that. I would not even be taking you as far as the river, except for the rope to get us across. But look, we should be heading into Seoul in a few minutes."

Earlier Lim had told me that two of our agents who had returned from a mission some days before, and had since been resting at the detachment, wished to draw their money for the mission and go on leave to Seoul. One was called Old Sobersides while his fellow agent named Soong was a quick, smooth-faced youngster who always managed to look well-groomed, even in the field. They were good agents, these men, the opposites in character and appearance apparently blending together. It was through their work that several large artillery pieces had recently been air-blasted out of existence, and I knew that some troops on our front, had reason to be thankful to them.

"It is some time since they were in Seoul," Lim said, adding with a thin smile. "I think Sobersides had a girlfriend there."

"Good for him," I said. "I guess they deserve all the fun they can get. Can you quickly get the trailer and put in a few beers? Make it a dozen or so cases. Throw in the usual amount of that more expensive booze and some cigarettes. And whatever else you think they may want to sell. Fix them some rations, of course. Enough for a month, is it?"

"Yes. And they will want to come back to us after a month in Seoul. It is an expensive, black market city."

As Lim turned and hurried away, I marvelled, as I often did, at the valuable information I was getting at so little cost. On the inflated black market the sale of whisky, brandy and cigarettes would be enough for our agent sellers to be in good financial shape for many weeks. The brothel-keepers were the buyers who wanted it for soldier customers on leave, anxious to forget the front in drink and fornication, men not apt to quibble over the cost of satisfying their immediate needs.

Sharp at mid day we drove from the detachment, Sobersides and Soong sitting in the back, Lim beside me in the front. With the trailer stacked high with all the things the agents needed, we headed south towards Seoul over dust-choked roads, on through the town of Ui-jongbu and the base units around it, and along the railway line which led directly to Seoul.

Three miles out of Seoul we left the railway behind and as the jeep mounted the last long hill outside the city I was touched as always by the indefinable beauty of the huddle of coloured roof tiles below. It was splashed here and there with white where a few of the roofs had been repaired and newly painted. But the tiles which always drew my attention were glazed and scalloped in intricate designs which recalled a more gracious period in a city now mostly a shambles, having been occupied, abandoned and then occupied again. Its streets were mostly gaping blocks of concrete, and in its centre not one house still stood. A shanty-town of straw and slat-wood was now the heart of Seoul, and vice and filth and hunger were parasites on that weakly beating organ.

Children who should have been starting school darted scrawny-legged among the soldiers hungry and persistent, pleading for money and offering in return the privilege of sleeping with their sisters or mothers. These the thin voices proclaimed in the only English words for which they had found a use had the firm slenderness of film stars, and they would cup their hands over the scrawny chests, and stroke their hips to simulate bodies to which any might buy access for the price of a meal or two. At first they cajoled the soldiers, whose presence they knew with childish wisdom was the cause of their misery and hunger and their sisters' shame and tears. But if ignored they would unleash a flood of un-childlike vituperation and turn away and run after the next soldier with their wares in the hope of staving off for another day the hunger which slept and woke with them.

Late in the afternoon I drove across a slender stone bridge which leapt across one of the water channels outside the city. The houses flanking it narrowed the road dangerously and the air was heavy with the foetid smell from open sewers and the stagnant green water. I turned the jeep off the first intersection to the right and stopped near an old looking iron-studded door which, when opened, gave entry to a clean gravel courtyard and the detachment house where our agents might spend a quiet leave, divorced from curious eyes. As the jeep stopped a wrinkled old man opened the door and called out a cheerful welcome to us.

The gear was soon unloaded and I swung the vehicle around. "I'm going up the road, Lim," I told him. "I'll see you about eight in the morning"

Lim knew that 'up the road' was a special British Intelligence Unit, which Hurgaard had mentioned when speaking of Colonel James and the Little Switch Operation, and while it carried out operations similar to mine, it did so on a much larger basis, for it dropped its agents by parachute into North Korea on special missions and took them off by boat. They were now involved in the Little Switch Operation because they wanted to know exactly which prisoners were held and in which prisoner locations. Colonel James was also responsible for letting me have appropriate and up-to-date identity documents which we carried when out on missions. I wanted to check that my present documents were still in force before we went out again. I also wanted to know if James or his men had any idea if peace was really brewing; if so, I might yet cancel our next operation.

As I alighted from my vehicle outside the administration hut, James, a big man, emerged and waved a meeting.

"Hello there, my Australian sergeant," he called out. "Glad to see you. Matter of fact, we were just talking about you, and up you pop. You staying over night?"

"I'd like to, sir."

"You're always welcome, you know that!" James was a ruddy-faced, strict man and, in the fashion of good intelligence gatherers, very capable. He drew back his shoulders as he began to speak again. "This is a Commonwealth show, so you're doubly welcome. And exactly what can we do for you, now that we have you?"

"I want to check that my identity documents, the ones you supply me with, are in good shape. I'm off for a long walk in a few days. Also, I want to check and see if the men close to this Operation Switch you are involved in believe that peace is near."

"I believe I can answer that, and tell you that peace is still a long way off. But I can let you talk to Captain Shaw, an officer who has been handling things on the legal side. Come with me, will you?"

We began to walk along the side of the drab-looking building, unconsciously falling into soldier-step as we went. "Tell me," James said. "How are things with you and your agents?"

"Just fine. Have you been told that two of my agents, Pak and Chet, got through? That now we're planning a long walk back to a place called Namsong-Dong? Hence my request that you check the papers we will be carrying."

"Yep. I know about that. I also know what you're planning and so I can tell you that before long we might have a stunt that could involve you and your men." James looked about him in a crafty fashion and lowered his voice confidentially. "Strange you should be here checking your documents and asking about that Operation Switch. Because of that we know for the very first time where some of our most senior and important prisoners are being held, and there is a burgeoning plan for a rescue. Because you and your men are getting a long way back undetected, we hope we might be able to get a prisoner out of his camp, walk him down to you, and you then lead him to safety, through the mountains and along that river you keep crossing. You know?"

"Walk a prisoner out?" I believed my tone expressed my amazement of such a plan.

"Yes! Yes!" James sounded impatient and annoyed. "But we cannot rescue anyone and take them out by boat. We might have been able to a few months ago if we had known where the prisoners were being held, but now the west coast is heavily patrolled by ships and we cannot move as once we could, dropping our men in and taking them off by boat. A walk out is the only safe way."

"Safe? But sir, the terrain is tough, a prisoner would be a weak and possibly sick man. It would be a tough ask. We might be able to put him in and rest him in one of my safe houses, but that would be dangerous."

"I know! Your predecessor Lavender never believed them safe at all, and they have been discounted!" He sounded even more impatient than before, but suddenly he smiled. "The other rivers are all deep, the cages men are being held in are a long way back, the mountains are high, the enemy is everywhere. No prisoner has ever escaped, but what a psychological boost it would be if we could pluck one out before this war ends, if ever. But it's just the germ of an idea and, as you might be involved, I trust you enough to tell you now what is going on. That's all, my young friend."

During our conversation we had come to a standstill on a slope outside the unit's mess. The camp around us was bathed in the late afternoon sunshine and the heat of it beat back at us from the wall behind. Vehicles passed up and down the road and men moved singly or in parties about the various missions of camp administration. It all seemed unreal. I a sergeant, standing there in the open with a senior officer, discussing a plan which, if it came to anything at all, would be first the subject of examination and argument by the highest brass behind those closed doors. I was proud that Colonel James, renowned as a close-mouthed officer, should reveal such top-level information to me.

"Come on!" James spoke suddenly, grasped me by the arm and propelled me towards the door of his unit's mess, which was shared by all members of the unit but with a small section set aside for officers. Once inside James pointed to a young officer, a captain, who was sitting comfortably and almost hidden in a big chair. James went over, the officer stood, and James introduced him casually to me as Captain Shaw. I instantly liked his clean look and the strength of his handshake. Shaw and I went to sit at the bar and he told me that his job, in a legal sense, had been an easy one so far, but he had been disheartened by the physical condition of many of the prisoners, none of whom were Australian. Most of those released were amputees who had been roughly treated and Shaw wondered if the doctors had ever been properly trained for such work or if they had gone at it with a hammer and chisel. The majority, though, were just plain sick with diseases, most of which had come from the soil. While we had been talking, darkness had fallen and the interior of the mess was bathed in the glow of several shaded globes. It was warm and safe and comfortable, with the clink of glasses, the muted hum of conversation and the smell of food being prepared, flowing soothingly over my consciousness. Shortly afterwards the gong sounded for dinner and when Shaw invited me to be his guest, we joined the general movement of people towards the long tables where we talked and ate and drank in ease. When, just before midnight, I walked through the silent camp to the tent to which I had been allocated, it was with a feeling of accomplishment and the knowledge that my detachment was recognised for its work, and that, unlikely as it seemed, I might later be involved in a prisoner rescue attempt.

The following morning on my return to the agents' house, I found only Soong and Sobersides, awaiting me in the courtyard. I noticed how guilty and furtive they appeared to be as they awaited me to alight from the jeep.

"Where's Lim?" I wanted to know.

Sobersides moved over to where I was standing and I noticed with surprise when we were face to face that he was sporting what I could only call a bonzer black eye. It was a beauty, of the sort I had never received in the boxing ring of my youth. I asked him what had happened.

"Police have Lim, sir," he volunteered.

"Why? What's up? Come inside and get it off your chest, will you!"

It transpired that after Lim had sold the goods I had brought in as payment for them, Soong and Sobersides went with him to a house on Moon Street that I knew. It was a mean, three-storied, old derelict which stood in the same fashion as its contemporaries: badly lit, sagging with age and ruin. The three agents were in high spirits when they entered, but that soon vanished when Sobersides, mounting the stairs to the second floor two at a time, found his particular and favourite girl busily engaged with another client. Sobersides told me that as the man was small and scared of him, he threw him out of a window naked into the street. Soong cut in to say the man pleaded for his clothes so he threw them out, but into the canal. The naked man then ran about shouting wildly in the street. So the police arrived. Lim hurried to the police and tried to explain what had happened, but someone belted him over the head and he was roughly handcuffed. Sobersides ran to remonstrate with the police and got hit in the face with a truncheon and he ran off. "And that is all there was to it, sir," he concluded.

I had a quick and vague idea that a man with legal training would be of assistance in trying to get Lim released from wherever he might be, and that man should be a soldier, helping to set the south of the country free from the communist north. Captain Shaw was that man, whose experience in Operation Switch must have given him some insight into the official mind, and how bureaucrats worked in this strange country.

An hour later I stood with Shaw in front of a desk occupied by a bulky Korean wearing the maple-leaf insignia of a Police Chief. His thick black eyebrows gave a threatening emphasis to the dark scowl perpetually on his badly pock-marked face.

During the last twenty minutes he had scowled, threatened and sulked, refusing all the time to release Lim. We were speaking in Japanese, with me interpreting for Shaw, when for the tenth time the chief snarled, "No!" However, Shaw was just as insistent, in his mannered British way, that Lim must be released, for what crime had he committed?

What crime? An innocent man's clothing had been stolen and he was forced to run naked through the streets appealing for help. To steal like that is theft. There were injuries to the men who arrested Lim who, even though handcuffed, had fought the police. To fight in that way was assault and what is more, assault of police officers doing their duty. What is even more, this creature Lim was armed with an American pistol, which at this time in a city under martial law was treason. Lim was in deep trouble and we, he said, could not get him out of the mess he had so stupidly made.

Shaw listened closely as I relayed the chief's allegations, then turning to the chief he spoke rapidly and I translated his words. He told the policeman that Lim had not assaulted any police officer and that when he went, in an honest effort to explain what had happened, he was roughed up and handcuffed. Lim carried a weapon because he was an important allied agent under threat from what Shaw called the forces of darkness, and that I as his superior officer insisted that he arm himself at all times. Also, right at this moment Lim was being readied for an important intelligence mission and he must be set free. If the chief would not release Lim, we would have no option but to approach a higher authority, even one as high as the president himself, Mr Rhee, who was our great friend. At the mention of the president the chief for a moment stopped drumming his big fingers impatiently on the top of his desk because Rhee, who had come from America to govern his country, was alleged to be a corrupt and vicious dictator who had ordered the execution of many of his former political enemies. He was now so powerful and wealthy that it was understood he would rule South Korea for years to come. I could see how Shaw obviously understood the way officials stood in fear of any authority higher than themselves, and Rhee, who had swept away many bureaucrats and destroyed those he hated, was a man to be reckoned with. I also understood that the chief was thinking very hard.

"It is most difficult for me to keep order in the city under such circumstances," the chief began, and the tone of his speech and his words caused me and Shaw to exchange a quick glance for we knew he was surrendering. "It is bad enough when common coolies run amok, but when a man like Lim, said to be a man of importance, causes disturbance, it worries me. My men were hurt too, but I know you will be generous with good things for them to drink and American cigarettes."

"That is understood," Shaw said, prepared to play the business out to its inevitable end. "We will make sure the things you want get to your men. We know you are all working for a free Korea. But could you tell me, sir, when will Lim be released?"

"At sundown. He will of course be placed on a bond. It will be discharged when my men receive all the things you have mentioned, their presents."

Shaw waved the condition aside, went to a telephone and spoke to Colonel James. When he was done and we walked from the place, he mentioned that as we had time to fill, he wondered if I could drive him out to see what was called the Old Wall, as he had seen so little of what was historical in the place. I took him on a long drive and on to where the road billowed out into the round about which fronted the Eastern Gate, a square cut sort of arch of triumph which straddled the road into the city, its sharp edges clearly defined against the back drop of a white-clouded sky. We passed under the black shadow of the arch and headed for the ragged looking, blue-tinted hills ahead.

Where the blue edged down the slopes to merge in with a necklace of green foliage, we could see the Old Wall. It followed a wavering line, threading in and out as it crawled along the spurs, topped the ridges and disappeared precipitately into clear cut re-entrants. I drove off the main road and on into the hill-country that led up to the wall: once it started its climb, the jeep began to whine as the track upward took us past small settlements of houses huddled where the sharp ridges of rock softened into flat, farmable tracts. Going on, we passed a few lonely straw roofed hovels which stood in isolation flanked by paddy fields cut out of the mountain slopes so that each house and its fields seemed to be embedded in a natural and lovely cameo of green and grey. At last, we came to the end of the twisting road and the green was replaced by flint-hard rock formations flaked and blackened by the suns and snows of countless centuries. Here I halted the vehicle.

As the rock terraces led up to the Old Wall, Shaw and I climbed up and stared at it, strangely awed by the almost tangible presence of the people who had tried to purchase their safety by hewing protection out of a living mountain. We sat, looking about us. Far below, in a smudge of grey criss-crossed pencil lines of roads, lay the capital Seoul. We stared at it for a long time before Shaw turned to me and exhaled deeply, as a man does when sometimes beauty catches at his heart.

"It's superb," he said very simply and the words conveyed to me everything he felt. "But what a tough people they must have been to come and live here."

"True. Tough but also cruel. Some no doubt like that mongrel bully of a policeman today, and yet a man scared witless when you said we might appeal to old Rhee, a corrupt and vicious man, very much like a former war-lord. I'm really fed up, too, hearing the stories of some of the men I work with. When I get their backgrounds it's a ghastly index of suffering: shooting, rape of young women, destruction of everything they once owned, a fear of the future with communism haunting them. Yet they are such brave men, if I might name a few: blokes like Pak and Chet and Lim."

"Lim?" Shaw cut in. "What about him? You went in batting for him, I must say. What's he really like?"

Keeping to the essentials as we sat comfortably together on that mountain, the story I related to Shaw was one I had heard partly from Lim himself and partly from people who had known him, as it was my job to know as much as possible as the men in my detachment. I had learned it in fragments: a word here, a reminiscence there, sudden confidences in our snug quarters, in dangerous ambush positions, in ruined places behind the enemy lines where just to hear the low voice of a friend was sufficient to keep fear at bay. I did not know the whole story, of that I was sure, but enough to tell Shaw that Lim had grown to manhood under the watchful eyes of the Japanese who had invaded his country years before. At seventeen he was recruited into the Japanese and Puppet Army, whose dream of conquest had already been realised in Mongolia, and they were poised to sweep on to the domination of China. For Lim there followed weary months of hardship and bitter fighting under the command of Japanese and Korean officers, crazed with power and success. He had to watch and endure a senseless reign of terror under the puppet officers, men of his own nation, competing with each other in the invention of cruelty to curry favour with their masters. For it was apparent, in those days, that Japan was a nation to follow and serve in a campaign which was a step in a broad plan as wide as the world.

Although Lim took no part in the terror sown around him, his heart was sickened by the misery he saw and he could do nothing to stop its perpetuation. He could only close his eyes to the cruelty and block his ears to the bedlam of screaming that shivered in every town, in every hamlet and in every home which lay in the path of the invaders: the hoarse animal yells of men, women and children gelded, burned, raped, spitted, gutted, or driven to screeching madness by what their eyes beheld. Lim could not evade the carnage, nor could he stop it. But he did live to escape it before his feelings hardened to indifference and beyond.

It was in a small village whose name I had forgotten that Lim became a warrior. Late one afternoon, on a day when the acrid smoke of burning straw houses hung low among the pines on the hillsides and when the invaders were immersed in a final debauch of drinking and raping before they quit what was left of the village, Lim paused on his way to the river below. It had been his intention to swim there. He had been down to the river on every opportunity since they had been in that place and now, as he passed a part-ruined cottage that he had come to know, his ears were assailed by cries of terrible agony. Lim paused and remembered that in this house he had observed a middle-aged woman who had once peered furtively at him through a narrow wicker gate. Once she had even smiled tentatively at him, and he had smiled back while giving her a courteous greeting in his own tongue.

The screams which had halted Lim rose and trilled, quavering like a demented song, hanging heart-breaking on the air. It was so terrible in its agony that it pierced the lack of interest which Lim had learned, to protect his senses. When coarse roars of laughter sounded above the agony Lim broke into a run, burst through the gateway and found himself in a courtyard ringed by straw dwellings. A heavy pole had been embedded in the earth in the centre of the courtyard and the woman who had smiled at him, had looked at him without terror from her gateway, was tied to it. She was naked, with the brown sheen of her breasts and belly streaked with blood and dirt. She writhed and screamed in a paroxysm of unbearable suffering as she tried frantically to dislodge a flaming piece of wood which had been thrust into her vagina. As he stared terrified at the woman, held immobile at the scene, one of the Japanese soldiers watching moved over and brutally kicked the woman in the face. In a searing rage, Lim with a powerful leap bridged the space between himself and a giggling Japanese officer, wrenched the snub-nosed Nambu pistol from its holster on the man's loose leather belt, and with one continuous motion wheeled and shot at the woman. Her screams ceased, her body stilled. Lim turned the pistol on the gaping officer, then with deadly yet cool haste on the other soldiers who in a struggling and confused knot were trying to reach their stacked rifles. When the firing-pin clicked on the empty magazine Lim, conscious of the shouts of a gathering crowd, made a great leap up to a nearby roof, balanced momentarily on a projecting loose beam, and at a crouch disappeared from view over the thatched huts of the courtyard.

Thus in one action he broke the ties which had bound him in a servitude whose violence he had never understood fully until he had thrown it off. When the invaders moved on they unknowingly left Lim in the safety of a resistance movement which was being nurtured from the wholesale brutality of the Japanese march into Manchuria. In the months which followed when he served that movement, and after on his return to Korea, he knew enough fear, excitement and achievement to fill many lives. When he eventually made his way back to his own country, the Second World War was over, so he went, hesitant but hopeful, on his way back to the north where he had been born, only to find that the Russians now ruled his country. They had moved in when they defeated the Japanese in Manchuria and propaganda, not force of arms, was their weapon. They preached a sort of brotherhood which was easy to believe in but meant enslavement. Lim was distressed to see that most of his people were accepting this new faith headed by Kim Il-sung, whom Lim distrusted because he regarded him as a man created from zero with a limited education. He was also an imposter with a heavily embellished guerrilla record. So Lim moved to the south which was under American supervision and in June 1950 when Kim Il-sung's forces invaded the south Lim fought against his own people. He was promoted to junior officer rank, fought in a number of hard battles and was decorated for gallantry. He was also badly wounded and was eventually interviewed by the British warrant officer Lavender, who was to set up the agent detachment I now commanded with Lim as my senior agent. I told Shaw that I believed Lim had been used sternly in war, both in his own country and in Manchuria, but with Lavender and me he was finding something of the fulfilment he had begun to seek in that village by a river somewhere in Manchuria, so long ago.

Dusk was beginning to throw its long shadows when Shaw and I entered a bare and cold waiting room at the police station. But I felt happy enough; I had passed a few pleasant hours with Shaw and Lim was to be released. I smiled to think of the anecdotes which Lim would probably relate about his term in the cells, and I looked up with a ready smile as I heard a noise a door nearby. But any pleasure I felt vanished when I saw Lim, for he was in a pitiable state. His puffed face was a mass of purpled bruising over which his hair hung lanky and clotted with blood and filth. He stumbled toward me, trying to speak, almost crying through his split and cracked lips.

"Lim…" I stretched out a hand and circled Lim's shoulders with my free hand. "What have they done?"

"Arrh! Arrh!" Lim groaned, "My back!"" He straightened up with difficulty and fixed me with a stare. "For every blow," he whispered, "I, Lim, will punish six. When Lim is well, the scum in here will be afraid, even in pairs, to walk the dark streets of Seoul at night."

"Jesus! I'd like to flatten that big, ugly bastard! That so-called Chief." I snarled, starting impulsively towards the closed door.

"No. Take it easy." Shaw laid a hand coolly on my arm. "If your so-called ugly bastard hadn't known he would get away with beating Lim, he wouldn't have done it. You can't do a single thing about it now."

"Can't do anything? D'you think….?"

"Yes, I do think," Shaw said impassively, "which is why I'm telling you to let the matter drop. Even from my brief time here I know this beating of people by those in control is a custom of this country, rather like eating rice. As a matter of fact, you can take what I say as an order: no more trouble here. Let's get out of this place. Come on!"

I caught his gaze and held it for a moment, anger boiling in me, but I knew Shaw was right, even if he had to pull rank on me to make his point.

"You're right," I said. "But I reckon this place, as you call it, is a fucking whore-house!" Without another word I turned and led Lim out of the chilly room.

We stopped in the car park and I raised Lim's thick woollen shirt from his back and almost dropped it in amazement when I saw the cuts and dried blood which marred the smooth muscles.

I heard Shaw behind me suck in his breath while Lim groaned anew.

"Rifle butts," he explained. "They made me kneel with a sharp board here." He pointed to the back of his legs behind the knees. "And they beat me. Many of them belted me, with rifle butts and boots. They kicked me."

"Why?" It made no sense to me.

"I was mistaken to carry my pistol into town, I admit that. I must be getting old and silly. But having the pistol, they said I must be Lim, and that I do intelligence work. They tried to find out exactly who I work for, where is our detachment, what success we have. They particularly wanted to know the names of the other two with me, not because they caused trouble tonight, but if they were with me, then they must also be of some security interest."

I stood immersed in thought, remembering that in this North-South war of brother against brother intrigue was rife, and the sentiments of few could be trusted. I knew that in Seoul in particular, many families kept two flags, flying them according to whichever army was in occupation. Perhaps the knowledge of any agent or intelligence formation would be invaluable to a police chief, if and when the armies changed again. Or perhaps he was merely a bullying thug or a sadistic animal who had to know the secrets of all luckless enough to come his way.

"Did you tell them anything at all, Lim?"

"I would not speak even if it had meant death to me," Lim replied contemptuously. "But as you know, sir, I have been through far worse than they would have had the brains to contrive."

"As I thought," I said, to Shaw who had been standing aside. "Shall we go and get Lim fixed up, sir?"

"Certainly. Let's get him some pain killers!" Shaw's mobile mouth moved into half a smile and he moved to help Lim gently into the back of the vehicle. "Let's get you to the hospital, old man," he said. "Get that busted-up back of yours X-rayed. Easily, now."

At the hospital, a converted warehouse in what had once been a crowded area of the city, I left Lim in the charge of a medical officer to whom I made it known that the best of medical treatment he could supply would be greatly appreciated. As we left, Shaw turned to place his arms about Lim and urged him to get well quickly. The medical officer looked on with an air of some disbelief and stared hard at the badges of rank on Shaw's shoulders, as if to convince himself that this man was an English officer.

Together we walked into the night, boarded our jeep and I took Shaw back to his camp before turning to go back for Soong and Sobersides.

Chapter Seven

By the time Lim returned to our agent's headquarters, showing little outward evidence of his ordeal but a few more scars on his face, all was in readiness for the mission to Namsong-Dong. Stores had been packed and were ready to shift, the route in and out minutely examined and committed to memory even though Pak and I had made the journey once before. It was all part of the preparation for the danger ahead and now we awaited only a dull night when the moon would rise late in the sky, a fragment of light, unable to show clearly the hill and valleys of any hostile ground we would have to cross. I thought of that scene, the panorama which I could see if I turned around and looked out of the window of my room: the valley, the river, the lacerated hills in which the enemy lived and patrolled. As I envisioned it, a small but dark cloud appeared and spread rapidly until it overhung the entire scene.

    I jerked my pack from where it lay on the floor, and strode out into the courtyard and after a few rough handshakes and advice, our jeep moved off with Lim driving, me beside him and Pak in the back with our gear. At the headquarters site of the forward battalion I was to pass through, some miles of yellow dust roads and two large rivers away from my detachment, I alighted from the jeep and ran up a steel staircase of empty ammunition boxes which had been firmly morticed into the earth. At the top of the boxes I entered a brown mud-smeared tent and as I appeared in the door way an officer looked up from his paper-cluttered desk and nodded.

    "Sergeant," he welcomed me. "Major Hurgaard said you

would be here about this time. You want our patrol policy for tonight, right? Sit here, will you?"

"I'd like to have a look at it, sir,"" I seated myself on a camp-stool beside him. "Don't want to get shot at by the goodies."

"No, you don't. But we've only got one group going out later this evening. Here." He leaned across his table and his fingers traced a route across a map on the table. Then he asked, "Will that affect you at all?"

"No. We expect to be over the river by then. As you know, we have to make it across the valley and the river before the Chinese get their patrols out."

"Of course. Word is out for our gunners, and especially for the tanks, to belt a few shells across at that time. Just to make everyone keeps heads down. But be careful. We all wish you well."

"There are three of us going to the river. One will be returning early in the morning. He is going out to get us across. Please have your blokes be careful as he comes back in."

"We have been well briefed by your Major Hurgaard. And, as I say, we do wish you well."

When the time came to move off, dusk had filled the valley with the luminous opacity of shadow and mist and I knew that for each of us waiting there our world extended no farther than the dim sight of a companion's back and the sour smell of our sweat. When we went on our course across the valley the three of us were tenuously linked only by our common purpose and our thoughts of caution and silence, even though it was a sometimes noisy world through which we travelled. From the rear a big gun sometimes roared, a machine-gun began to mutter and the slow sigh of a mortar bomb could be heard as it arched along above us in a whisper of sound. I was thankful to that officer who had said he would keep a few enemy heads down. It was keeping ours down as well, but we kept pressing onward. We were hidden by the darkness and the mist while the voice of war reached across to prompt us, it we needed any such reminder, of why we were there, creeping across the valley to the bank of a river which was our final safe boundary. Beyond it lay a massed enemy and a possible death.

We halted near a gnarled old tree, the same one we always used as a crossing point. Here we squatted, searching the gloom while Lim unwound the knotted nylon rope from about his body. He spoke to me and I reached out and took one end. I tied this about my waist, then, in a motion of deep friendship I shoved out both my hands to grasp both of Lim's broad shoulders, whispered a goodbye, and stepped down the steep bank and into the river. I shivered as I stepped into the cold water. I crossed quickly just as I had done many times before and soon Pak joined me. On a jerk of the rope from me, Lim hauled it back over the river and once in the cover of the brush, a few yards from the water's edge, Pak and I sat down and removed our footwear. We squeezed the cold water from our socks and replaced them, tied up our boots, checked our weapons once more, stood up and continued our advance, all without uttering a word. We moved with infinite care. When a thick bank of foliage or a crooked overhanging branch or a rounded boulder stopped our way, Pak or I crouched on our knees, exploring with our hands the nature of the ground over which we would have to proceed.

After a couple of hours of this torturous progress we were forced to rest. The air in the confines of the thick scrub was warm and close and the nagging weight of our packs, constantly becoming entangled in the undergrowth above and on either side of us, wore us out. We sank onto the ground and retired each into our own personal lair of exhaustion and anxiety, our heads drooping wearily over our hunched knees. I sucked on a dry piece of wood, my eyes closed, the drag of my pack burning into my spine.

When the sweat on my body began to cool and stiffen, we moved on. I at times leaned back and touched Pak who would take the lead position, assuming responsibility for finding the least dangerous route through the brush. Except that the darkness began to thin and that my weariness had increased to the point where my muscles screamed for release from the strain of tensed and wary movement, time ceased to exist for me. It was almost with surprise that, on hearing a whispered caution from Pak, I looked up and saw three soldiers in Chinese uniform silhouetted against the sky on the first anti-tank ditch. Dawn could not be far away.

After the river, the ditch was the second major obstacle in our way. We crouched side by side in a leafy recess and watched as the soldiers paced up and down on the lip of the ditch. They remained there for some time before turning to patrol back away from the river and towards the hills their armies had occupied months before. Pak and I went forward, our progress easier but countered by the need for even greater caution in the thinning darkness. The flat pistol crack of a snapped twig could halt us motionless for minutes, wanting to run, almost afraid to breathe, until the imagined reverberations of the sound died away.

We continued our slow walk until we reached the right-hand edge of the huge ditch, big and deep enough to stop any tank even a sixty-ton British Centurion, I reckoned. We craned our heads forward and peered into the blackness of the opening which, in my fevered imagination at least, might hide more than a hundred Chinese soldiers. I could not tell if any were close and there was only one way to find out. I was first to go across the wide mouth of the trap, with Pak hurrying on my heels. We halted together at the far end, breathing noiselessly but deeply, plagued by insects which, attracted by the stink of our sweat, hovered and attacked in the stillness about us.

Now that we had crossed the river and the ditch and done it so easily, I almost felt our mission was over. That was for a moment only and the quick elation died, stillborn beneath the smothering tide of apprehension and worry of the menace of our surroundings which immediately reoccupied my mind. We were still on the first leg of our venture, still in the first few hours of a term which could encompass many days and nights of peril and discomfort before Pak and I could once more cross the Samichon to that gnarled old tree and the safety of our own lines.

We crept through the thicket with my mind moving restlessly through the accumulated experience of past patrols, seeking for guidance on this present undertaking. All the time one part of my consciousness remained sensitive to every footfall, every swish of every branch as I passed it, every cry of the night birds and the constant mutter of the faraway guns, some I knew firing directly over the country we were now passing through. Pak suddenly halted, bringing my thoughts tumbling back, like beleaguered forces to a breach in the wall.

"Ambush position about fifteen minutes from here," he told me.

"Good man. I thought it was a bit further on. We're making good time. But if it's that close, let's rest up here for the coming day." I moved to my right, worming deeper into the dense undergrowth until, in what seemed to be the heart of the cover, I squatted down. Pak came to join me and we both hunched our weary frames into tight bundles and soon Pak's breathing took on the regulated rhythm of exhausted sleep. Misty rain began to fall, I shivered where I sat, my ears alert to any noise, my eyes roving the gloom. I envied Pak's swift escape into sleep but was comforted to know that he trusted me so completely as to instantly find sleep. I wondered again about Pak's background and the equally harsh backgrounds of so many Koreans I now lived with. As I did so, my mind embarked on one of its favourite excursions: in an instant I had crossed the sea and the mountains and stopped at that lovely stretch of water, the Murray River at Buronga. I saw so many stars and those huge silver eucalyptus which the white people must have admired when they settled there. I also saw the hessian shanties on the ridge, particularly the one Martin had built with pine uprights stuck in the sand, wrapped all about with bag and covered with galvanised sheeting. I saw Mary and went under the rickety veranda to knock on her front door. It remained closed although I knocked very hard. The sullen rumble of a big gun firing from miles away broke my vision and I shook my head, shivering as water trickled down the front of my shirt. I glanced at my watch and started guiltily. Two hours had passed. Surely I couldn't have dropped off? I shook Pak gently and without a sound or a movement, he was awake beside me, as instantly and completely as when he had fallen asleep.

"You sleep, sir." Pak told me and I curled my body into a tight ball on the wet ground. I rested, my head on my arms until I sank into a fitful slumber which brought me once more to the closed front door of my grandmother's place. I saw her red coloured geraniums blossoming like hard-won trophies against the sagging walls and although I knocked on the door, just like before, it would not open, probably because both my grandparents had died years previously. I stirred, then slept, knowing that Pak was watching beside me.

I was awakened by the coldness of the dawn and I stirred, embracing my knees. A glance at Pak revealed that he was wide awake. I grinned at him, then sat thinking about the Elder at

Namsong-Dong, a venerable sort of man known to me as Old Kim. He had an outstanding command of the Japanese language but a hatred for what the Japanese had done to his country during their long years of occupation. When they were driven out in 1945 and a triumphant Russian Army moved in to occupy North Korea, Old Kim hoped that life would return to what it had been in his youth, but for reasons initially incomprehensible to him he was accused by the Russian NKVD of being a rapacious land owner, an exploiter of the peasant, a person whose elder brother had gone to America for schooling. This at a time when the Japanese were in control of Korea meant that his family must have co-operated with their enemy. Yes, Old Kim was an evil man. As he had told it to Lim, who in turn confided the story to me, it was at the end of a long day of horror that he stood in a daze of grief and fear, listening to the people of his own village, urged on by other village elders, calling for his death; but some were people, he said, to whom he had given sweetmeats when they were children and golden persimmons from over one of his orchard walls. Despite all that, as he stood in a shallow ditch just outside the boundary of the lands which had once been his, almost every male and female member of his clan lay dead in blood and dust and filth. He knew finally that only his youngest son Kim had survived. His life was spared when a senior Russian officer discovered that a number of villagers, hoping that they could be allocated his huge property, had concocted some evidence against him. He told Lim how he had sunk to his knees, a stream of blood caked over his face, his one pure white robe dark-stained with refuse when he was told that his life had been spared.

My recollection shifted as bugles and whistles sounded from several points about us, for the dawn that had come to our bushy hideaway had also aroused the enemy. Day was upon us and with it the dangers which attend the light. Almost at the same moment, as if each of us had been prompted by the same instinct, we reached out and began to cover our bodies with dried leaves and twigs, not so as to cover the body entirely but just enough to break up the outline of a person lying prone.

As the sun rose higher, Pak fumbled about in his pack and took out a cloth-wrapped parcel of thick rice cakes which had been sprinkled with chopped meat and herbs. He passed a portion to me and we savoured the taste while taking water from our canteens. It was our sustenance for the day; towards evening would we eat again. As the sun climbed we dug hip-holes of sorts and dozed in warm contentment in the heat of the sun until I was suddenly jerked into wakefulness by a loud noise. I glanced inquiringly at Pak who nodded at me. We listened and it came again: there was no doubt it was laughter, as incongruous in that quiet yet menacing place, as can-can music in a cathedral. We both peered through the brush with our field glasses and saw two men laughing and splashing in the shallows of the river about one hundred yards away. Another Chinese, closer to where we lay, clambered down the bank of the river and began to wash his face. He lay prone, then drank deeply from the running water before standing to relieve himself at the very spot where he had just drunk. He then glanced up and down the river before disappearing from my view. Well, I thought, if the buggers are swimming and piddling in the open, they must reckon no one is about, watching them.

Four days of hiding in the undergrowth and three nights of making our way over escarpments and depressions to the north had passed; we had quit the watercourse to evade an ambush position set along the bank of the river and kept as often as possible to what we hoped were unguarded mountain trails. During our patrol a number of artillery shells had pounded the hills about as the nightly business of war, of confining our enemy to his pits and trenches, was under way. Both Pak and I understood we were safe enough from any bombardments for they were a pre-arranged fire pattern, designed to keep the shells away from our area of operations and to keep the enemy confined if possible.

During the day when we were hiding, the sun had been hot, the oppressive air hung heavily over us, sapping our energy while we waited, often dry-throated, in low timber. Apart from draining our energy, the heat left us wet and stinking but there was consolation in that we were getting close to our destination. The next walk would bring us close to the mountain range overlooking Namsong-Dong and the home of Old Kim. We pushed ahead, finally going down from the high ridge until our descent was halted at the raised edge of a paddy field which indicated that the village was close. We lowered ourselves into the squared area of land and felt our way across the hard furrows. At the far end we scrambled over to drop into a narrow ditch which paralleled a faintly discernible stretch of road. At last! We had arrived at the further-most limit of our mission, the path that led to the main intersecting roads of the village. The home of Old Kim, once the largest in the village of which he had once been the wealthiest man, lay separately at the end of the place, hemmed in by many paddy fields.

We followed the ditch for some time, crawling in the mud on hands and knees, until I heard a sound up ahead. Raising my head to peer cautiously over the lip of the ditch, I ducked back with a hiss of alarm to Pak. I saw two dim shapes on the road and heard the grating of their boots as they moved along. We grasped our weapons, waiting, each of us congealed in his own personal mould of fear: we resented that fear and hated the mud in which we knelt. But we knew that if we wanted to get out of the danger we were in, we would just have to stink and wait in the mud, simply bearing it. The *slap-slap* of the footsteps came closer, sounding clear as they neared us. Coming close enough to sprinkle a shower of light gravel down onto the back of my neck and hands, the soldiers passed without speaking and receded into the gloom. Pak and I moved again, *slush, slush,* hand and knee, *slush, slush.*

We halted when we came to a culvert which ran under the road and I turned to Pak, indicating that we would have to go under the road, with him leading. He went ahead, squeezing his small body into the opening, forcing a way through. When I wedged my way in, following Pak, the muck in the bottom of the culvert stank horribly and a threaded maze of cobwebs, left by Pak's passing, clung to me in a revolting way. Gritting my teeth and cursing obscenely beneath my breath, I went on until I was at the far end of the tunnel. There I drank deeply of the clean, fresh air.

The danger of the intersecting roads had been passed and Pak, as had been planned, left me just outside the culvert in the ditch. Silent as a weasel, he disappeared in the direction of Old Kim's place. In a surprisingly short space of time, he returned, looming soundlessly above me as if by magic. He led me to the front door of the house which opened protesting in a squeal of wet timber. Pak went forward and I followed him, feeling the movement of tatami matting beneath my feet. 'We've made it!' I thought and elation filled my chest close to bursting, flooding away the memory of the journey in and the realisation that there still remained the long and hazardous walk back to our own lines.

Suddenly a hand reached out from nowhere and felt my arm. I pulled back but a whispered word from Pak reassured me, saying it was Old Kim.

"Lao Kim?" I queried, using the honorific. "My boots are

filthy on your tatami. Forgive me."

"You are a thoughtful man," Old Kim complimented me. "You have come on a long and dangerous journey and you honour my home. You and Pak are doubly welcome here. Come with me. Rest now. Later we will talk."

Old Kim then led me forward but I ducked as I cracked my head on the top of a door. I spat a curse in Japanese and for some reason repeated it in English. Suddenly I was in another room, my whispering companions close behind me. For a moment all movement ceased and even the sound of restrained breathing died away. The darkness was then shattered by the scraping of a match followed by a flash of fire transferred to a large candle. The light of the candle lit a bending old man, with a pleasant face topped with a mass of white hair. Old Kim looked just as he was when I had first met him some months previously. He was, I thought, elderly but ageless.

"Time has been kind to you," I complimented him.

"And to you also," he smiled. "But as you say, you are dirty. Come now, you and Pak, to my humble bath. I will give you clean robes and prepare a meal for you. Then we can talk, briefly. Later I will prepare beds for you both. Then you can sleep safely here for many hours."

Pak and I later sat at a low table with Old Kim and his son, introduced to us as Young Kim, although I guessed he was in his forties. The food was good; in fact, compared with the food we had eaten in the past four days, it was scrumptious. A thin pungent soup, thick glutinous white rice, kimchi, that peppered dish of beef which is served on every Korean table and green vegetables. Lastly we drank hot tea from thick small cups. Then we talked. Old Kim, always seeking information that might be useful to Lim, whom he had first met when Tony Lavender had recruited him into his agent network, told us that he always gave the impression that he was friendly to the Chinese soldiers serving in his area. He often had them in to drink, to smoke, sometimes to eat, and he had learned that the Chinese were deliberately stalling their peace talks so that they could take the feature called The Hook. They were building up war supplies and massing troops in this area. Many new divisions had arrived and his son had identified most of the new regiments about the place.

This was first-class information and, if accurate, would be graded A1 because The Hook was a feature on which the enemy had lost thousands of lives. It was the springboard to the gateway to Seoul, a small hill manned by stubborn English and Australian soldiers with New Zealand artillery in support who had refused to be budged from a thorn which for so long had needled the enemy. The Hook was in fact the only Allied held mountain feature over The Samichon and north of the 38th Parallel: similarly, it was the southernmost point of advance reached by the Chinese Armies. It barred the road to Seoul and the Chinese wanted it to honour the way their armies had fought and died in desperately attempting to win that hill. They now allegedly did not want peace until that goal was won.

Several times they had almost succeeded, but casualties, lack of supplies, and the stark ferocity of the defenders had always beaten them. Still, never forgotten and always feared by the Allied commanders, there was the possibility that if the enemy could stock pile huge stores of war like materials, then the sheer weight of added fire power and men might swamp the defenders and let loose a ravening flood to pour southwards. And what a good position that would be if peace negotiations should come after that Chinese win on the battle-field!

I told Old Kim that his information was first-class and certainly worth travelling to him to hear. He went on to explain that as a charcoal gatherer he had been able, along with his son, to climb many of the hills and big ranges about his home and they knew the location of most of the important storage areas. He suggested that Pak with his son should go the following day and record the exact positions of those dumps if our aeroplanes wished to destroy them. He then asked if Pak had the necessary identification and ration cards which all civilians in North Korea had to carry. By way of answer Pak felt in his jacket for his waterproof wallet. He flipped open the lid of the pouch and took out four cards which he passed to Old Kim who examined them closely in the candle flame. He pronounced them to be very good, praise due to Colonel James and his special unit in Seoul which specialised in printing such cards while making sure the details were all current and would pass inspection.

I noticed that Pak's head was beginning to droop and Old Kim with a compassionate glance at him quit the room. He returned with two thick quilted blankets which he spread nearby on the tatami matting. He indicated that he and his son would be on the alert in the case of any untoward happening. Both men bade us good night and left us alone. I lay down with Pak and he was asleep almost instantly. I leaned out across the low table near me and extinguished the candle noticing that the first glimmer of the awakening day, with thin greyness, was beginning to soften the night's gloom. I lay back comforted. We had arrived and all was well.

The following morning after a quick breakfast of congee rice mixed with a special meat and dough Pak busied himself changing into ragged black trousers and coat, left over garments of Young Kim. I watched as he tugged the coat over his lean shoulders and with an air of studied bravado hitched his trousers a little higher and went with Young Kim to where two A-shaped wooden carrying frames leaned against the house wall; each gathered a frame and disappeared in the direction of the nearby hills. There was nothing I could do but await Pak's return and hopefully get some news and information from Old Kim about what was happening, as far as he knew, in North Korea.

He knew among other things that the Chinese volunteers, as they were called, who had entered North Korea as friends found they were not welcome and their battle victories and the way they had pushed the Americans and the South Korean armies out of North Korea in late 1950 was never applauded or accepted. The North Koreans claimed that under their beloved Kin Il Sung, they alone had chased the invaders out of their country and the Chinese armies had simply rendered some assistance. The huge number of Chinese dead and wounded was never mentioned in radio or press.

Old Kim also told me that the Chinese hated the cruel way the North Koreans treated their captured and wounded men. The shooting through both hands of prisoners, their imprisonment and starvation, their freezing to death in winter in miserable camps under malicious commandants and sadistic guards, their being dragged away to execution. There was great friction between the two armies with much mistrust and bitterness. I mentioned the case of a captured American colonel shot down over North Korea. He was the most senior American pilot captured and the Chinese were desperate to interrogate him about American air strategy and developments about which such a senior man would have knowledge. It happened that the American was sitting in his cell waiting to be interrogated when a top North Korean general entered his cell: a small self important man, dressed in splendid gear, with polished boots and accessories including a red scarf, a confection of medals and honours, and a polished cane. He expected the prisoner to leap to his feet and stand in rigid attention but the American simply sat and looked in mild amusement at this visitation. In response, the insulted general had a placard hung around the American's neck saying that as an airman he had confessed to dropping biochemical agents in North Korea; anthrax and cholera germs had been spread and many parts of the country were devastated. The general then ordered the prisoner to be dragged out into the street where a crazed mob beat him to death. When the Chinese interrogators arrived to talk to the American they were handed a bloodied, broken corpse. Old Kim said he had heard of this and that later the general concerned had another medal pinned on his chest by the president.

I needled Old Kim further and noted his replies, for I knew that information was of great value. It was exploited in the unending psychological warfare which was being waged in the civilian and soldier alike, being disseminated by pamphlet, by front-line broadcasts, and by microphone from circling aeroplanes. And if the information was true, how much greater would be the value and the impact on the listener. What was not true were the claims that American pilots were engaged in biological warfare, and if it could be shown that an innocent man was dragged out into a dusty street, allegedly for being engaged in that warfare when the case had never been proved against him, so much the better.

Thinking yet again of the hardships the Korean people had known for years past, I felt a sudden well of companionship that made me, for a brief moment almost revere Old Kim. His white hair, his lined, patient face, the quiet way he smoked from his long, thin pipe, all spoke of some inner strength that engendered trust. He had suffered greatly and even as I spoke to him in Japanese I had to accept it was a language he had been forced to learn. From what I knew of this old man it must have been a time of bitter schooling. So it was that when he asked hopefully if his brother would be rewarded for the good intelligence he was providing, I could only say that I hoped he would be well compensated.

That evening after Pak and Young Kim had returned from a long day in the hills, and had washed and eaten, we sat together with a field map on the low table, transferring the day's intelligence to marks on the paper. All the supply dumps dug into tunnels and camouflaged, the guns protecting them, the hidden barracks and quarters for soldiers were scribbled and pencilled in at Pak's direction. Almost an hour passed before the job was finished, and Pak and I looked down on the map with satisfaction.

"Good!" I exclaimed. "Now we can get out of here. It's too dangerous to wait any longer. We have all the information we need."

"I would like to get away, sir." Pak confessed. "There are many soldiers about, too many for comfort."

"Yes." I grinned at Old Kim and he smiled in return, knowing that secrecy was paramount in this curious war of ours.

Pak and I left the safe house late that night. This time we did not have crawl in mud or burrow under a culvert, for Young Kim showed us the way along a secure mountain track, and there he left us. Moving fast we made our way along a high crest, halting at intervals until we felt safe and rested. Although peaceful, the place was bunker cut and had apparently been fought over during that period of the war when such positions changed every few days. Now the war was static and armies were dug in on other ranges of hills many miles to our south where neither side could attack because defence was imperative. As I looked over this old battlefield I wondered if the Chinese would really attack The Hook in great force as suggested by Old Kim, merely to straighten their defensive lines.

We waited until nightfall, sitting near old bunkers and trenches, dusty and long disused, and I wondered about what sort of battles had once been waged in such a brooding spot. The trees, the rocks, the very clods of earth could tell of men who had died in their efforts to storm the hill, forcing the defenders from the crests, and of those who had stayed to fight and were wounded or killed in that defence. It was a quiet, lonely and to me in a way, a lovely place. But here, men had once waited, tense and fearful, for the shock of cannon bursting into the ravaged earth in prelude for a massed attack; they just had to sit it out, then fight, for there was no place to run.

We hid in an old bunker during the day, speaking little, each occupied with his own thoughts, then with darkness we moved on again. In places, sharp fir cones and the coarse boles of trees hindered our searching hands and feet. In other places, large rocks with little sand and shale covering afforded scant security for our footsteps but we struggled on, a star and a south bearing our only signposts. We stumbled and fell on occasion, cursing and miserable, our clothing torn, our muscles bruised, our only comfort being our companionship. Pak truly was my friend and supporter that night, my brother-in-arms.

During the day we slept in turns, the air about us still, and even the annoying small insects were injected with drowsiness to the point where a feeling of security seemed to cloak us all around. That was until we were both jerked rudely awake, shocked and wondering, as we heard the nearby blast of a gun. We stretched cautiously to our knees to see three Chinese soldiers and a Korean in civilian clothing advancing toward us. Two of the soldiers had shotguns and as the Korean hills abound with pheasants, their intention was obvious. They were out looking for birds to shoot, but if we were not very careful I knew they would certainly shoot us instead. Pak and I looked at each other and nodded: a pity, but there was no place for us to hide. We had the element of surprise and all we had to do now was use it cunningly. "You take the one on the left," I whispered to Pak. "I'll get the one on the right. Get rid of the gunmen first, then the others. You left again, me right. Got that?"

Pak nodded grimly. We eased our safety catches forward and waited. The hunters were still down near the bottom of the hill but only forty yards or so from where we were hunkered down watching. They worked up slowly, fanning the tall grass about them and occasionally the sound of a voice drifted up towards us. They were closer now. One was whistling carelessly and I was about to kill him. The other man, the one with the second shot gun, spoke loudly in Chinese, *"Che li mei yo!"* "There's nothing here", he commented.

"Not bloody much!" I growled to Pak. After so much stooping and slinking and crawling about and being scared for a lot of the time, the prospect of action now almost thrilled me to the point of forgetting the known consequences of revealing our presence. I felt the muscles of my thighs and stomach tense in what I was surprised to recognise as eagerness. "You silly buggers," I thought, "I'll give you pheasant hunting! Don't you know there's a bloody war going on?"

The soldier who had been whistling stopped the tuneful notes he was making and started searching about in his pockets, meanwhile balancing his weapon. He was standing so close to us now that I could see the red-and-white cigarette packet he finally extracted from his pants. I knew from experience it was that beautifully painted Picasso dove with the Chinese letters *Ho Ping*, meaning 'Peace' written boldly across it. The smoker lit his cigarette and with his companions turned left; they all casually walked away from us.

I gazed incredulously through the tall bars of grass confronting me, feeling exalted, amazed, distracted by this macabre change of events. I had looked at death on the battlefield before, but this was different. I felt cheated yet relieved as I continued to watch the retreating backs of the hunters for several seconds. Then I turned to look at Pak and I could not tell whether he was relieved or pleased; he had missed a killing but he had not run the risk of being killed in return. I put the safety back on my gun, placed it in the ground nearby and settled back in the grass. Feeling less secure now, I was just dozing off when Pak came crawling up to me. As he got into position beside me he looked me full in the face and asked very quietly. "I have been told you speak Chinese, sir. I know you speak Japanese, as you do with all of us, but where did you learn your Chinese?"

"I did an army course in Australia for a year."

"What is it really like there?"

We spent a long time there in the grass, watching for the enemy, while I told Pak about part of my life in Australia. I understood from Pak's question that he had been more shocked than I thought about our experience with the hunters and he was now seeking some reassurance from me, some re-affirmation that I would get him out of trouble, because I was equipped to do so. I went on then to relate that growing up in the Australia of the 1930s had been tough but we had never known invasion, pestilence or the terror this land, this Korea, had known for so long. We had sent our men off to fight wars, but it had always been on other land, never ours.

I told Pak something about the life I had known on the Buronga Ridge with its bag shanties: how I had worked on the forge with my grandfather, had been on a milk run, had worked on the vineyards with my mate Clarrie, had fished in the Murray River with the old professional, Shoofty, and how we had once caught the Big Feller, that legendary fish which inhabits all great rivers. As big as a whale, as sagacious as Moses, king of the river, older than the first settlers and even the Aborigines, he'd been half-caught a thousand times and talked over on fishing trips all up and down the long waterway. Even people who never got to within cooee distance or feel of him, still claimed some close acquaintance. But Shoofty at last, caught him on one of his heavy cross-lines which spanned the river at several spots. They had been baited with witchetty grub, once sought after by the Aborigines when they had lived in tribes scattered along the waterway. Having landed him at over eighty pounds he was the biggest old cod ever taken from the river. Shoofty stared at the prize we had struggled so hard to land for a long time, and I guessed he was sorry to think that never again would he think about his cross-line, and wonder about that catch, now dead by his boat. In his death the Big Feller had taken a huge slice of the river's history with him, Shoofty's too. And mine as well, I remembered, as I related it to Pak that day.

I told Pak about how Enzio Clemenza had arrived in Buronga from his native Italy and the way I had picked grapes on the his property, land he had taken up along the river where he had grubbed out a place for his vines. The soil he first worked was so poor that some of the locals said he would never make it but he did and what was more, he gave me a wonderful farewell party when I enlisted. I remembered the people invited clustering about the glowing barbeque pits, shielding their faces and arms while sawing of portions of the juicy meat they most fancied. The place was fragrant with the fat of a whole pig and a sheep being cooked over glowing coals of Murray River wattle.

When I ran out of anything more to say, Pak was silent for a long time. Then he said very quietly, "Could you describe again the smell you said came from that pig and a sheep being cooked?"

Nothing more came to disturb us for the remainder of the day and when darkness came we felt safe enough to move on again. We left the low area and made our way up into the higher hills, hopefully divorced from sight or sound of our enemy. At about midnight we encountered a telephone wire which ran from the crest of the hill we were advancing along down somewhere into the valley. Pak was in the lead at the time and he motioned me forward and showed me the wire. We both knew we were above the Samichon River, about four miles from our crossing place by the old tree with only the tank trap and the river itself remaining to be crossed. I wanted to be over by dawn of this very day.

We went on resting and walking until my watch showed four o'clock, and then with the silence of long practice we moved downwards. The descent was easy enough but as we continued, friendly artillery began smashing into the hills to our right and I understood that Major Hurgaard and I were right on schedule. He knew that we should be moving in and that the only relatively safe way out for us was through this valley and along the river which followed the lowest portion of the landmass. Occasionally the whine of a near shell made us crouch into pockets of earth until the threat was gone. We moved on until I heard the river, the most dangerous area on our way back. We crossed the face of anti-tank ditch unseen, and beyond that point, which was free of trip wires in the river, I told Pak we would swim down to the old tree. He was to stay beside me until we got out at that point.

The water was cold and swift and with Pak hanging onto my belt I was swept downstream, with him clutching at me. We half swam, half pulled ourselves along together. After awhile, I saw the old tree dark and silent, naked of leaf but somehow clothed in security, standing tall on the left bank. I groped for a hold but the stream carried me on ruthlessly until I was smashed into a rocky ledge. Pulling the gasping Pak close to me, I managed to halt our progress and we were able to splash our way to the bank. From there we made our slow and careful way across the valley towards what we hoped was the British standing patrol position.

Chapter Eight

Major Hurgaard was delighted with my report on our patrol and said that our information confirmed radio intercepts and the breaking into Chinese codes indicating a large enemy build-up in the area from where I had just returned. A massive air-strike was being planned which could now also target the tunnels and dump areas which Pak had reported and which I had mapped. The strike was ultimately delayed for some days because of heavy rain, but on a Sunday morning relays of planes were sent screaming up the valley in the direction of Namsong-Dong. They were laden with bombs and napalm and were in groups, like eager terriers darting in to harass a pack of rats. I hoped the pilots would avoid the village which I had marked in blue and only destroy the tunnels and the dumps represented by red crosses. I wondered grimly about the chaos being wreaked all about where Old Kim lived and even as I thought about it, I could hear sullen reverberations from somewhere behind the hills. But I could not be sure about the noise: it might have come from a newly-gathering storm prowling over the high ranges of oak and cedar out there.

When it was all I went to see Major Hurgaard. It seemed that the entire valley where Divisional Headquarters was located had been drained of sound. I found the major pale and drawn, while the lips of his generally humorous looking mouth were set in an uncompromising line. I knew he had worried over the airstrike, but now he was obviously worried about something else. I knew what was troubling him and I appreciated his concern.

Because our agents had been getting safely through the enemy front and as I could produce photographic evidence of our penetration, the plan for a prisoner-of-war rescue attempt, the one mentioned to me some weeks previously by Colonel James, was now operational. Operation Switch, that exchange of sick prisoners begun in early 1953, had revealed where other men were being held and the location of Lieutenant-Colonel Carne, the former commanding officer and survivor of the Gloucester fight, who later surrendered at Kapyong in mid-1951, was known. A plot to walk him out and get him down to me was being put in train. Captain Shaw, who had determined where Carne was being held, told me one morning over a cup of coffee that the treatment afforded many prisoners was heartless. He talked about some who had survived and the unmarked graves of many who had not. He wondered about the brutality, the scabs and the bruises, the stench, the filth, the caked blood and the tattered rags of clothing many had worn since their capture some months previously, and of the men who felt they were living in a nightmare from which they hoped to one day wake up and find themselves at home. He said that the top planners of the rescue operation hoped that Carne who, as he put it, was an acclaimed hero, might now be taken from his camp, walked down to me and taken out to freedom. The safe houses were not being considered because their security was suspect. I was to wait in the hills and settle into the bunkers I had found when the pheasant hunters almost came upon us. The spot had, for convenience, been named Pheasant Hill.

It was known that Carne was in solitary confinement, as he had been for the nineteen months of his incarceration. His five chaplains had died in captivity from brutal treatment and Carne was only allowed out of his hut on a Sunday morning to briefly conduct his own church service. When he talked and prayed with the men in attendance, he carried a small wooden cross he had carefully carved in his hut, out of a small oak branch that he had found somewhere.

We wondered what solitary confinement meant to a soldier like Carne. We knew he was brave enough, with a DSO from the Second War and now a Victoria Cross as proof of his fearlessness and determination when being overwhelmed in battle. We also knew from men who had served with him that Carne was a lonely, introspective person. Psychiatrists and other specialists in behavioural patterns believed that his solitary existence for such a long period would affect him far less than one who was extroverted and seeking company. For all that I could see it would be difficult for a man like Carne, given his weakened physical condition, to walk to safety even while being assisted, over one hundred and fifty miles, the distance from the Yalu River to the 38th parallel. Also it was mid-year, a time for typhoons, torrential rains and swollen rivers, many of which Carne and his rescue party would have to cross.

It was this which was troubling Major Hurgaard, hence the hard line of his mouth that morning. But his features softened as he reflected, "I can only hope this next assignment goes off as well as your last one. I reckon that you and those tough Koreans you have with you could crawl through hell and not even get your hair singed. But the prisoner? He's probably sick and weak. And the peace talks? They just drag on! Is a resolution close? But you and your men will be safe enough. And the chaps who have been chosen to jump in are tough as ancient boots, with medals galore. I have no qualms at all in that regard. I worry only about the fitness of the prisoner. But we've been ordered to get on with it, and that's what we have to do. And if we pull it off, what a coup! Colonel Carne would be the only soldier ever to escape, and the man is a hero! Well, *carpe diem,* as someone once declared: *seize the day!* Let's get on with it, hey?"

The two men selected to assist Colonel James in the rescue attempt had been flown in a hurried manner from England. They were parachutists, top men from the secret spy world of the last war. One was a warrant officer named Chris Evans. He was a Welshman, a compact, powerfully built man who wore a Military Medal with Bar ribbon pinned with a number of campaign ribbons above his shirt pocket. He had a thick moustache, a powerful baritone voice, and such an air of supreme confidence about him that he inspired everyone involved with him in the operation. His partner was Sergeant Tim Wallis, a lanky Scotsman with that quiet air of authority that seemed to be a part of every Scotsman I had ever met. He had a DCM medal heading many other ribbons. He was the radio and communications expert.

With fifteen members of Colonel James' special unit, the three of us directly involved in the rescue an Australian, a Welshman and a Scot practised with our weapons until the knife and gun were as much part of us as an arm or a leg. We tumbled and swung and parried in murderous unarmed combat until we were as quick as Korean squirrels and tough as their great oak trees. We went on long walks through the black hills at night until the heavens and their guiding stars were as familiar as simple stories written for children. Evans and Wallis, when they had a free moment, studied such elementary phrases of the difficult Korean language that might, in an emergency, get them out of trouble.

The reason we trained with some of the other members from the Special Services was that Colonel James, appreciating that both sides in this war had intelligence services, threw as much of a false trail as possible and with a large number of men, to hide the fact that anything special was to hand. He thought that if word got out that two decorated and highly trained paratroopers had suddenly been attached to his unit, some perceptive enemy intelligence operator could start thinking about what might be taking place especially as prisoners recently returned in the Little Switch Operation would be bringing back with them much previously unknown classified information about POW camps: their location, guarding methods, prisoner identity and many other facts.

The physical condition of the prisoner was worrying to everyone. Captain Shaw had informed us that Carne, although a senior officer, had like all other prisoners been on a steady diet of millet and boiled rice with few vegetables, meat or fish. He would therefore have known a disruption in what Shaw called the circadian cycle, the metabolic and glandular rhythms, which occur once or twice a day and are central to normal living. Carne would have a massive iron calcium deficiency and he would need acid found in spinach, liver, onions and plain salads. So the men designated to rescue him were to carry masses of vitamins to strengthen and bolster his bodily needs.

Because Evans and Wallis had to jump close to Carne's camp in North Korea with an extra eighty pounds of equipment, it was essential for them to make a number of day and night parachute drops to ensure they could handle such loads, and that the food and drugs in the heavy canvas bags would not break or be damaged on impact. I understood that Evans had been trained to set up an intravenous drip and give Carne a couple pints of glucose saline within the first two hours, keeping the vein open with a pint of Hartman's solution. Evans would also start him on oral fluids with fruit juices and Lucozade.

To maintain the fiction that we were all going through the same training, everyone did four night drops by parachute and four by day, all from a height of about fifteen hundred feet. Evans and Wallis experimented with the canvas bags full of supplies, making sure they could hold them so as to hit the ground rushing up below them, without them bursting open. I earned my parachute wings but the drops only reinforced to me the danger Evans and Wallis were going to encounter when they dropped at night into North Korea.

It never entered my calculations that Evans and Wallis might never drop with their precious bundles and, having rescued Colonel Carne, be unable to make it all the way down south where I would be waiting for them. For one thing, we were all too busy to think negatively and for another, we were being indoctrinated subtly, through our hardening bodies and the proficiency of our training, with the army maxim that admits no fear or thought of failure by fit, competent men. I had not yet decided who I would select to accompany me as I went through the enemy lines again, and I had not even told Lim that I would soon be going out again or the reason why. I only told him that my superiors had asked me to train with a number of Colonel James' men and to do parachute training as it might be useful at some later date in my service life. On the need-to-know principle of security work there was no need yet to tell Lim or anyone else what was being planned. I had seen what the Korean police had done to Lim in an attempt to extract information and, while he had not talked then, he just might at some more vulnerable or painful period of his life.

While we got on with our training I spent a long time with Evans and Wallis in a stuffy secluded barracks going over maps and sand tables studying the land surrounding the prison camps where so many men had been incarcerated in a haphazard fashion in buildings surrounded with barbed wire. The terrain, hostile villagers and distance to the west coast had inhibited

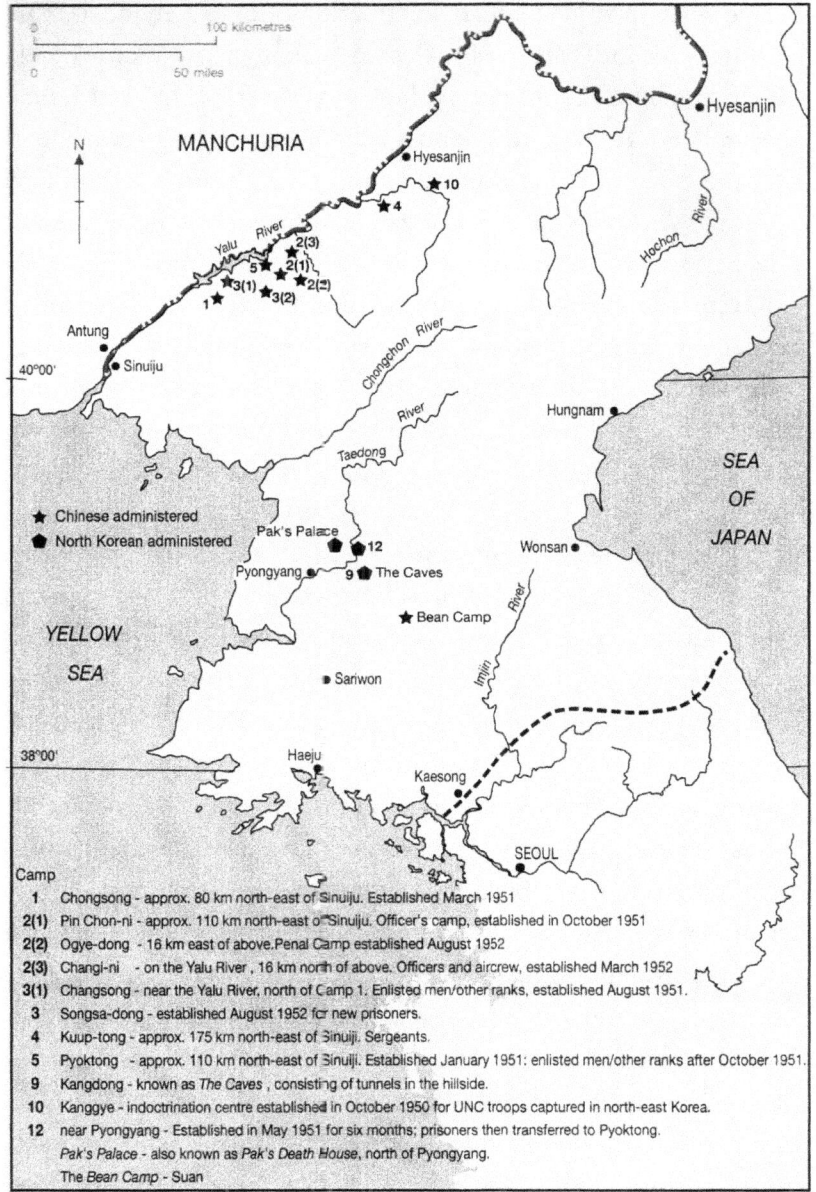

Map of North Korea with Prisoner of War Camps noted.
Courtesy Clive Baker War Book Shop.

escape attempts; a few had tried but none had made it. One prisoner, Major Farrar-Hockley, the former Adjutant of the Gloucestershire Regiment, had escaped several times but he had always been apprehended and badly beaten when returned to his captors. Looking at the main camps set out on the sand table we could see that Camps One to Ten were set out along the Yalu River, stretching from Antung in the West to Manpojin in the east. Colonel Carne was to be rescued from Camp Two and to be helped somehow across many fast flowing rivers, over high mountain ranges, and finally down to me. It seemed like a tough assignment, but knowing the calibre and courage of Evans and Wallis I believed it could be accomplished, but it would be a hard endeavour.

A couple of days later, though, I had reason to make a re-assessment of the plan, for when Evans, Wallis and I were looking over the sand tables, Colonel James came in to the hut and looking down with us on the depiction of the country to the north, he looked over my shoulder and muttered to Evans, "Thank God he's agreed to this, eh?" Evans immediately coughed very loudly, cutting across anything else the colonel might say. Glancing into James's face, I saw how embarrassed he was for having made what he must have instantly known was a stupid comment, a serious lapse in his security training. I also understood that he had unconsciously put into words the fact that he was worried about the rescue attempt but also, that as Carne had been contacted and agreed to escape, there must be a network of James's agents in North Korea who were to participate in the rescue. They were obviously in place to help Evans and Wallis take Carne out of the camp, get him, perhaps by bicycle and the use of A frames, down the many roads before them, to have boats ready to cross rivers and escort him down to me. I always knew that I was involved in a huge operation, why else would two experienced paratroopers by flown in from England when many other paratroopers were serving in Korea? I also accepted why I had not been informed of the scope of the plan, for there was no need for me to know. I even wondered if Major Hurgaard had been given the full picture, for he seemed concerned about what he knew of the operation.

I had no idea how James had been able to establish a network of agents in North Korea but, as the Americans had been briefly in North Korea before the Russians arrived to occupy that part of the country in 1945, it was possible they had set up a network of agents and that Green had later taken them over. Or perhaps he had infiltrated his own men into that part of the country. He was regarded as a top intelligence officer and almost anything was possible, given his background. I knew for certain that I was working under and commanded by a highly competent officer. All we were waiting for was the green light to make us operational.

The green light came in the second week of July 1953. The armistice that many wondered about seemed as improbable as ever. In fact, the defences of The Hook area to the left of my crossing point on the Samichon River had been coming under increasing and sustained attack by the Chinese. It was still apparent that even though peace was hopefully near, the enemy wanted it on their terms, one of which was to have their defensive line running all along the bank on their side of the river. But The Hook, which bulged out over the river, denied them that straight defensive line. The Australian 2nd Battalion RAR was fighting desperately to establish their defensive positions after a recent heavy battle endured by the Duke of Wellington Regiment which had fought so desperately to hold the place. Because of what the regiment had faced there, The Hook was gaining a reputation as one of the bloodiest bits of rock in the Korean War.

Colonel James, becoming worried about the increasing numbers of Chinese patrols in that area, asked me to go out there once more. I was to ascertain if my way through was still open and if the hills above the known ambush spot were clear. I told him I would organise a patrol which would take me and one man past the ambush position. I would also send another two man patrol up along the tank ditch and follow a telephone cable known to us, and have them go up in the direction of Pheasant Hill. They would make sure that should the rescue party get there, I would be waiting and we would all have a great view of the valley below and of the Samichon River which would be all we had to swim across to safety.

Chapter Nine

It was in the dusk on 2 July 1953 that five of us were huddled just outside the communications trench of a forward British Company. It had been raining heavily for days past and this was the first opportunity I'd had to go on the mission requested by Colonel James. Just then a tank on the reverse slope of a hill behind us began firing directly across the valley in the direction we were planning to take. Its big gun smashed heavily, jolting the air above us. The trajectory of the shell, a red ball which blazed fiercely for a moment, lessened gradually to a spark and was suddenly snuffed out. The tank, firing on fixed lines, also sent regular drumming bursts of machine-gun fire, with every few shots being interspersed with tracer. These too arched across the valley and died in the distance just as another tank in support from a knoll on the right flank took up the fire-task when the first grew silent. Several mortars were firing, the spluttering whistle of their shells murmuring through the air. After dark the cacophony of war never really ceased but on this night I was not concerned with what they might hit, or even where the gunners aimed, as long as they kept enemy heads down. That was important along the river to my right where, once I had moved off, the shelling and the mortar fire would be directed at some other point.

With every crack and smash of the shells, each of us on the exposed ground near the trench instinctively hunched our bodies into tight bundles, then relaxed them cautiously to watch the flight of the missiles. A slight mist began creeping across the valley. The soldier's last light was at hand and at a whispered word from me we all stood erect and went along a small track and through a disordered pattern of barbed wire entanglements. In a small pit at the base of the hill we had just descended, we went on through the mine-field gap and into the deepening mist. Once outside the gap we took up single-file, about three feet apart. Keeping to the edges of the paddy fields, we made our way across the valley. The shells from the tanks along with their machine-gun bullets continued to gash through the night above our heads while our canvas covered feet rustled and whispered among the deep wet grass along our way. After about twenty minutes of rapid advance, I called a halt. Lim moved up to me from the rear, his face glistening with perspiration in the pale gloom, and I told him we would rest a while. He nodded his shaggy head and turned back for a whispered consultation with Pak, Chet and Soong, the other three members of our team. We hunkered down, motionless except for the slight movement of our hands as we brushed away the hordes of mosquitoes which buzzed and circled above our heads.

Apart from the sound of shells thudding into the far-off enemy positions and the incessant whirr of insects, quietness generally possessed the still, hot air. I stood erect, gazing back towards the friendly lines, my thoughts dwelling briefly on the security that lay behind them, the safety of my own small headquarters village and the stark contrast of my present position. It was something which a small part of my mind still did of its own volition, even while the main focus of my thoughts was engaged on the men with me and the patrol ahead. I glanced at them, smiled, swung my head around and looked at the big old tree, my crossing place at the river. I gestured and they arose; we gathered together momentarily, not saying a word but each feeling the comfort of the others' nearness. I wondered what they were feeling or thinking, and if, like me, their minds had been centred on a warm cave somewhere else, anywhere but the enemy-peopled darkness about us and in to which we now moved.

Our advance was extremely cautious, stopping frequently to listen to the noises in the murky darkness, but our progress continued and we soon came to a white patch of sand which glistened in front of us and here I expelled a gusty breath of pleased exclamation. The sand indicated we had reached the first point of our patrol, the bank of the river. We moved forward over the pebble-strewn place to the old tree. Under its gaunt limbs we gathered together, almost protectively, as though our nearness was our safety.

We knew what we had to do, having rehearsed our procedures. So Soong stepped forward, working at the rope about his waist then handing one end to me. I sat to remove my canvas shoes, tied them about my neck, made sure my grenades were secure, that my Burp gun was in its water proof cover and stepped into the river. The recent heavy rains had swollen it and I struggled in deep water, spat some of it out, was buffeted hard against the rocks and at times was fully submerged, with the rope dragging hard at my waist, before I made it to the big boulder that formed part of the small island in the stream's centre. I rested there briefly, secured the rope about the rock and continued, fighting against the high water level until I was on the far bank, thoroughly wet and exhausted.

On previous crossings, it had not been necessary to secure the rope about the boulder and I was able to tug on the rope to signal that I was across. On this occasion, however, with the river in spate the agents knew that once the rope was tight they could cross. By the time my breathing had normalised, and I had checked my equipment and tied on my shoes, Lim had come to stand beside me. He was closely followed by Pak, then Chet. They sat nearby checking their weapons, dragging wet shoes back on their feet, making sure they were ready to move. Everything was done so quietly and with such an economy of movement that I believed Pak and I would easily make it up the river, get past the anti-tank ditch, the ambush point, and make it back by dawn.

When the rope was jerked away from where I had been watching it, I knew Soong had made it to the centre of the river where he untied the rope from where I had secured it about the rock, had made it back to the old tree, gathered in the rope and was gone into the tall grass where he would await our return. It was planned we would all go back together at daylight to our own lines.

I had never mounted a patrol with more than two men but, as I had to carry out Colonel James' orders, I had decided to take Pak with me to the ambush point near the anti-tank ditch and send Lim and Chet into higher country in the direction of Pheasant Hill. The four of us moved off, all without uttering a word, Lim and Chet moving to their left, while Pak and I went along just up from the river. We moved with the skill of long practice, going forward until we rested, often in anxiety and exhaustion, our heads drooping. Then we crept on again with the lead position changing after each halt. I knew we could not be far from the anti-tank ditch when Pak, who was in the lead, turned suddenly, put his hand on my chest, and pushed me backward, while hissing, *"Mochi buse!"* He was standing upright, staring up to the ridge on his left hand side.

'Ambush!' Pak's word registered, and even as I looked to where he was standing close to me, a murderous blast of fire came from the darkness: six pinpoints of red flashed out in a circular pattern of fire from a submachine gun. I heard the slugs drill into Pak's body, he sighed, ever so gently. I knew he was dead even as I reached out to grab his body to pull him back, and an awful emptiness of loss over a man who was my youngest brother-in-arms, hit my heart. As I fell to the ground, with Pak part-covering me, new blasts of gunfire smashed at our position in the darkness.

Bullets hit Pak again but missed me. Then I heard the hiss of a grenade very close. I pressed my body close to Pak's and, while small bomb spat and burned my hand went quickly to my belt for one of my own grenades, a Mills 36. I knew I must try and warn Lim and Chet that we were in trouble, which they would understand when they heard a Mills grenade explode. My intentions were stalled when the Chinese grenade, a concussion device, went off; my head shuddered as though I had been clubbed and my ears set up a huge ringing noise. Another grenade was burning nearby and when it went off I felt its fragments hit my right thigh and hand. I knew I must fight back to live. Lurching to my knees I drew the pin from the grenade, waited for three seconds and lobbed the bomb high and arched to where I had seen the Chinese weapon fire. Even as I readied to throw the second grenade I heard the first one explode.

The Mills 36 grenade is a fearsome weapon, exploding a full roar of sound. It is shaped like a hand full of serrated potato and when it tears apart the flying toothed steel is adequate, or so its devotees claim, to stun and halt a rogue elephant. Following the bursting apart of the first small bomb I had thrown, I heard shrill cries that told me that, while I might not have worried any elephants, I had surely given my enemy cause for alarm and fright. My second grenade was immediately on its way, causing more enemy distress. But my main worry was whether Lim and Chet had heard the noise those grenades were making. I had a Burp gun with me and I could have fired that, but as it was an enemy weapon the sound would have been meaningless to those agents. I also had that Luger pistol given to me earlier in this war. I had always had it in my possession but I had never used it, except on a practice range. It was a deadly weapon which made a strange *'whack'* of sound when fired, one I knew Lim would identify. I now aimed it in the general direction of the ambush point and fired the whole magazine.

A number of enemy were shooting from the bank above and grenades were exploding all about me. Some were fragmentation but like all grenades in Chinese hands they were not nearly as lethal as the Mills grenade. Concussion devices were also being hurled down about me but they landed too far away to bother me. It was obvious that the enemy were confused about our location and they probably were not aware that Pak was lying dead beside me. In an attempt to further confuse them I put my Burp gun on fire and hurled it with all my strength to the right hand side. When it hit the ground it released a long burst, then apparently jammed and stopped. But the deception worked for I heard a wild yell in Chinese: *"Tso pien!"* "Left side!" Firing and hand grenade activity immediately shifted in that direction and I knew I could get away by moving to my own left-hand side away from the enemy. Before going I stripped two grenades from Pak and put my hand to his chest to find he was bleeding profusely in a sticky, hot, uncontrollable flow. I knew that his cup of happiness, the one I sometimes thought about, had been brutally emptied. All I could do was mutter to the dead body, *"I'm sorry son, sorry."* The words kept repeating in my mind, a poor and inadequate farewell, but they encompassed everything I felt for this brave young Korean soldier.

I grieved for Pak and the shock of his death, but in the midst of my own immediate danger my brain had become strangely self-possessed; it seemed as though the ambush had not happened to me or even to Pak but to somebody else and I was in a box seat watching the circumstance unfold. I was able to plan my every move and think with clarity of each action and plot its result. The probability of my own imminent death was not even a consideration. The extreme danger all about me had produced a feeling of strength and there was no fear, no pain. There was only a deadly coolness and a plan which my mind fashioned calmly as I went: moving to my left, knowing that my enemy were scurrying to their left, firing as they ran and widening the distance between us.

All of a sudden I was at the bank of what I thought was the river. I edged my body down the slope and dragged my bloodied hand over a protruding rock. Groaning with pain I slipped over the edge and fell splashing into the water. I heard an excited yell as the sound of the splash must have carried to the group which had ambushed us but it did not matter to me for I believed I was in the river. All I had to do was make for the fast-flowing centre and I would be away, out of sight and sound of whoever wanted to kill me or worse, take me alive and interrogate me, possibly using drugs to break me down, a constant fear on any of our missions, and the reason I had touched Pak to make sure he was dead. I could not have left him there alive.

I groped my way from where I had fallen, my feet floating off the bottom of the river, my knees turning in a sliding, lifting motion. The depth of the water was just up to my chin when I felt the rocky base slope upward and my chest scraped against another bank. I realised then that I had dropped into the narrow creek which ran parallel to the main watercourse. A small stubble-covered island loomed in front of me and I raised my head like an animal sniffing the wind; the friendly rustle and swish of the strong-flowing main stream came to my ears as I edged onto dry land.

I knew the enemy would be aware that I had dropped into the creek and not the river, also that I would now have to try and cross the small island. I was just beginning to crawl across many rounded pebbles and small rocks when a grenade plopped into the soft mud ahead of me, exploding sharply. Another grenade blew up somewhere to my left, showering me with bits of stone. Everything seemed directed towards my destruction and I knew I must reach the main river and sink into its protection. Almost as I thought of it, my left hand, which had been digging gravel and rocks and some sort of stinging nettle, met water. The contact flashed a wild elation in my pounding heart.

In a quick, crabbing fashion I crawled into the wide stream with grenades crashing behind me. As I progressed deeper the tug of the water became stronger. I felt my legs being dragged away, twisting and bending from the trunk. Steadying my body I lay still, clutching a smooth rock. The water swirled in freshets about me as I looked back, but a sudden burst of enemy fire made me aware that I was still far from safety. I released the rock and the water engulfed me in its strong flood and carried me swiftly downstream.

A sandbar loomed ahead in the tumbling river and, as I tried to steady my sweeping progress, I was smashed feet first into it. I lay there, floundering, spitting and cursing as a foam of white swirled about me. Above the tumult of the river I could hear the wild stuttering of a Burp gun, but the sound was fainter. The enemy was still firing in the area where they had last heard me and I knew they were wasting their ammunition in the darkness. It was possible also that they were venting their spleen on Pak's shattered body because someone had evaded their ambush point. With daylight they would be astonished to find a body dressed in Chinese uniform, carrying Chinese weapons and with a number of valid identity documents in his pocket. They would think at first they had killed one of their own people, possibly coming back from some sort of mission downstream. But where was the person who had carried the Burp gun which had been thrown away? And the British grenades, who tossed them? And a pistol which had been fired: I wondered at the puzzle for their security people and nodded to myself in some satisfaction at their bewilderment. Releasing my hold on the sandbar, I was borne downstream. I half swam, half drifted along, keeping to the bank, quickening my progress by digging my uninjured leg into the sandy bottom. I had explored the wound in my leg to find that while my trouser leg had been ripped open, the wound appeared to be only deep cuts with no bone injury.

After a while I saw the old tree on the left bank and I made my way out of the river at that point. As I trudged towards the white strip of sand nearby, a thick column of red soared out of the blackness from the direction of the friendly lines. A tracer from the tank shell floated in a slow graceful arc behind; I thought it looked beautiful and welcoming. All I had to do next was locate Soong and go with him back through the mine gap and up to the British ambush point ahead. I hoped Lim and Chet had heard the sound of our gun fight and would soon follow me home.

Captain Tony Shaw visited me in hospital the following afternoon. He was anxious to know how I was, if Pak had carried any papers on his person which might jeopardise any future attempt to rescue Colonel Carne and the importance placed on Pheasant Hill as a meeting place, should another rescue go forward. I told him that Pak was clean and that like Lim and Chet, he knew nothing of the rescue plan. When he was leaving Shaw took my hand very hard and thanked me for what I had achieved, sad as the death of Pak was to me.

My wounds were not serious, lots of stitching in my right hand and leg. When Lim came to visit me three days later I was walking about. Lim informed me he had heard my fight at the

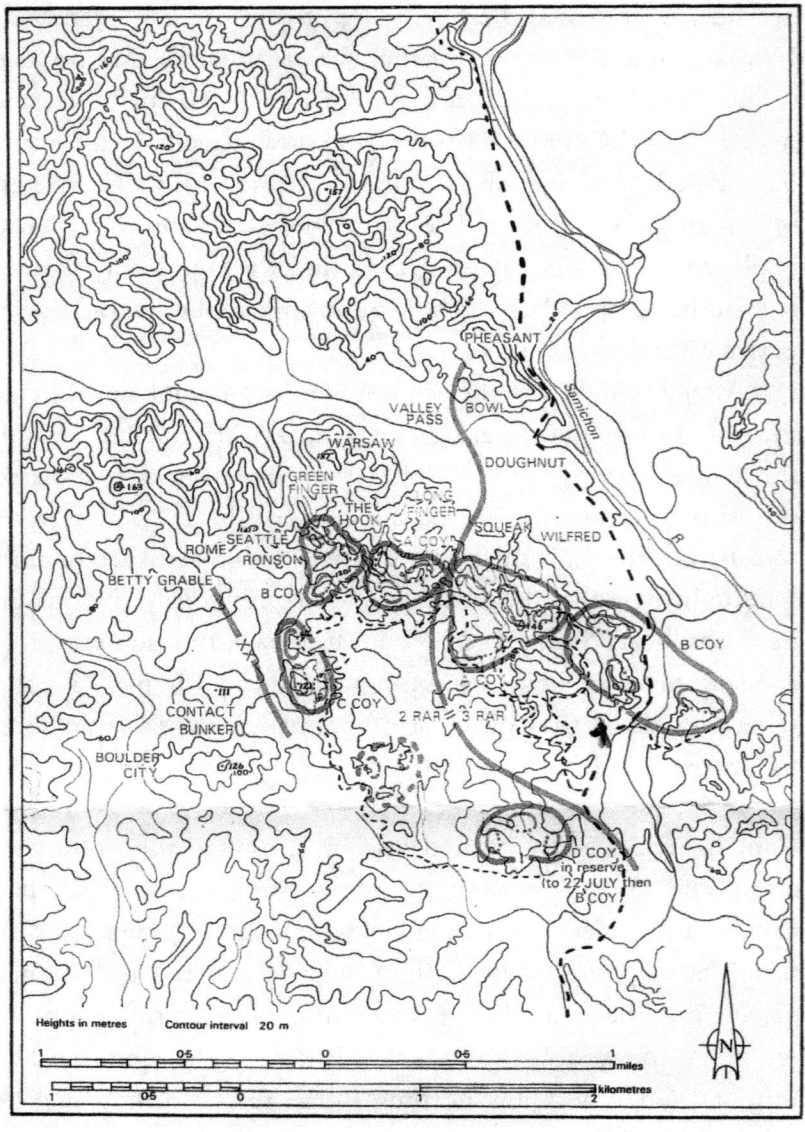

Map showing The Hook where 2RAR and 3RAR fought so bravely in 1953. Courtesy Clive Baker War Book Shop

place where we had been ambushed and he had taken evasive action luckily for them, as he and Chet found the place they were heading for well guarded. They had hidden in the hills beyond the Samichon River, narrowly avoiding capture by the Chinese forces who had apparently built up their numbers all about the place.

When Lim was preparing to leave he reached out impulsively and took up my bandaged right hand. He held it gently against his big chest and with tears streaming down his rugged face he muttered brokenly that he was sorry about Pak. "He was my best young friend. I am sorry he is dead. You are my best old friend. I am so glad you are alive." With that he dropped my hand and strode away from my bed and out of the ward.

Upon my release from hospital Lim drove me back to our agent detachment and we waited to see what would take place next. Major Hurgaard had visited me and he mentioned we might wind up our operation or we might have other missions to fulfil; it all depended on the Chinese. It seemed that they wanted peace, but it was also obvious that they were going to launch yet another huge assault on The Hook. In fact they attacked the Australian-held sector ferociously on the nights of 25 and the 26 of July but were forced to recoil with huge losses. An official report on the action reads: *The floor of the valley between The Hook and the Chinese positions was almost covered with dead bodies…on the immediate approaches to the Australian position bodies literally carpeted the ground to three deep…most of the bodies had been there for two or three days and in the humid weather, had commenced to putrefy. There was a strong and nauseous stench of death.* So it was that the monstrous pile of bodies in front of The Hook could not be taken away until there was a ceasefire, which came about on 27 July, the final day of the war in Korea. It was said that it took

Chinese stretcher bearers five days to clear the battle field, while the Australian soldiers above, looked on.

On a lovely morning early in August I stood with Lim at the bottom of one of our paddy fields just below the houses to our village. We were shoulder to shoulder, taking in the green balance of the land when I turned and told Lim about the proposed rescue of Colonel Carne, and the reason of Pak's death. Lim listened closely to what I had to say and he was very quiet for a long time. He then asked me. "This officer, who would have been released by now seeing that the war is over was contacted, and agreed to escape. Despite his physical condition? Despite the danger? He was safe where he was, he had survived. Why did he agree to put his life at risk?"

Why did Carne agree? I had thought about it, and there was only one answer. "He was a soldier," I told Lim. "A good soldier."

"Seems so," Lim agreed. "But was it also a good war, sir?"

"Strange question?" I queried. "After all, it was your war, my friend, not mine. I did not come here fighting for home and hearth, as we call my country. But it was good in the sense that I met some great soldiers, you included, of course. Still, no matter how hard we fought we never did win all of Korea for you and get a happy reunification of this country. But at least, we prevented the North and Kin Il Sung from imposing his dictatorship on all of you in the South."

"Indeed!" Lim cried, his dark eyes flashing his happiness. "And can we shake on it, as you say?"

I thrust out my right hand while saying, "I might just give you a big hug, as well!"

Chapter Ten

The winding up of my detachment took place over several days, and while I was disturbed at what I thought was the cavalier treatment of Lim and the agents who had worked with me, and earlier Lavender, there was nothing I could do about the decision made. It had been resolved that, as Lim and the others were mercenaries, no mention was to be made about their work behind the lines. They were to be paid off, at a rate considered very fair, disbanded and their work was to go largely unrecorded. There would be no mention of their bravery, or of the way they had worked at great risk against our enemy. I discussed the matter with Lim and he was very sensible about it, saying the authorities were probably correct, in that the money they were to get would help most of them start anew, and besides, none would want their names to be on record as having helped the Allies against the Chinese or the North Koreans. But once the south was secure, both in a political sense as well as with military power and protection, Lim thought that he or one or more of the others might write about what they had done.

As I waited for my own re-posting I took it easy about our detachment village: walking in the hills, going to the divisional mess, visiting those security friends of mine in Seoul and, to put it simply, just relaxing. When I heard that a large athletic event was to be held at division I decided to go along with Lim and see what transpired. I had been a good athlete when serving in Japan, competing in the middle and long distance running events. When we got to where people were seated or standing about waiting for the games to start, I heard my name being called and

I was then taken in a huge hug by an officer in an Australian uniform.

"Sergeant Harris!" he declared. "Don't tell me you are going to compete!"

Far Eastern Sporting Championships, 1949.
The author being awarded a trophy for winning the one mile race.

It was David Butler, my former platoon commander. We had been together all the way from Pusan to Chonju where I had been wounded in late 1950. Then a lieutenant, he had been awarded a Silver Star by the Americans for his bravery at the fight at the Apple Orchard. He was now a captain. A handsome man, he looked fit and happy as well as being pleased to see me. We had been good friends, understood each other, had worked well and fought together.

I introduced him to Lim, explained in part what I had been doing with the divisional agent detachment. Butler in turn told me he had heard about an Australian soldier going through the British front on patrol behind the enemy lines, but he had never guessed it might be me. He went on to tell me that he was a signals officer with the Second Battalion and that he was serving on The Hook. He told of the recent battle they had fought, and how the Chinese had been badly beaten.

As it was hot, dusty and very noisy in the athletic arena I suggested we should go back to my detachment where I could give him some good food and a beer. He said the beer sounded like a good inducement so we went to my place and with Lim and some of the other agents in attendance we had an old-soldier reunion. I sent him back to his unit at sunset. When Lim and I were driving away Lim said he had listened closely as Butler and I had discussed our army service, much of which he did not properly understand. He noted that I had never mentioned what I had done on my first tour in Korea. All he knew was that I had a badly shot-up left hand. I felt I owed Lim an explanation and besides, so much was stirring in my memory that I wanted to talk. So I let my mind, lulled by its own urgings, indulge in a little relaxation and recalled for Lim, that other time for me in Korea.

The war then, did not seem particularly dangerous in late 1950 as our 3rd Battalion, RAR with two British battalions forming a brigade, roared northwards on trucks with tanks chasing the retreating North Korean army. The place was dusty, the roads were narrow and packed in many places with refugees herding southwards fleeing from the north. The Allied Eighth Army, part of the United Nations force including Australians, was poised to drive on to Pyongyang, the North Korean capital.

By October we had reached a town called Sariwon and there we came upon large numbers of North Korean soldiers waiting to move on for the defence of Pyongyang. When our brigade came upon them, they thought we were Russians come to help them.

They began exchanging cap badges and cigarettes, but fighting soon broke out at close quarters and over two hundred enemy soldiers were killed. Darkness had fallen and Major Ferguson, our battalion 2IC, who was waiting in an apple orchard for the arrival of some ration trucks, heard the thump of approaching feet. He flashed his torch to see who was approaching. An officer at the head of an enemy column of men called out 'Ruski?' and Ferguson knew he was facing his enemy. One of our tanks was nearby, Ferguson jumped aboard, and told the enemy through an interpreter that they were surrounded and should surrender. This brave bluff worked and nearly two thousand enemy laid down their arms. The battalion, however, was still without food and Ferguson ordered Lieutenant Butler of 9 Platoon C Company to drive trucks into Sariwon to solve our problem. I heard Butler ask Ferguson what we should do about enemy still in the area, most probably on the road that led back to Sariwon. Ferguson dismissed Butler's concerns by telling him that the enemy had probably all surrendered. What followed, though, had surreal overtones as we later drove on through what must have been an entire regiment of North Korean soldiers who had not relinquished their weapons or their apparent will to fight. They were lining both sides of the road and our trucks drove straight past them, headlights blazing. Many of the enemy waved to us, shouting something as they must have presumed we were friendly, possibly Russians. Nearby, a long line of blazing railway carriages was billowing fire and smoke, lighting the place about us with an eerie glow; we hurried along until just short of Sariwon I saw a tall officer in an English uniform standing in the middle of the road, a revolver in one hand a large walking stick in the other. He was wearing a strange looking bonnet and thrusting his walking stick at us, he demanded we halt. Our lead truck screeched to a halt before him, Butler dismounted, had a quick discussion with the officer, jumped back into our truck and told me he had just spoken with Captain John Slim, Adjutant of the Argylls. Butler said he knew Slim was the son of General Sir William Slim who had defeated the Japanese in Burma. Later he was promoted to Field Marshal and served as Governor General in Australia. According to Butler, though, John Slim was a worried adjutant who did not know what happened to his battalion commander who had earlier gone by jeep to make a reconnaissance of the area. Captain Slim had halted our convoy to inquire if we had sighted a jeep along our way. Looking from Butler and towards Slim I saw his long frame melting into the night. He was waving his stick about while clutching his revolver. The red tassel on his curious looking bonnet bobbed along as he went from us. We were later to learn that Slim never did find his CO that night but he turned up the following morning to report that his jeep had driven into the enemy we had passed earlier. The jeep was fired upon and the driver accelerated to the safety of a large haystack where the jeep was covered with straw. There the group in the vehicle spent a worrying night under piles of bad smelling straw.

It was a chilly morning on 21 October that we crossed the Taedong River at Pyongyang. As we passed through the capital city I was reminded of parts of old Japan with its clean streets, tidy homes, colourful roof gardens and walls of terraced rock. As we moved through the centre of the place I saw many impressive imperial-style buildings; that was to be expected, given that Japan had occupied Korea for so many years. But unlike Japan, much of which had been destroyed during the last war, Korea was untouched and its buildings with their surrounds still retained an old and lovely reminder of a past heritage.

We were not given time to rest or even to wash in the river at Pyongyang for our brigade had been ordered to advance to the town of Yongju and relieve the American 187th Airborne

Regiment which was in serious trouble. General MacArthur had ordered the parachute drop across two main roads leading northwards from Pyongyang in the hope of blocking the withdrawal of major elements of the North Korean Army. The drop was made on 20 October 1950 but the main enemy force had escaped the trap. They had left behind a force of 2,500 men who had been ordered to fight a delaying action. With a good eye for a battle ground their commander had chosen a high position in the vicinity of Yongju and his force was grinding down the 800 Americans who had been dropped in to fight him.

On the morning of the 22nd our Battalion advanced through Yongju to lead the brigade northwards. Charlie or C, my company, was leading our battalion because it was our turn, and we were certainly ready, having come to full company strength by absorbing reinforcements from the new K Force arrivals. This K Force comprised men who had come from a successful recruiting campaign in Australia, when 1000 ex-servicemen were chosen to spend three years in the army, including one year in Korea. Most had seen service in the last war and they helped give us an edge in experience. One such man was Teague, known only as 'Teagie' who had been a warrant officer. He was a determined and forceful man who claimed he knew what war was all about, having fought, as he sometimes boasted, in some of the most dangerous campaigns in Africa. He carried a holstered Luger pistol on his hip, a trophy he claimed of his war in Africa.

Teagie was in the leading truck with me when we first came under fire from the direction of many apple orchards set above the road beyond the town. The trees looked beautiful with their trunks bound with straw in anticipation of the arctic winter to come. It quickly became apparent that we had driven into the rear of our enemy, then forming up for a mass attack on the Americans. We had radio contact with the Americans and, knowing they were in serious trouble, we scrambled from our trucks and swung into action. Platoons 7 and 8 were ordered to attack the apple orchards on the high ground to the east of the road while 9 Platoon under Lieutenant David Butler was to proceed directly down the road. It was then that I realised that Teagie had been, and still was, a good soldier. Showing us all what to do in those crucial and confused opening moments, he was the first to fire and give support to the two platoons running for the fruit-laden, heavily leafed apple orchards. He was constantly on the move, shouting for us to cover him, ordering riflemen where to aim, every action quick and definite, every order precise. He was also protective of our young soldiers and I was proud of the way they reacted to danger and to Teagie's appraisal of the situation.

My expectations for our young soldiers had been high, and once they got into the fight, bayonets fixed in what was to become known as the Apple Orchard Fight, they justified all my hopes. The three section commanders, who had all fought in New Guinea, were splendid in the way they handled their young charges. They gathered their men together, all at proper drilled distances and kept them moving on to set objectives. They made good use of cover, probed for weakness and exploited any advantage quickly. But for all that, it was a confusing time, with the enemy bobbing up all over the place to our front, from the paddy fields to our left hand side, and in the apple orchards above the road to our right. None of us had much understanding of what was really happening all about us. I, for one, was in ignorance of anything beyond my immediate field of sight. I was not at all concerned about my safety, though, knowing I was well protected by all the young men gathering about me.

Sergeant Bandy of 8 Platoon which went into the apple orchard above the road later told me that the enemy must have fought a furious battle with the Americans the previous night for dead and dying soldiers littered the orchard and the hills above. Looking down at 9 Platoon moving along, Bandy reckoned we had the great good fortune to be able to make protective use of the deep stormwater drains which ran down both sides of the road. We were also able to make use of the dominance of the road itself, for it allowed us to attack directly into the unprotected backs of the enemy just then forming up for their final assault on the paratroopers without knowing we were behind them.

The Americans by this time were almost out for the count, with huge numbers of dead and wounded. A sergeant who saw the Australians arrive later told Bandy that he sat and cried, knowing he would be saved, when he had expected to die that very morning. The enemy, he said, had been attacking with a brutal and rampaging fury and in huge numbers. Bandy, an experienced soldier described in a later history as 'a redoubtable warrior', believed that if the enemy had formed a defence across the road and forced us from the drains, we would have been in for a hard battle. The enemy were massed in such numbers, they should have made it nearly impossible for us, without heavy supporting fire securing our flank by the open paddy field to move so easily against them.

Having initially been asked to protect the platoons attacking over the hill beside the road, 9 Platoon moved forward once that attack was successful and the positions were stabilised. But the fighting generally had grown much heavier and Captain Denness, our company commander, who had made his way forward, decided we would have to proceed with the Sherman tanks we had in support. When they saw those steel monsters lumbering up the road towards them I presumed that the North Koreans must have realised, perhaps for the first time, that they were suddenly up against a large and combined enemy.

The commander of the leading Sherman was anxious to proceed down the road and link up with his countrymen for it was obvious that the Americans were in serious trouble. Enemy dead littered the sides of the road and the paddy fields, apparently from the previous night when the Americans had been heavily engaged. When he saw the bodies all about the tank commander called out that he could not go down the road until he was sure that the culverts ahead had been cleared of enemy or mines. Lieutenant Butler asked me to get on with that clearing and I ordered Teagie, who was still busy shooting at anything that moved, to help me inspect the culverts. I told my runner named Robinson to come with me, we would take the left side, Teagie would be on our right. Going ahead down the water drain, we got quickly to the first culvert. I told Robinson to watch for Teagie at his end of the culvert, stooped down low and saw Teagie's leg appear. But even as I turned to speak to Robinson to tell him it was clear, he fired a shot directly past my face. Immediately Teagie screamed.

"You've shot Teagie!" I cried. "Jesus man!" I was astounded, for apart from hitting Teagie, Robinson must have missed my face by the thickness of an eyelash.

"No! No!" Robinson stammered. "No!"

Lurching to my feet I hurried across the road to Teagie and taking my bayonet from its scabbard I ripped open his pants at the outside of his thigh. When I saw what a .303 bullet can do to the bone in a man's leg, I knew I was looking at the merciless side of war, for the exit wound was as large as my clenched fist. I looked at Teagie whose face was drenched with globules of sweat, his eyes were bright with pain. "Don't put me down as accidentally wounded," he said, speaking to me very quietly. "I went through a lot in the last war and my missus would kill me if I went back looking like a fool. Please. But I'm finished now, so take my Luger pistol, will you? It's been useful to me, may it be to you."

Taking the holstered pistol I yelled for a medic as Lieutenant Butler came up to tell me to get on with clearing the other culvert. Just then I saw one of the section leaders, Rowlings, coming towards me and I asked him to get on with the job, for I had noticed that while our two-inch mortar team was getting ready to fire into the hills to our front, the tank commander was shouting for them to stop as they might hit the Americans, not the North Koreans who were fleeing into those same hills. By the time I had sorted out where the mortar should be firing and directed the Bren gunner to another target, I saw Rowlings, a huge man, come striding back. He was carrying a very small and dirty child while a number of civilians were coming along behind. He had a big grin on his big face and he told me that when he got to the culvert he could see there were people inside. Yelling for them to come out and they did not, he was getting ready to throw in a grenade when first the small child appeared, followed by the others. I thought that with the child in his arms and the others gathered behind, Rowlings looked comical but magnificent and not at all warlike.

I called the first tank forward and it came on, savagely flinging bit of road behind it. As the tank moved with some of our soldiers sitting ready for action on it, I saw that a horse and cart had stopped on the road, right where it would block the tank's progress. I ran forward with Lieutenant Butler constantly on the move, hurrying along with me. On reaching the cart we found six badly wounded enemy soldiers stacked inside, like bloodied lumps of timber. Don Parsons, another section leader, came up with a number of his men and they got the hurt men out. All together we tried to pull the cart to one side along with the horse, but the animal refused to budge. I noticed it had been wounded, its broad white chest had been hit with many bullets, while its reddish flanks were sliced and opened by deeper bloodier cuts, probably from mortar or artillery fire. Given my youth at my grandfather's forge and my love of horses, I tugged at the reins while looking directly into the animal's liquid brown eyes, speaking softly to the distressed animal, when I noticed over the horse's head a North Korean soldier pulling himself slowly out of a hole in the ground. He was dressed in a grubby uniform and he moved so slowly that he seemed to have awoken from a heavy sleep, probably one close to exhaustion after the previous night's engagement with the Americans. He must have been aroused by the clamour of the tank and the noise 7 Platoon was making as they moved through the ground above him. He was struggling to get his Burp gun in position and fire at the men above his head. Dropping the reins from my left hand, I slipped my .303 from my shoulder, aimed and shot my enemy through the upper part of his body. As he fell and thrashed about, a 7 Platoon soldier leaned out over the high bank and riddled the him with a short burst from his Owen machinegun.

Several members of 9 Platoon on a Sherman tank at 'Apple Orchard'.

Following the Apple Orchard battle.
Above, left to right: the author, Private Renshaw,
Lance-Corporal Dave Wilson.

A dead North Korean machine-gun crew. Phil Hobson collection

I turned back to the business of moving the horse, for the tank commander who had drawn very close was shouting that he must get through. But, try as we might, we could not move the animal. Ordering us to remove the cart, the frustrated tankman drove his machine directly at the badly wounded creature. A Sherman tank is a massive piece of mobile metal and when it hit the horse side-on, one of its legs got wedged between the front track and its flat side. The tank shuddered and snarled, its great tracks shivering in agitation. Suddenly, it lifted the horse clear off the ground and smashed it, full-bodied, into the nearby paddy field. The thud of that heavy body hitting the ground at great force shocked me, but the horse looked at us in a dazed and puzzled way, then lay back, appearing to rest.

The resounding 'thwack' of the dumb animal hitting the ground with such force must have been enough to startle a North Korean soldier who had been hiding in a nearby small stack of rice stooks, as they were known, and he raised his head very slowly to take a look while pushing his weapon out. I took him with a snap shot through the head. As slowly as he had raised his head to look, he now dropped it from my sight, dead.

The tank, cleared of its obstacle, moved forward. Some enemy were running away, some surrendering, a few standing to fight. Much of it took place in the paddy-fields where the enemy had hidden in the rice stooks scattered all about. Many were hunted out and killed. The battle was not over until mid-afternoon but miraculously, we had suffered only seven wounded while the enemy dead numbered over one hundred, with eighty wounded. We had also rounded up over six hundred prisoners. The disparity between our few wounded and the many enemy dead was because of the way we had attacked, with two platoons taking to the heights above the road, while 9 Platoon had gone down the road. Accurate firing had also come from the

American-held positions, and the tanks which supported us.

Our link-up with the Americans, however, proved to be quite extraordinary and the headquarters of what we were from then on to call the 3rd Battalion, 187 Airborne Regiment, was a shambles, with officers and NCOs scrambling all about the place. One of their senior officers had apparently broken down under the sustained pressure of the fighting and he had been taken away. A top NCO who had won acclaim for his courage and leadership, was on a stretcher with most of his face shot away, and many young soldiers were grouped about, weeping bitterly. Many had not expected to survive the battle and they hated General MacArthur for having ordered them dropped into a nearly impossible military situation. Some of us tried to talk to the Americans, to applaud what they had done, but they neither wanted to talk nor listen to us. We did learn, though, that some American soldiers, thinking we were Russian soldiers from the thick winter greatcoats we were wearing, had attempted to surrender to us. And now, whatever the reason, the Americans were not in a welcoming mood.

I, Lieutenant Butler and several soldiers moved to an area where we could eat and where I noticed a number of the Americans were moving in and roughing up some of the surrendered North Koreans. It was later suggested they may also have shot many of them, but war is unreasonable and if prisoners were executed, the Americans may have thought it was pay-back time. It was noted that in the early months of the war, when the poorly trained and badly led American soldiers were in panic withdrawal, some who surrendered had their hands tied behind their backs before being shot or bayoneted. In violation of their surrender, others were shot in the palm of each hand, and a rope or a piece of wire was threaded into the hand. They were then dragged away, sick with horror and apprehension, into captivity or death. It was understandable to some of us that many Americans would have an exquisitely sharpened hatred for the North Korean enemy. That background aside, they probably would have been mostly wiped out that very morning, had not help miraculously arrived.

Just then, as an example of how some Americans regarded their enemy, a long column of supply trucks pulled up near where we were waiting for our rations. I noticed the drivers were African Americans with a support driver sitting alongside. The truck halted where many North Koreans were coming in large numbers across the paddy fields to surrender. When the first truck halted, the driver scrambled down from his vehicle. He was a huge and muscular man. In his right fist he carried a Colt revolver. He strode to the edge of the paddy field and roared at two surrendering Korean youths to come closer to him. He was furious, his mouth saliva-flecked, his huge body tense as a coil. Gesturing he indicated that the two young men strip naked. Trembling with fright in the cold morning, they did so. They then held up their hands in a kind of supplication, palms forward, trying in sign language to plead with the man with death in his hand. Unresponsive, he shot one directly in the chest who was flung hard to the ground. The other when shot fell down beside his companion. Naked and dead they looked pitiful lying in a furrowed field while their killer shouted himself hoarse about what the North Koreans had earlier done to captured American soldiers.

The other trucks in the convoy had come to a halt and many African Americans came to join the one who had killed the youngsters. They stared at the naked dead, patted the killer on the back and he relaxed, holstering his pistol. I looked at Lieutenant Butler, wondering what we could do, but he signalled in a placatory fashion that nothing could be done. I knew he was right for how could this furious man be disarmed and held to account? If he was, what would be the reaction of his many fellow soldiers, all armed and excited?

Our food had not arrived and. wanting to check on my platoon, I went about to see that everyone was in good shape. On the brow of a hill I came upon Captain Denness urging one of our Bren gunners to take out some white-robed men walking in file about two hundred yards below his position. Denness told me that with his binoculars he had seen that they were wearing army boots and he reckoned they were North Korean army men out to infiltrate our position. The Bren gunner, however, was having trouble with his weapon, so taking it from him I carried out what we call IA, which means immediate action when the gun stops or fails to fire. It was a procedure of only a few seconds and we could do it blindfolded or in the dark. I then adjusted the sights to two hundred metres, fired a short burst and the first two men in white dropped, presumably dead, into a ditch by the road. The others turned and fled. Captain Denness thanked me as I handed the weapon back to the gunner.

When I got back to Lieutenant Butler about an hour later news correspondents were arriving and our soldiers were happy to relate details of a few real and a couple of doubtful feats of military endeavour. I was to find Butler had been hit in the waist by a spent bullet that had slightly penetrated his web belt, but which had also cushioned the impact of the bullet. He was bruised and slightly cut. While I quickly cleaned him up we discussed some aspects of the fight and how we could probably now push on to the Yalu River because our enemy was withdrawing. Butler then commented that Captain Denness had suggested that I be put in for a gallantry award because of the way I had handled the platoon. Butler said he could not commend me as he believed that the battle generally, and our few casualties, did not justify any awards. But things, he thought, had gone well. Our battalion had at least, seen some action. I agreed, but I was thinking of the poor mangled horse with the appealing brown eyes, and two young North Koreans lying naked and dead in a paddy field nearby.

Chapter Eleven

Talking to Lim I went on to tell him how the following day the brigade moved forward and entered the town of Sinanju in a yellow and late autumnal morning. Most of the townspeople welcomed us, bowing from the waist, and shouting the Japanese *'Banzai'*, meaning another ten thousand years. Some stood to the rear, throwing apples to us. We were happy to eat them, for the late harvested fruit made a succulent crunchy sound and had a taste that was mouth-watering. A short while later our battalion was ordered to lead an advance on the next major town, a place called Pakchon, some six miles to the north on the Taeyong River. Our commanding officer, Lieutenant Colonel Green, had already ordered an air strike and American F-80 Shooting Stars had strafed and bombed the high ground on the west bank of the river. A bridge there had been destroyed by the enemy, but a fording place for the tanks had been found.

Later on in the darkness soldiers of A and B companies began clambering over the broken bridge. They quickly occupied positions on top of a bank on the far side. By midnight they were dug in, glad to be working and trying to keep out the freezing winds creeping in from Manchuria. The most bitter winter in decades was just beginning and as yet we had no proper winter gear to ward it off. We were all sleeping in the open with our main protection being our bulky greatcoats. We also wore clanking hob-nailed boots whose steel could quickly refrigerate any feet they encased. We were not too concerned about it, though. After all, the enemy appeared to be in full retreat, and we expected to be back in Japan by Christmas, living again in heated barracks.

By midnight our men across the river were under heavy attack. Several had been killed, some were wounded, and it was decided to send 8 Platoon of C company across the broken bridge to reinforce them. Bandy of that group, had observed 9 Platoon's progress along the road by the apple orchard. A fine parade ground soldier, straight as a gun barrel, was the sergeant in charge. He came and told me he was taking his platoon across the river and that he would find a comfortable spot for me, should I also go over. We had been friends for the past four years in Japan and I jokingly told him not to stand tall, but to lower his impressive height. He said he would hug the ground, patted me on the shoulder and the warmth of his hand persisted even after he had disappeared into the night.

When we crossed the bridge the following morning we had to walk past a number of our dead soldiers. They were lined up alongside a road with their heavy, muddy boots sticking out from under their ground-sheet covering. It was an ugly reminder what war was about, and I could not but wonder if Bandy was lying there. I discovered he had survived, but Bluey Wilkinson, a red-headed fine-looking young man, had died right next to him. He was the battalion joker and a fine musician, able to pick out almost any tune on a piano. But the capricious fortune of war had stilled whatever potential he may have possessed.

Bandy explained that he, Wilkinson and others had taken up positions in shallow weapon pits the enemy had previously dug. Wilkinson kept popping his head up and down, trying to see what was ahead. Bandy saw movement in a small bush ahead of him, told Wilkinson to keep his head down and also quietly called out to his men nearby, telling them where he had sighted the enemy soldier. Wilkinson said something, raised his head again and, just as one of Bandy's men fired his rifle and called, "Got him, Sarge!" Wilkinson collapsed beside Bandy who found he was dead, shot clean through the forehead. He had apparently decided to have one more look just as the enemy soldier fired and killed him, but the enemy was in turn shot dead by the man who had, "Got him!"

Wilkinson was later buried with others in a small Christian churchyard at Pakchon, a place we quit on 27 October, finding that the road ahead and the area about had all been heavily bombed. We counted many enemy dead, along with several destroyed tanks and self-propelled guns. On 29 October our battalion was the spearhead of the brigade and, as was often the case when the Australians were in the lead, we encountered strong resistance with the force facing us, estimated to be several hundred strong with tanks and guns in support. Spotter aircraft reported on some of the enemy dispositions and air-strikes were called for. They destroyed nine tanks and several self-propelled guns.

Colonel Green had ordered D Company to attack along the road, supported by American Shermans and the tanks played a vital role in delivering close and heavy support fire for the attacking infantry. Also supported by tanks, A Company went in to attack along the ridge line north of the road. C Company was placed in the rear of the battalion to serve both as a reserve and as a protective unit against small parties of the enemy roaming the hills on both sides of the road.

As darkness fell the North Koreans launched a strong counter-attack against D Company. They had brought up substantial reinforcements, including tanks and self-propelled guns. The main attack fell in 10 Platoon but the platoon commander ordered his men to hold fire until the attackers were only a few feet away. In the morning close to forty enemy dead were counted about the position.

The North Koreans made a furious and determined charge against A Company in the evening and mortar and artillery fire

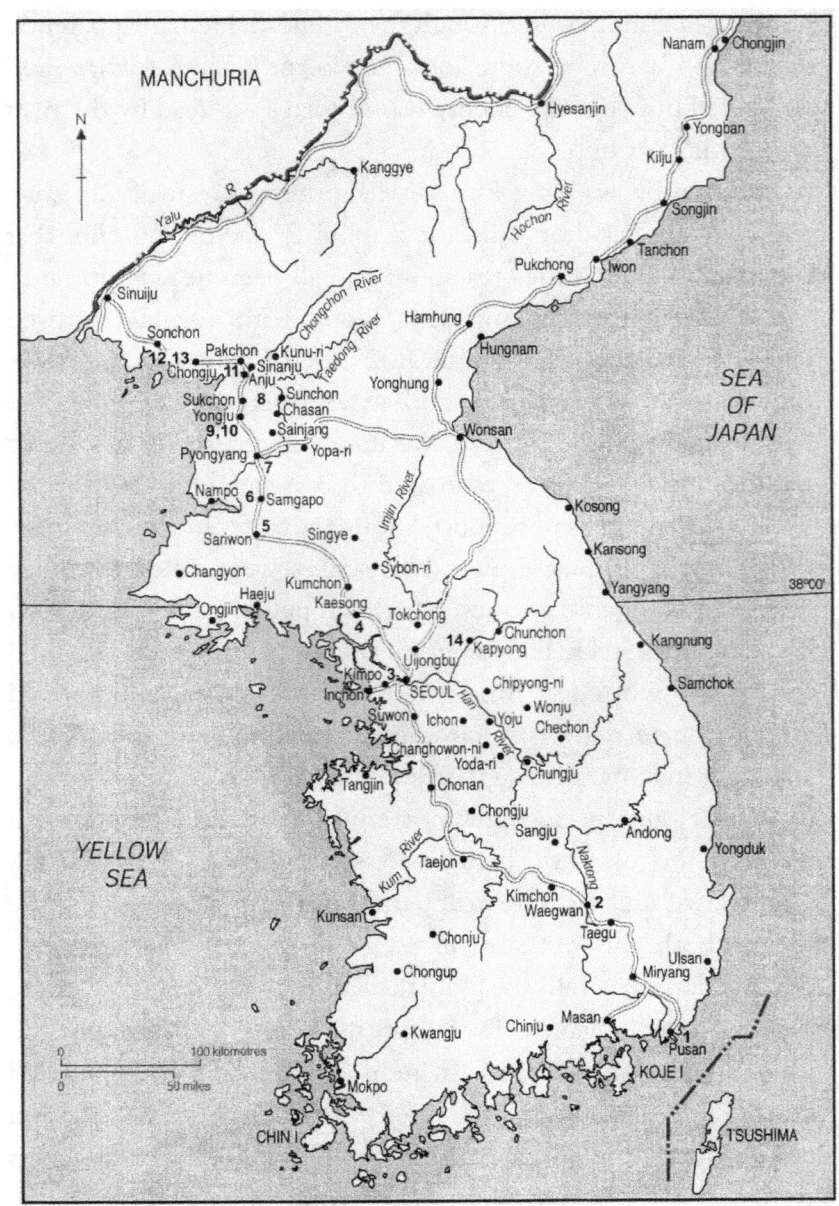

Korean Peninsular showing 3 RAR operations,
28 September 1950 to 30 June 1952

from supporting Americans was called in.

It fell only a few yards from where the company had dug in. The enemy attack was broken up, and during the battle the rocket launcher team destroyed three T 34 Russian tanks. The following day 150 enemy dead were counted about the battalion's position, which showed that the battalion was becoming very professional in the conduct of war. But our own count of 17 dead and 59 wounded was mounting after the brief fight at the Apple Orchard, another at Pakchon and now, this one at a place called Chongju.

Chongju is a small town located about 60 miles from the Yalu River and was the farthest point north of our advance into North Korea. Our battalion proudly entered it on 30 October. There was a widely-held belief that, once we had lustrated, that is, performed a ceremonial washing, in the Yalu waters, or more practically after some American general had pissed in it, the war would be over, with North Korea forced into a humiliating surrender. A belief, however, is not something necessarily true and it proved so for me, for Colonel Green and for our battalion, who came to experience first a battlefield sense of great loss, and later a sense of shame when we were forced out of North Korea when the Chinese forces entered the war.

On the morning of that late October, I was sitting on a hill enjoying the coming day after making sure that our platoon position was secure, when an American soldier came pounding up the hill from the valley below. He was a tall, skinny, highly agitated man and he shouted to me that there was a self-propelled gun moving about below us. Having yelled this information he simply disappeared from my view, waving his arms and shouting.

Lieutenant Butler had gone away to discuss something with Captain Denness so I told Corporal Parsons who was sitting near me that I would go down to investigate. I asked him to organise the bazooka team to go with me and for him to get his section into place, giving me covering fire if necessary if we should come under attack.

We were well equipped with American bazookas, having trained with them in Japan, and knew they could punch a hole straight through several inches of metal and were lethal against self-propelled weapons. The two-man team of Paull and Hunter who handled the gun were quickly beside me and together we hurried down the hillside towards the valley, cleared of rice but covered with stooks of straw. We skidded about as we ran, enveloped in noise and dust, our heavy boots smashing into the brittle surface of the stony ground. I was in front, my rifle gripped in my right hand, the team close behind, when we came near to a ruined village close to a raised paddy field wall. I saw movement, possibly a head behind the wall, and turned to warn the others when a huge blow to my left hand spun me around and threw me flat on my back.

There was no immediate pain but the dead weight of my arm along with the screaming agony which flowed from it seconds later forced me to sag on one side. I lifted my hand to see I had taken a bullet in the gap between my thumb and the first finger. The entry wound was small but the lead had taken all my knuckles away and the exit hole, where the smashed bone had been blown out, was horrible to look at. Stupidly I thought that I would never fight in the ring again, even if should I keep my hand. I looked about for the bazooka team to see that Paull, whose remarkable nickname was 'Blossom', was standing in full view on top of the paddy field wall. His body was shaking but he was preparing gamely to fire his launcher. I yelled at him to be careful, to get down, that I had been shot from there.

Paull looked over to me, nodded, then bravely fired his launcher. There was a massive blast of sound and a long thin column of fire from the rear of the launcher as the missile was fired. The shell struck the house to Paull's front and simply disappeared in a great cloud of dust and timber. But I could not sight any self-propelled gun which Paull apparently presumed could have been hidden behind the house.

Some of Parson's section were quickly gathering about me and a medic was pressing morphine into my arm while speaking quietly to me. As I struggled with him and another soldier back up the hill I heard the bazooka fire one more time and I hoped Paull had done some damage to the gun we had been seeking. I was stretched out on the ground and made comfortable while waiting to be taken to hospital, when Lieutenant Colonel Green appeared and spoke to me. He put his hand on my shoulder, hunkered down beside me and said he was sorry to be losing me. Also, that I should have come to him and he would have called in an air strike to take out the alleged gun. I was astonished that our colonel could have come to talk to me because he would have had a busy night, and must hardly have slept during the battle which had cost us our dead and wounded.

Soon I was stretchered out on a jeep, ready to be taken away and I wept, asking not to be taken from the men I had been with for so long. They were fine soldiers, younger brothers to me, men to die for, yet here I was being carted away with a ruined left hand. As I was driven from the battalion site I saw Colonel Green standing with a group of men on the brow of the hill. He raised a hand to me, I waved back, soldier to soldier. Then I fell asleep.

Blossom Paull did not take out the self-propelled gun that crazy bugger said was in the valley; Colonel Green did not call in an air strike either. That agitated American soldier had seen the gun, but he had it in the wrong position because at dusk that evening six high-velocity shells fired from a self-propelled gun somewhere in the valley, hit near our battalion headquarters which was protected by being on the reverse side of the hill. Five of the shells exploded harmlessly on the forward slope of the ground, but the sixth cleared the crest, hit a tree and tore apart close to Green's tent. Asleep on his stretcher, he was badly wounded in the stomach by shell fragments. His batman who was in the tent with him was not injured and he reported that all Green said when he looked at his awful wound was, *"What will happen to Olwyn?"*. His mind was obviously fixed on his wife, the woman he loved, and knew he was losing. Along with one small child, a daughter.

Green was taken to the army hospital situated in a town called Anju, where they had already saved my hand. They could not save Green, however, and he died the following morning. Had he lived he would have read a message Major General Gay sent to him the following morning, noting that Three Battalion had travelled thirty miles in twelve hours to deliver to the enemy what Gay called 'a disastrous blow'. Green was later awarded a posthumous American Silver Star for his courage and leadership. A country lad, he was educated only to Year Eleven but he became one of the youngest battalion commanders in New Guinea where he was awarded a DSO for bravery and his skill in commanding. He was discharged from the army at the end of hostilities but in 1950, when a student at the Australian Staff College, he was appointed to serve in Korea with the Third Battalion, the Royal Australian Regiment or 3RAR, as it was commonly known. Green always had a desire to own a farm and it was said that shortly before his death he had written to Olywn, saying they would soon have money enough to buy the farm they had both cherished.

I had related most of my background 1950 story to Lim over a number of sessions and following more visits of David Butler to my agent detachment. Now in July 1953, my new army posting had come through: it was to go, as a Chinese language interpreter to the armistice talks being held at Panmunjon, a small town in Gyeonngi Province, in what is called a de facto border between North and South Korea. While I waited I considered how things which seem to be disruptive or even disastrous were not what they appeared to be, and often every wound, every hurt, every mistake, can turned to be to one's benefit. When I hurt my shoulder in the Merchant Navy and joined the army, I entered into a new and wonderful phase of life. With a partly ruined hand I was returned to Australia, desolate, thinking my army life was over, but when I heard that a Chinese language course was taking place, I wrote to the School of Languages setting out my background in Japanese, and I was accepted to study Chinese. On graduation, I was seconded from the army to the Australian Security Intelligence Organisation whose acronym was ASIO. It was there that I met Norma Robinson, later to be my wife. She was a young lady with a clear-cut mouth shielding good teeth, dark challenging eyes, and a nicely moulded figure. She had dependability, forbearance and a sense of reality which appealed to me. We had some lively discussions and, later, intimacy. Her mother, "Call me Jean," liked to act the duchess when she poured tea elegantly, passed sandwiches, and talked softly. There was a pleasant warmth in her kindness, and good sense. She did not mind her daughter being interested in a soldier with no wealth or much education and who had fought in a war in Korea, one most Australians were not much interested in, or even talked about. She did once remark one Easter time, that she recalled a previous Easter when the Australians in Korea had fought bravely while a British Battalion, the Glorious Gloucesters as the newspapers had it, had been overwhelmed and forced to surrender. Jean had been born in London, hence her interest in the Gloucestershire Regiment, and I told her that fight had taken place at Kapyong, a battle which took place after General MacArthur had been recalled, and as though to prove they would never surrender as he had once stated, the Chinese mounted their attack, one estimated by intelligence reports to be of a force of hundreds of thousands and with its main thrust driving directly for Seoul. The 1st Battalion of the Gloucestershire Regiment were deployed on high ground over-looking the Kapyong valley and they believed one of the main obstacles to any Chinese forward movement was the Imjin River, some distance to their front. Unfortunately for the defenders at that position, the wide river was fordable at many points and the Chinese struck with great force at midnight on 23 April, cutting a gap between the Gloucesters and the Fusiliers of the British 29th Brigade. The Gloucesters fought desperately on the 23 and 24 of April against enormous odds. Many attempts were made to relieve them. One was made by a Philippine battalion but it was ambushed and cut to pieces. One group led by three tanks was getting close but the driver of the leading tank had not closed his hatch cover and a Chinese mortar bomb landed directly into its interior. The tank burst into flames, swung about and hit a cliff face, blocking the road. There was no way around it because there was a sheer drop into the river on the other side. The Gloucesters then tried to fight their way out but their enemy forced them back. Some of the survivors gathered on a small knoll. Attempts were made to supply them and evacuate their wounded but all failed as the Chinese held the high ground above.

During the night the British brigade was ordered to withdraw but as the Gloucesters were surrounded their commanding officer Lieutenant Colonel Carne gave his company commanders orders to fight their way out. Carne with his medical officer and his chaplains remained with the wounded and were captured. But the stubborn resistance of the Gloucesters over two days and three nights had held up the Chinese in that sector sufficiently to allow the other battalions in the brigade to withdraw safely in order and establish a new defensive line. Carne, I told Jean, was awarded a Victoria Cross for his leadership and courage.

Jean had listened without once interrupting me and when I had concluded, she said, "Wonderful soldiers, those men from Gloucestershire". Quietly, she then poured me another cup of tea. "I hope you are finished fighting there?" she asked with a smile.

"Sure," I said, adding. "My days of so-called derring-do are over." It was not be, though, for a few months later I was involved in what could have been a remarkable feat of arms, the attempted rescue of Carne from his prison camp deep in North Korea.

In early 1953, after only a short period in the Sydney office, ASIO sent me to New Guinea to look for the "Red Peril" among the Chinese there. I could find none, and knowing that I was wasting my time, I wrote and told Norma I was bored with the job and that I was going to contact the Director of Military Intelligence offering to serve a second tour in Korea if he would get me out of ASIO. I was quickly moved but before I left, Colonel Spry of ASIO asked me to come and see him on my discharge from the army, as he thought he could make good use of my background. He agreed that the New Guinea posting had been a mistake. Norma was pleased with my decision, believing that I would take on some sort of administrative position in Korea, as I had been declared unfit for infantry service, and that the future ASIO offer looked promising, as did our future together.

On my return to Korea early in 1953 I was posted to an IPW or Interrogation of Prisoners of War Team but, as there were no prisoners, I went to Divisional Headquarters and requested an interview with the GSO 1, a colonel. I told him of my infantry background and languages and although I had no notion of it, he was just then looking for a soldier to post to his agent detachment. It was a miraculous stroke of luck for just as I accidentally popped up, a warrant officer, Tony Lavender, who was running the detachment, was on reposting back to England. So by sheer chance, I met and worked with Lim and Pak and many others.

Evdokia Petrov being 'escorted' back to Russia in April 1954.
Courtesy of ASIO.

And now, as my discharge date from the army was only a few months away, I intended, after my service at Panmunjon and on my return to Australia, to approach Colonel Spry and work again in his organisation.

I never explained to Norma what I was doing in the agent detachment and when I wrote to her assembling plain words on paper, I cursed myself for not saying what I wanted to say and tell her that sometimes fear lay like a cold knot in my chest. I knew anyhow that trying to tell her what I was doing behind the enemy lines was like trying to explain the sky to someone who had never seen the colour blue. In the meantime my usual letter: *'Hi there love, nothing much doing. The war's dead as usual. Peace seems to be on the way...'* So when Pak was killed and I was wounded I was able to cable her before someone in the army was sent to tell her about it. All I could say was *'Slightly hurt...safe in hospital.'*

But Norma's later letters and some newspaper cuttings with photographs, the ones discussing the defection of a Russian diplomat named Vladimir Petrov on 3 April 1954, had been stimulating, especially as Norma believed that this defection had given ASIO a sort of glamour, and its future as Australia's top security organisation was assured. My hoped-for job with them in the future appeared marvellous. A good, clear-thinking writer and a serving member of ASIO, Norma was able to give me a concise account surrounding the defection, especially about the story of Evdokia Petrova who had not forsaken her country at the same time as her husband. In one long letter Norma described the extraordinary scene which took place under harsh floodlights when Evdokia, a small woman, the last on board, was physically lugged up the aeroplane steps by two burly Russian couriers, labelled thugs by many, who had been sent from Russia to escort her back to her homeland. They were so alarmed by the overt hostility of a massive crowd who had waited about the airport for hours, that they dragged the helpless woman along by her arms until one of her shoes was rudely ripped off by the sharp edge of the stairs. Unconcerned about her tear-wet face and a lost shoe, the couriers thrust her brutally into the aircraft. That red shoe, declared by many journalists to be the hated colour of the communist flag and its system, became, according to Norma, an iconic symbol of the Petrov defections.

The surging mass of people, who had gathered with the express purpose of rescuing Evdokia and who had unnerved the couriers, were mostly immigrants from Eastern Europe. They shoved about, yelling and swearing, trying to push forward with massive force, waving their fists, some brandishing blunt weapons, for they honestly believed that Evdokia was being taken back to Russia against her will, and that death awaited her. It was only the mustering of a large armed and committed police force, all brandishing batons, that held them back.

As Norma described it to me and according to talk in the Sydney office, the drama continued in the aircraft when a hostess who had been briefed by ASIO waited nervously nearby until the courier who had been beside Evdokia had eaten and drunk wine with his food and gone to the toilet. The hostess, not noticed by the other courier who had been allocated a seat to the front and was strapped in and eating, quickly slipped into the vacated seat beside Evdokia and told her that it was known her first husband had been arrested and executed for unknown reasons, and that on her return to Russia she might easily follow him. She surely understood the way officials in Russia thought and behaved with their obsession about so-called civilian evil, and the eradication of countless millions of Russians whose views were alleged to be counter to those of Stalin. ASIO she was told, had already given five thousand pounds to her husband. More would follow, they would be guarded at a safe house, and economically their future was assured. She should take this last chance, while flying over Australian territory, to defect.

Evdokia, who had listened closely, said she would think about it. The hostess then hurried to the flight cabin to talk to the captain who had been briefed by ASIO and he radioed Darwin to say that when he arrived at the airport for refuelling, a Russian woman passenger had indicated that she might consider remaining in Australia. He reported the hostess had advised that the two Russian couriers were armed and suggested the Darwin police be informed as the situation was dangerous.

Norma went on to write that at Darwin Airport the Administrator of the Northern Territories escorted Mrs Petrov to a private room where she spoke by telephone to her husband, and it was then that she decided to defect. Meanwhile a sergeant of police, stronger and taller than the Russian couriers, quickly disarmed them in a nearby room. They had refused to hand over their weapons so the sergeant simply wheeled the first one about, thrust one of his arms cruelly up behind his back, tore a pistol from a shoulder holster and threw the gun to a nearby officer. He took the other one in the same fashion and swiftly had his gun. A Russian diplomat, based in Australia and who had accompanied Mrs Petrov on her planned return to Russia, protested at the courier treatment, and the way she had been taken from his custody. Some time later the plane continued on its flight to Russia, with the couriers denied their weapons. A short time later Russia withdrew its Embassy from Canberra while the Australian Embassy was closed in Moscow. Norma summed up the incident in a couple of descriptive words: *"She's free!"*

Norma continued to write and by the end of July, when my transfer to Panmunjon became effective, I knew among other things that despite Petrov's junior rank as Third Secretary at the Embassy, he was a colonel in the KGB, the Soviet secret police, and that his wife was a ranking Soviet intelligence officer. They had been sent to Australia in 1951 by the Soviet security chief, Lavrentia Beria. A cruel and depraved man, but one trusted by Joseph Stalin, he was arrested and shot following Stalin's death in March 1953. Vladimir Petrov evidently feared that if he returned to the Soviet Union he would be purged because he had been a confidante of Beria. Petrov's wife had initially elected to return to Russia because she believed that if she defected, her sister Tamara and her parents would be victimised. But the ASIO briefed hostess who spoke to her on the aeroplane was persuasive enough to make her decide to defect after she had talked the matter over with her husband.

I only spent three months at Panmunjon where during discussions with "Our Side" and "Your Side" I found the Chinese negotiators to be reasonable while the North Korean were black-faced, shouted a lot, were bloody-minded and seldom agreed to any proposals "Our Side" put forward. I was disappointed when it was agreed that The Hook, with its bulge into Allied territory, would be handed back "Your Side" to make for a straight demarcation line. Given the rigid defence of the Commonwealth Division and its dead and wounded and the many thousands of Chinese who had perished in futile efforts to take it, I wondered how a pen drawing a line on paper could so simply decide the final outcome of such a bloody battle.

But the war at last was over. Australia had 340 of its soldiers killed, with another 1,600 wounded. The most significant battle took place at Kapyong when the Australians were holding a position close to the Gloucestershire Regiment who, after a fierce encounter with an overwhelming force of Chinese soldiers, were forced into surrender. On the 23 April 1951 and well into the following day, the Australians fought vigorously as the Chinese force had attacked in great number but they were never able to overwhelm the Australians and they finally retreated, leaving many of their dead on the battlefield. I was to learn that among the Australian dead was a soldier named Lenny Lenoy; he was an Aboriginal who had once challenged me to a bare knuckle fight. It was a late summer day going towards evening, in 1948. I was sitting in a train, returning to my battalion after a visit to Hiroshima when Lennie, a slightly intoxicated private soldier came up and challenged me to fight him when we got back to our base area at Kaitaichi. I did not want to fight but Lennie said that, as I was supposed to be the best fighter in the battalion, he was out to prove that I was not and he wanted to get on with it. Later we stood on the station platform and did indeed, get on with it. I found Lennie to be simply a brawler while I, who had learned to fight over a number of years and had boxed professionally, easily countered Lennie's wild punches. A clenched bunch of bones, referred to as a fist, is a harmful weapon when snapped accurately into a man's flesh, and Lennie was soon a bloodied mess. After some time, while Lennie hung on bravely and we fought under the train lights which the driver had turned on for us, Lennie pleaded with me to knock him out with a right hand-blow. I told Lennie I did not want to hurt him any more, and finally he gave up. We then walked back to camp, sergeant and private, close together in the comradeship of fighters who have tried to batter each other senseless, but who find after the battle that they are both good blokes, following all that fury.

I got to know Lennie very well in the months to follow and I was pleased when he was promoted to lance corporal, then corporal. When I heard he had died a sergeant at Kapyong, I was deeply hurt. Later I thought about a writing a novel set at Buronga, blending Lennie into that story along with what I knew of Captain Reg Saunders, the only Aboriginal commissioned in the Australian Army. He fought at Kapyong but was never promoted although he stayed on in the army until his retirement.

It was at Panmunjon however, where I had a lot of spare time between sessions of interpreting, that I began to work on a fictitious story about my work with the Agent Detachment. I provisionally called it *The Tall Man*.

Chapter Twelve

On my return to Australia I was discharged from the army in mid-1954, got into civilian gear, and went for an interview with Colonel Spry. I had talked about him with Norma and checked some records to find out he was born in 1910, had graduated from Duntroon and had served in India for a year before the war. He had won a DSO in New Guinea and, like me, but on a different level he had been seconded from the army to ASIO four years previously. Following the defection of Petrov he had resigned from the army and was appointed as a civilian to head ASIO. A virulent anti-communist, Spry had already established an extraordinary influence in these early days of Australian intelligence, just at the time when Australia was feeling for an independent path in the world, clear of the scandals of MI5 and MI6 and the Cambridge Group who had spied for Russia.

Colonel Spry was just as I remembered him from our earlier meeting; his well-cut countenance radiated a friendly glow beneath his balding head. Under his thick eyebrows his dark eyes glowed. He had a manly handsomeness, and a good sense of dress. I was to find that when a subject interested him he would show excitement, then in a twinkling, he would be nonchalant again. He was facing a window overlooking St Kilda road in Melbourne with its many trees and fine parkland, when his secretary ushered me to his room. He stood up, shook my hand firmly, and indicated a seat for me with a good view to the front.

Spry told me he was glad to see me and that he had a spot in ASIO for me. I was to be given the rank of Field Officer and to be stationed in the Sydney office. He told me that a Royal

Commission on espionage was to be conducted in Sydney and I would be assigned with other ASIO officers to guard Vladimir Petrov and his wife during their attendance at any commission sittings. I would also be stationed at the ASIO safe house at Palm Beach where the Petrovs were being held under ASIO protection. Spry talked easily while ticking points off with the forefinger of his right hand. He went on to tell me that most ASIO officers were ex-policemen and people from the armed service who had been intelligence officers. The public service, however, had recently told him that he must appoint university graduates, but how a graduate would talk to and control a wharfie under-cover agent, he did not know, he said and laughed. But what he did know was that I must consider going to university to get a degree in Chinese studies. He noted that a Faculty in Chinese was soon to commence at Sydney University. He understood that I had left school at Year Ten, but having checked my army records he knew I had completed some correspondence courses through the army education service and that, coupled with the study I had done in Japanese and Chinese should be sufficient to allow me to study for Year Twelve and be admitted to University.

At this point Spry signalled for coffee and as we drank it and nibbled at biscuits Spry told me that it was expected that the commission on espionage would last for several months. Many witnesses would be examined, stacks of papers were to be read, many exhibits would have to be handled. He was going to hand me a sheaf of documents, classified secret, all to do with the Petrovs and some background people. I was to read them, the better to understand Vladimir and Evdokia, who he said, someone had called Pee-Wee, after a small bird, and the name had stuck. Spry also told me that ASIO would be questioned at the commission and that ASIO's advisor was a noted Queen's Council, Sir Garfield Barwick, whom the communists had named Sir Fishwick Barfly.

Spry caressed his bushy moustache and laughed slyly at the way the noted barrister had been caricatured by his enemy.

Spry then pressed a buzzer; his secretary appeared and was asked to give me the papers that had been made ready for me to read. He then noted that some of the background material, particularly on Beria, Michael Bailoguski and Petrov himself, made interesting reading. He stood, brushed a hand across his full moustache, shook my hand and welcomed me again, to ASIO.

Norma and I were living in her mother's small apartment in Darling Harbour while I waited for settlement on a war service loan to buy a small home we had located at Revesby, a working-class suburb some miles out from Sydney. The loan could be obtained following active service in the army and had a mortgage repayment of only 3%, which was very attractive. But at present I was flat broke after eight years as a soldier. As a sergeant, I had been receiving only fifteen shillings a day, most of which I had sent to Eileen, my mother. I had retained only enough to pay my mess bills, for Bonnie had told me that Eileen had been going through a rough on-and-off relationship with Jock, mostly problems of her making. She had lived with other men, but briefly, for such relationships were becoming harder and harder for her to find, what with her heavy drinking and what Bonnie described in a telling turn of phrase as her age and the thickening of her body.

While waiting to take up the task of guarding Petrov at the safe house I worked in the ASIO office set in an old mansion called Agincourt at the far end of King's Cross, overlooking the naval dockyard. It was there I was introduced to Ron Richards, deputy director-general of ASIO. He was a handsome, strongly built and friendly man; as was Jack Gilmour, a senior officer who had worked closely with Richards for endless months, scheming

Petrov's defection. I also met Roger Hollis, later to become head of MI5 and be knighted for his service. Hollis had brought with him a famous Russian interpreter who with great skill was able metaphorically, to get Petrov to spill a great number of beans.

ASIO had its own Russian speakers but their sessions with Petrov were not very productive. Under the skilful persuasion of a new man however, Petrov developed an eloquent tongue, telling firstly that a man known as Kisliysyn, then attached to the Russian Embassy in Canberra, had been responsible for settling Guy Burgess and Donald Maclean in Kuibyshev, a large city located on the Volga river a long way upstream from Stalingrad. Burgess and Maclean, formerly described as diplomats had 'disappeared' from England in May 1951. This was the first time their whereabouts were known, and they had come back to notice.

David Maclean came from a distinguished family and was, according to Kisliysyn, teaching English in Kuibyshev. He was happy in Russia. Maclean, in another life, had worked as secretary, then head of Chancery in the British Embassy in Washington, D. C. He was also appointed as secretary of the Combined Policy Committee and Atomic Energy and he was privy to highly classified intelligence in that field. Later, as head of the American department at the Foreign Office in 1950 he helped formulate Anglo-American policies during the Korean War.

Guy Burgess however was not a happy man as he was spending considerable time in sanatoria located on the Black Sea. Dependent on alcohol, Burgess often got into fights and one night, many years previously, he had been involved in a brawl. He was knocked down a flight of marble stairs and suffered multiple skull fractures from which he never recovered. Early in 1951 he was recalled from his post as second secretary in Washington and asked to resign because of growing disorderliness in his life. A few weeks later Burgess and Maclean fled England and mysteriously vanished.

At Cambridge University Burgess and Maclean were part of a group of privileged young students who shared a fashionable disdain for capitalist democracy. But recruited as agents by Soviet operatives it was now believed they must have been providing great quantities of information to the KGB from their respective posts.

The second great disclosure from Petrov though, was that Kisliysyn believed that a third man had persuaded Burgess and Maclean to run and indeed, had organised how it could be done. The Third Man now became an international celebrity; many years later he was identified as Kim Philby, formerly a senior officer in MI6 and the most famous double agent of the Cold War period. He was a ruthless operator, responsible for the deaths of the many Western agents he betrayed over a ten year period. But an event which could have appealed to a writer of suspense-fiction took place at the end of the war when Philby found himself close to exposure, and a possible death sentence for spying. It was August 1945 and Konstantin Volkov an NKVD agent and Russian vice-consul in Istanbul approached the British vice-consul in that city and he requested political asylum for himself and his wife, who appeared with him. For a large sum of money Volkov said he would name three Russian agents inside Britain, two of whom were in the Foreign Office, and a third who worked in counter espionage in London. After an incredible series of security blunders, with schemes proposed then aborted, Philby was appointed case-officer in the Volky case. It was planned that he would fly immediately to Istanbul and interview Volky, a man Philby knew he had to silence. Managing to stretch out the time needed to get to Istanbul, Philby was able to warn his Soviet controller who in turn alerted Moscow. Specialists were then sent by military aircraft to Istanbul. Volkov and his wife were summoned to the consulate where they were sedated, tied to stretchers, and carried to the waiting aircraft. Flown to Moscow they were both later interrogated, tortured and shot. When Philby finally arrived in Istanbul he was met and taken to the British Consulate. From there, according to reports, he became frantic trying to talk to Volkov, only to be told he was no longer available. He telephoned so often that finally the consular officials refused to speak to him. Philby finally concluded that the information allegedly passed on by Volkov was nonsense and the defection request was a Russian attempt to embarrass British intelligence formations.

Nearly ten years later, following Petrov's revelation and with doubts in some intelligence officers minds about the truth of Volkov's disappearance, and his known close friendship with Burgess and Maclean, Philby was placed under investigation. Few could believe though, despite mounting evidence, that this distinguished English gentleman and cricket devotee was anything but a warrior in the war against Russian communism. But Philby, feeling under threat, defected in 1963. He settled in Moscow, was cared for, and later decorated by the KGB. He died in a Moscow hospital in 1988. Allowed a splendid funeral with a KGB honour guard in attendance, he was later commemorated on a Russian postage stamp.

Apart from his discussions about Burgess, Maclean, and the third man which prompted a hunt for him, Petrov brought a mass of information which included details on Soviet cipher, agent networks, and the names of hundreds of KGB officers. He was manifestly a smart and observant officer and no doubt when ASIO soon publishes its two volume history to be called *Spycatcher* he will be applauded. But Petrov was not a trained intelligence officer as was made clear when he recruited a Polish doctor and musician named Michael Bailoguski to spy for him, when Bailoguski was in fact an ASIO agent. Formerly an intelligence agent for the Commonwealth Investigation Service, when that service was disbanded and merged into ASIO, he was recruited into that group. Bailoguski was a member of the Russian Social Club and because he seemed to have the background to be a spy Petrov recruited him and gave him the code name Grigori. So it was that Bailoguski became the hunter and Petrov his target, with his objective to persuade Petrov to defect. It was known that Petrov was having trouble with his associates at the Russian Embassy. He was, as noted, concerned about the execution of Laventi Beria, once the second most powerful man in Russia. Because he was a 'Beria Man' Petrov would most likely be executed when he returned to Russia. Persuaded by Bailoguski, Petrov sought defection on the 3rd April, 1954.

The information on Lavrenti Beria, the longest lived and most influential of Joseph Stalin's secret police chiefs, the man Petrov had worked for, was chilling. Beria was born in 1889, trained as an architect, became a Soviet politician, a Marshal of the Soviet Union, Chief of Soviet Security, and a Secret Police chief under Stalin. He administered vast sections of the Soviet state and served as Marshal in command of the NKVD, the Soviet secret police agency responsible for anti-partisan operations on the Eastern Front during the war, as well as the apprehension of what were called cowards, turncoats, deserters and suspected malingerers. They were executed in their thousands. Beria also administered the vast networks of the Gulag labour camps. He played a decisive role in coordinating Soviet partisans and he developed an impressive intelligence and sabotage network behind the German lines. After the war he administered the communist takeover of the countries in Central and Eastern

Europe. His uncompromising ruthlessness in his duties and his skill at producing results culminated in his success of overseeing the Soviet atomic bomb project. That it was completed in under five years was partly due to the clever Soviet espionage organised by Beria. Klaus Fuchs, Beria's man, a German physicist and spy, was arrested and convicted in 1950 for giving vital American atomic research to the Soviet Union. McLean could also have been Beria's spy.

It was Beria's confidence in his position after Stalin's death which led him to misjudge the feelings of many of his associates, some of whom had relatives in prisons following Beria's activities against them. One man who hated him was Rossokovsky, a soldier who later became a Marshal of the Soviet Union; at the time of Beria's arrest he proudly exhibited his hands from which Beria personally had wrenched out all his fingernails when under interrogation, although he was innocent of any crime. In 1953 during a coup led by Nikita Krushchev assisted by military forces, Beria was removed and arrested on false charges of treason, but the full politburo convicted him. Following interrogation when a towel was stuffed in his mouth to halt his screaming, Beria was shot, along with most of his trusted associates.

It was then disclosed that Beria had been an evil and sadistic man. He was declared to be a womaniser whom power had distorted into a sexual predator. It was said he was a familiar sight on the streets of Moscow, cruising about in his armoured Packard with two burly Caucasian bodyguards who were ordered to get out and seize any woman Beria fancied. Many were brutally kidnapped and raped. There was also a story about a famous actress who was taken to Beria and told that her father and grandfather would be released from prison. That information was supposed to keep her quiet after he had raped her, although he knew at the time that both men had already been executed.

But the woman was let go, she talked, was arrested and sent to solitary confinement in Siberia.

I was assigned to the safe house in September 1954. By this time the commission of espionage had been going on for some months and guarding the Petrovs had become a routine and, for some, a boring time. When I met them I found Vladimir to be a paunchy man with a large face. He had small, tobacco-stained teeth, a morose demeanour and he liked strong alcohol. His spoken English was excellent as he proved when being questioned by the commissioners. He appeared to be a man used to authority and command. Evdokia dressed nicely, was small in stature, had blondish-coloured hair and remarkably clear blue eyes, set in white. Her marriage was obviously one of convenience and she and her husband acted like strangers to each other.

A much happier Evdokia Petrov now that the Royal Commission on Espionage is over. An ASIO officer is beside her. Courtesy of ASIO.

When on guard, which was four hours on and eight off, just like a seaman's watch, we walked about the large and lovely garden with the Petrovs, played cards with them, flung a few darts at a board, attempted our skill at Monopoly and tried to pass the hours comfortably. Both Vladimir and Evdokia were good cooks and they liked to prepare what the Russians called palmeni, which was finely cut meat, seasoned with herbs, wrapped in thin rounds of dough and quickly boiled. It was delicious food and we all relaxed when eating it, while talking and laughing happily. When they appeared at the commission, however, they went there nervously and came back annoyed and exhausted. One night a depressed Petrov having a drink and being guarded by Jack Dodds, put aside his glass of whisky and, picking up a nearby shotgun shoved the barrel into his mouth. Dodds was a former British sailor who had served in the Arctic convoys on the run to Mermansk and had been decorated for his skill in detecting a German submarine, one of which had sunk nearly ninety merchant vessels and sixteen Royal Navy warships. A man used to panic and tense situations, Dodds quietly lied to Petrov, saying he knew a man who had shot himself through the mouth, but he had blundered and blew only half of his face away. After considerable surgery he looked terrible, lost his wife, lost his children, and it was thought that he had retired into a religious order in Tibet where he was often buggered. Petrov stared at Dodds for a few moments, then took the gun carefully from his mouth. He shook a stubby finger in Dodd's face, laughed mockingly at him, and picked up his glass of whisky.

I took Vladimir fishing on the Hawkesbury River many times and on one beautifully clear morning he hooked and almost landed a huge flathead. That was until I picked up the net and attempted to land it. Unfortunately I put my weakened left hand to the side of the boat and under my weight it folded under me. I fell forward, the net took the fish in the head, the hook was ripped from its mouth and the fish slid back into the water. It lay there, looking at us until its tail began to move and with a splash it disappeared. I turned to Petrov. "Sorry, Vlad," I said. "Sorry! Sorry!" and he shouted at me, "What use is your bloody sorrow to me?" He remained in a leaden and poisonous mood for some time but eventually we had a laugh together and ultimately became not friends but had an understanding of each other.

The Petrov defections came shortly before the 1954 Federal elections and Dr Evatt, leader of the Australian Labor Party, accused Menzies of having arranged the defections to coincide with the election date for the benefit of the ruling Liberal Party. The defections became dramatic when Menzies alleged that Petrov had brought with him documents concerning Soviet espionage in Australia and the Royal Commission, which continued for the rest of 1954 and beyond, uncovered some evidence of espionage for the Soviet Union by some members and supporters of the Communist Party of Australia during and immediately after World War Two. But no one was ever charged with an offence as a result of the Commission's work, and no spy ring was ever uncovered.

Evatt's loss of the election and his belief that Menzies had conspired with ASIO to contrive Petrov's defection, and his appearance before the commission on behalf of two of his staff members, led to criticism within the Labor Party which was compounded when Evatt wrote to the Soviet Foreign Minister, asking if allegations of Soviet espionage in Australia were true. When Molotov replied, denying the allegations, Evatt read the letter out in Parliament, inviting amazement and ridicule from the Liberal Party. The Labor Party did not win office again for another eighteen years. Menzies always denied that he had knowledge of Petrov's defection, but he agreed he had exploited it.

The Petrovs spent eighteen months under ASIO guard at Palm Beach but by mid-1956 I was carrying out surveillance and other duties in and around Sydney. Norma and I had married, by which time we had bought a cottage at Revesby, I had been accepted and was studying for the Year Twelve examinations that year, and I was working hard to finish my novel, *The Tall Man*. The Petrovs were no longer under ASIO guard once the commissions findings were released. They simply disappeared into obscurity under ASIO supervision.

In late 1956 I was advised by the Australian Army that because of my part in the attempted rescue attempt of Lieutenant Colonel Carne, I had been awarded a Military Medal for gallantry. I was told I could travel to England and have the medal presented to me by the Queen or in Australia from the Governor of New South Wales. I chose the latter and accompanied by Norma we attended a church service. I was later called to a podium where the citation was read, the document was handed to me and the Governor pinned the medal on my lapel. Afterwards we attended a reception in the gardens of Government House where I was photographed and interviewed by a newspaper reporter whose comments were printed the following day.

I no longer have that document but Robert O'Neill's Australian War Memorial official history of the Korean War reports the following:

'*The rain caused acute problems for those responsible for the infiltration of intelligence agents into enemy territory. Sergeant A. M. Harris, an Australian attached to the headquarters of the Commonwealth Division to command the Divisional Special Agent Detachment, decided that the only way he could, at that time, ensure that his agents crossed the flooded Samichon River and no man's land was to take them himself. He set out with a group of three agents at 9.30 p.m. on 2 July and he swam across the swiftly flowing Samichon, taking a guide rope which he used to help his agents across. He divided his party into two groups and set off for a Chinese anti-tank ditch, one and a half kilometres behind the enemy front. On reaching the ditch, Harris and his companion were fired on and grenaded by nearby Chinese. The agent was killed; Harris was wounded in the hand and thigh. He realised that the other group might still be proceeding successfully, without detection by the enemy and he decided to help them cross their difficult area by creating a diversion. He threw grenades and fired his pistol at the Chinese until his ammunition was exhausted. Enemy counter-fire grew heavier and Harris withdrew to the Samichon, dived in and allowed the current to carry him out of range. The other group was able to penetrate the Chinese defences and returned later with urgently needed information. Harris was awarded a Military Medal for this, and ten other journeys into enemy territory.'*

The urgently needed information was of course the fact that my previously safe route through the enemy front was no longer secure, and Colonel Carne could not be escorted back to safety on this, the final leg of his escape from captivity. I have often thought how wise someone, possibly Colonel James, asked that someone be sent out that night. If I had not gone to check the route, Carne would have been released from his prison camp by the paratroopers, walked all the way south and, not finding me waiting on Pheasant Hill, would have probably have gone to the same ambush point where Pak had been killed. It was a matter I had discussed with Captain Shaw when he had visited me in hospital, but it was not mentioned in the report about that particular crossing of the river for which I was decorated. As far as I know, that plan to rescue Lieutenant Colonel Carne has been under security wraps up to this very day.

By the end of 1956 I had completed *The Tall Man* and I gave it to an army friend of mine to read. He told me he liked it and asked if he could show it to an author mate of his, one he had served with in New Guinea. That author turned out to be Tom Hungerford whom I had never heard of, although I was to find that he was already famous as the author of *The Ridge and the River*, a prize-winning work about his time in New Guinea where he had been a sergeant in a commando unit. In the company of my friend I met Tom in a local pub and found him to be a big and happy red-haired man with arms as muscled as a wharf labourer. Tom was a journalist and, apart from his work and his success as an author, he was also a poet of growing repute. He had told my friend that he liked my book, wanted to meet me, and over that first discussion, helped along by several beers, he suggested some changes, all of which made sense to me, a struggling author. I met Tom on a number of occasions and had him home to dinner. Norma liked him and he was to become a lasting and true friend to us. He suggested, when I had finished with *The Tall Man*, that I enter it into the 1967 Sydney Morning Herald Literary Competition. When the winners were announced in mid-1967 I found I had won a prize worth five hundred pounds which, to me at that time, was a mountain of money. I immediately sent half of that loot to Eileen, then back living with Jock. I had, through Bonnie, invited her to my wedding and though Bonnie attended she did not bring Eileen with her as, according to Jock, she had gone out on what he called a walk about. He knew she would return to him at some time and when she did, she wrote me a long and wonderful letter of thanks over which I grieved as I read.

That was a good year for me for apart from that success with the book I passed my Matriculation Exam and had been accepted by Sydney University as an Arts student. I was to take

Chinese, English, Philosophy and History as First Year subjects, later concentrate on Chinese and go finally into the Honours year. I did not expect problems with the university courses for in my Matriculation examinations I had done so well that one of the newspapers, with what I took to be a miraculous piece of research, for how else did they know, described me as a 'Brave Sarg with A's in his Examinations.'

I did not mind a bit of publicity for it helped me with a promotion in ASIO and letters of congratulation from Colonel Spry, one for the book, the other for entry to university. I worked diligently for the colonel and all of us were constantly mounting surveillance operations on Australian Communist Party members, carrying out set tasks against visiting foreign communists, and running our own agents in many sections of the community, including some trade unions.

While I was busy at work and at university I set about writing my second book which I called *Grains of Sand*. Set in Korea with a fictitious me, Lim and Pak, the concept was that we were all like a handful of sand which had been scooped up, pressed together tightly, then scattered, the same grains, but never the same again. Like *The Tall Man* it was published by Cassell, an English company, and also by Farrar Strauss in America who wrote to me in 1958, asking if I would agree to *The Tall Man* being scripted for a film with Gary Cooper in the lead role. I was offered several thousand American dollars if the deal went through. Naturally I agreed, only to receive word back that Cooper had died and that the idea of a film script had been shelved.

Some time later and when *Grains of Sand* was in a second impression, I received a letter from an American film company, Aldrich and Associates, offering me several thousand dollars if they could produce a film script on the story. I agreed, was paid, and never heard from that company again. But I gave up writing early in 1960 when I was summoned to Melbourne, entered the office of the now Honorary Brigadier Spry's office, to be told that I was being posted to Hong Kong, to be attached to the Trade Office with diplomatic status to work undercover as an Immigration Liaison Officer. My main task would interviewing some of the many thousands of Russian immigrants, mostly living in Harbin, China, being forced out of the country as unwanted citizens. I was to assess which families could enter Australia, and determine if any might work for ASIO once settled in various parts of our country. I had been selected for that position according to Spry because early in 1960 I had received an Arts Degree from Sydney University, with Honours in Chinese. He also noted that he liked my book and later Robert O'Neill, our war historian said of *The Tall Man* and *Grains of Sand* that *These two volumes are the most significant contribution to Australian literature to have come from the Korean War.*

I returned to Sydney, Norma and I got ready to rent our home and I managed to sell a battered but faithful old Ford which I had bought from my half of the prize money I had received for *The Tall Man*. One evening though, I received what I can only call the worst news of my life when Bonnie called to say that Eileen had been hit by a car and that she was so seriously hurt as to be close to death. I immediately flew to a Melbourne hospital and when I was ushered in to see Eileen, after being told there was no hope that she would survive, my heart felt like a cold and heavy fist on my chest. Bonnie told me the police had said Eileen had been drinking heavily, she had walked into a park in St Kilda Road and there she had slept. On awakening and apparently not knowing where she was, she had gone out onto the busy road where a motor vehicle had hit her, full force.

As I sat by her bed I thought that Eileen's face looked very pale and lovely, and it seemed that she was just comfortably sleeping and would soon awake and smile at me. I took her hand, pleaded with her to press mine if she knew I was there and when she did, my tears flooded out, but silently so that Eileen might not know how hurt she was, how upset I had become. She died while I was there beside her, and I cursed the man, my father, whom she had loved so much and who had deceived her rottenly, ruining her life. I hoped he would cart shit forever!

A Gerard Henderson impression of Hong Kong painted in 1962

Chapter Thirteen

Norma and I arrived in Hong Kong in July 1960, a few days before I turned thirty-five. This a was when the Colony was still being engulfed in a flood of refugees from China seeking the freedoms their revolution had been mounted to achieve so many years previously. I was told by the ASIO officer I was replacing that shoals of desperate runaways were arriving with nothing but the clothing they wore, and most disappeared into slums already bursting with unwanted scores of thousands. Others, wanting their own refuge, built flimsy shelters on perilous land and rock-sliding hillsides. They used flattened-out cans, tar-paper, hessian bags, strips of this and sheets of that. From such mean hovels the Chinese went down into the city to work ten-hour shifts, seven days a week in factories that were often as basic as the places where they lived. But they undertook any sort of work for any sort of wage just to stay in Hong Kong with even the remote, and sometimes almost impossible, chance of creating something for themselves and their children, a life at least free from the bleak embrace of communism.

Walking and looking about me, taking in the meanness of many refugee places, I reflected on my early years in Buronga and the bag shanties many people had lived in, but where many women kept small gardens of hardy shrubs and some had trailed climbing geraniums to blossom against their calcimined, sagging walls. That was in the 1930s when times were hard with much unemployment. But the Australian government had been wise enough to introduce a form of social engineering that provided enough dole money to keep people fed and hopeful about the future. It seemed to me now, that while Chinese communism may have been faceless and harsh, the Hong Kong capitalist system appeared to be quite uncaring about the countless thousands of desperately unhappy and hungry refugees living within its border, not that I could do anything about it.

Meanwhile my own standard of living had taken a huge upward curve for wonderful accommodation was to be ours at a place called Stanley set on the long wooded peninsula to the south. The apartment had four bedrooms, two bathrooms and a great porch to the front overlooking a cultivated expanse of lawn. There were excellent quarters out back for the two servants we were to take over. The man had been a seaman and was a good cook. His wife was a pleasant woman and spoke some English, which pleased Norma. But she did not want to sit about and be waited upon so she quickly obtained a job as an accountant with the Shell Company. He mother Jean was an accountant and Norma had studied accountancy but had then switched to take a secretarial course, hence her job with ASIO, a connection which seemed to help when she applied for the position with Shell.

My office, within the Trade Commission premises, was situated on the corner of Pedder Street overlooking the lovely, colonial-era post office with its massive granite columns and beautifully fashioned red-brick dome. I was to work with Nesta, an English secretary, and Gloria, a woman with a Russian background and she was to interpret for me during interviews with the many Russian families I was to process, according to Australian immigration requirements and my ASIO brief. I was also introduced to the MI5 and MI6 officers, the CIA representatives with whom I was to liaise, and to Director John Prendergast, the head of Special Branch. A man of considerable repute, Prendergast had been awarded a George Medal for going alone to discuss peace with the Mau Mau terrorists in Africa at the height of their brutality. It was arranged that I would meet once a week with Prendergast to discuss my work. I appreciated the opportunity to talk with him, for I knew he had a searching mind and a keen intelligence. He was a tall, fit-looking man, stern and aloof, with a shock of white hair. He never sought friendship with people junior to him in rank or position.

I worked hard with long hours, kept company, wined and dined the English intelligence representatives, the CIA and the Federal Bureau officers. Pleased with what I was doing, and with some good results, Brigadier and now Sir Charles Spry extended my first three-year term. But I resigned from ASIO towards the end of that second term in 1965 because I was enraptured by the place and the appeal of Hong Kong with its surrounding beauty. I wanted to live and work there. Besides, according to an uncompromising letter I had received from the office of Sir Charles Spry I had made a serious error of judgement early in 1965 by telling a visiting Public Service inspector that the ASIO office, because of a diminishing work load, could now be managed by my secretary, Nesta Gray. Reading that letter I knew I had not only shot myself in one foot but in both feet, and that my future promotion prospects in ASIO had probably vanished. But on a personal level I had inherited a cocker spaniel. He was named Copper, and I had come to love him. I had found, though, that I could not take him directly back to Australia should I return. He had to be sent to England and be impounded for a couple of years. Once returned to Australia, he would be placed in pound again, for another couple of years. I could not allow that to happen.

As luck would have it, the Myer Emporium was hoping to open a Buying Office in Hong Kong and after many interviews and discussions I was appointed to a good, well-paying position with that distinguished company. I found space, recruited experienced staff, learned quickly what I had to do, and the Myer senior executives were soon pleased with the result. However, my marriage began to founder, as Norma having worked for ASIO for a number of years in what was her first job, was committed to that organisation. She would hear nothing wrong about Sir Charles, and she at first disliked and then discounted what she called rag-trade people who were central to my new position. My office had outside accounts with Alexanders of New York, a Jewish company, and Steinbergs of Canada. They paid a commission on all their shipments, money which helped keep my office financially secure.

Looking for a new place to live, we at first rented a place at Shatin in the New Territories, and when a lovely old stone house set in an acre of so of garden became available at Tai Po Kau, a village even further out, we rented that. The place lovely with great walks to be had in the surrounding hill for me and Copper.

At this time, dangerous feelings had been growing in Hong Kong with much talk about corruption and rottenness in high places. The police force was accused of corruption on a massive scale and an Englishwoman named Elsie Elliot, a compassionate missionary with an equally kind husband who ran a small English teaching school, constantly complained about how bad things had become: of young women being forced into prostitution by the Triad Gangs, girls who were said to gang-raped into submission, and if they did not agree, a bottle was thrust brutally into their vagina. Also some Triad members committed crimes for which they were never convicted, while other men were paid to sit in prison for years in their place while their families were well cared for on the outside. Elsie, derided by some as a silly old eccentric expatriate, typical of many who lived in Hong Kong and Peking, was abused by others, and particularly by many police officers who described her as being a paranoid, meddling crank because she was so vocal about corruption in high places, particularly the police force. Elsie was constantly in the news; her photographs sometimes showing her with her hair pulled back and tied into a bun at the nape of her neck. While such a hair style might have given a kind of severity to her features, it instead softened her face. The child of missionary parents, born in China and speaking excellent Chinese, she had a look of gentility, of good manners about her. But she constantly raised her concern about opium divans, massage parlours and the huge and corrupt gambling syndicates all ignored, she alleged, because the police were paid to let them be. Sometimes people listened to her and read what she had to say, and many journalists found her provocative remarks to be excellent copy.

Incidental to Elsie, discontent swelled and late in mid-1966, when the Star Ferry decided to raise the fares in the lower deck by five percent a young student went on a hunger strike at the ferry concourse and riots began. The student had a placard set before him, showing the balance sheet of the previous year with its huge profit result, along with a declaration that he would die, if necessary, unless the price increase was repealed. A few journalists of the communist press interviewed the young man. Other members of the press corps also gathered and he became the nucleus of what was soon a considerable crowd. Some reported he was some sort of lunatic while others, pointing to the Star Ferry profit line, said he was much more sane than those who would simply agree to any fare increase, either for the upper or lower decks. As time passed, others came to sit with him, some dropped money into his begging tin and a few left him food and drink, which he refused to touch.

Gradually the jostling heated crowds about changed into a surly mob. More and more came to stand and sit with the student. Many stayed the night and into the following days. Placards denouncing the Star Ferry, smeared with large black and red Chinese characters most abusive to government, appeared beside the student's and the air began to resound with chanted slogans, progressively more abusive of the police and government, bold and bolder yet, in advocating no fare increase. The mood of the mob grew increasingly restless, with some of the younger onlookers heckling the police; inevitably arrests were made. Newspaper reporting, particularly in the communist press became more challenging to the government. As a consequence, according to newspaper accounts, when a group of protesters marched down Nathan Road they were immediately supplemented by hundreds of youths looking for trouble, seeking an excuse to fight and, if possible, loot and burn as well. When they got to the ferry concourse the enraged mob wildly smashed anything in sight, fighting the police and bystanders, and even among themselves. With the concourse in flames, taxis and public light buses and private cars burning and looters running wild, the police anti-riot squad, which had been on stand-by, marched directly into the centre of the huge crowd, which quickly dispersed under the batons of the superbly trained young policemen. Praise for them was well-founded but the communist press through its Hsin Hwa, the so-called official communist news-sheet, declared that the British in Hong Kong could not put down the Chinese with such impunity, and that the weight of consequences would finally crush them.

A commission to investigate was established in December and the young student who had gone on his hunger strike was arrested and sentenced to three months imprisonment to be spent in an open compound on the island of Lantao, lying beyond Hong Kong in the South China Sea. Elsie Elliot was censured by the senior judge who said that because of her reckless and unsubstantiated allegations, particularly about the police force which had put down the rioters so gallantly, she should, as he put it, be censured at the bar of public opinion.

Elsie Elliot was shattered by such an attack and she wept when being interviewed. But bravely she challenged the judge, saying that she could not be deported from Hong Kong as she was a British subject. Later the judge was criticised, the matter was shelved, and Elsie continued her crusade against the police, saying that while the riot squad youngsters had indeed been gallant, she had no faith in some of the older senior policemen.

One of my best friends in Special Branch was Bob Richards, a Senior Superintendent who was being groomed to take over from Prendergast. I believe he kept in close touch with me because, as I had now opened an office in Taiwan and would in time be working out of China, I might be a useful source of information to him. He told me over a confidential lunch the details to a question I had posed. It was about the publicised drama of the deportation to China of a senior policeman who had been sent back over the border, accused of being a Chinese spy. John Prendergast was central to the deportation issue because, ever the hunter and seeker of information, he had visited the train station at Lowu, the crossing point on the railway line between Hong Kong and Canton, and when talking to a couple of his officers stationed there, he was suspicious of the way one man, in a group of labourers or coolies waiting to board for Hong Kong, was trying to keep from view by huddling to the rear. Prendergast ordered that all the labourers be taken away, have their clothing removed and searched, including their shoes. The job was done quickly and effectively and a coded message was found in the unscrewed heel of a shoe worn by the man Prendergast had been wary about.

That man was put under close surveillance and was followed

until he met up with a senior Chinese police officer in a Garden Road park where something was passed over. The coolie left but men watched him while the officer was followed to his home and later arrested while decoding the message passed to him, on a One Time Pad. Charged with spying, to which he confessed, the officer said he had also been corrupt, that the police force was largely corrupt, and if given amnesty he would name all the people he knew to be involved in corruption, Chinese and European officers alike.

It was to take Prendergast's men many weeks to unravel all that was known from their subject. While some of Prendergast's officers at first indignantly wanted to tear his force apart on charges of wholesale corruption, Prendergast was worried about the way the operation had unfolded so neatly, with a senior police officer being so easily exposed. Concerned that the rebellious Red Guards were causing destruction all over China, might not the Chinese have deliberately exposed one of their top agents with the aim of discrediting, and indeed, destroying the police force, one way or another?

He went to his commissioner with the facts and his concerns, stating among other things how the anti-riot squad had so easily beaten back the raging mobs at the Star Ferry in late 1966, and that the Chinese security service may have set out to discredit the police force. If action were now taken against many of its members charged with alleged corruption, what sort of police force would Hong Kong possess if the Red Guards in their madness decided to invade and wreck Hong Kong? Look at things in China, he declared. He had information about three hundred thousand rich farmers and landowners being arrested in southern China alone. Such people had everything taken from them and they were unmercifully beaten. With many bureaucrats it was even worse. In a number of cases senior officials, hoping to protect themselves, had sacrificed their juniors, but all were ultimately persecuted. Many people were committing suicide and some of the most beautiful homes along with shrines and temples in Hangchou and Fuchou were in ruins. Young people were running crazy, destroying priceless art objects simply because they were old and beautiful and were getting sledge hammers to break anything in their way. They were no different to Chairman Mao who was out to crush and ruin, in many cases to destroy, his old former friends, now his enemies, because many opposed his so-called social revolution. Mao's Red Guards were central to his movement and they had already taken Macao with the Portuguese government already agreeing, in a document signed in December the year before, that the colony of Macao be returned to China. In that case the Red Guard demands had been met, and they were now known to be gathering just beyond the Hong Kong borders. They were running wild, with thousands of people being beaten and murdered. Rape was being widely reported. The Hong Kong police force must not at this stage be investigated on charges of corruption. The officer who had laid so many allegations must be deported to China to shut his mouth. And so it came about.

In May 1967 Hong Kong faced its greatest danger since the war when riots flared in several parts of the Colony. They were carried out by committed cadres, professional trouble makers, hard-core communists and the equally determined thugs of the various Triad societies, all of them wanting to bring down the government institutions they hated. They were also joined by the many thousands of workers whose grievance was against the government's apparent lack of concern about the dirty, exhausting, degrading and poorly paid grind of their daily lives. The last to participate were the desperate hordes packed into slums and lumped together on dangerous hillsides, all in the belief that their only hope for a better life lay in joining the mob in a concerted protest of wholesale destruction. They had also been given a rallying point, a martyr. He was a youngster who worked in a factory where the owner had locked in all his workers for twenty-four hours and made them finish an order destined for shipping overseas. The boy, determined he would not be forced to work, had escaped by squeezing through the bars of a small window. Apprehended by a brutal, stupid guard, he was beaten so badly he died on the ground below the window. News of his death inflamed the mobs to new violence but journalists reporting on events, many with photographs, detailed how bravely the police tried to control events as the violence fluctuated in intensity, then faded to a curious lull, expertly orchestrated to keep the city in a nerve-wracking expectancy of the crescendo to come. The police seldom attacked, for they were ordered not to make any more objects of compassion for the rioters' cause. They had simply to confront any violence with as much restraint as possible and work behind their riot shields, with only that and a baton as protection. Having spent some time with the police at points of havoc, I could see that the security forces were sorely frustrated and intimidated as, lured into old slum areas by well-trained bands of agitators, they were met by bottles of acid and heavy objects dropped on them from tall buildings. When they entered the ramshackle, rubbish-choked rookeries in pursuit, their assailants would disappear with cries of mockery up choked stairways, and over plank-joined rooftops.

Through all this, watching, listening and reading many reports I had to modify an earlier opinion that the bravery and discipline of the police force might just be in defence of wholesale corruption, amounting to hundreds of millions of dollars each year, which the deported police officer had alleged, and which provided so many with a hugely bountiful second income. Now I knew there was something of much greater importance they were fighting to preserve, and during those violent weeks I became certain that they were struggling for their right to live where they chose, and that no matter how corrupt and, at times, how sordid it might be, this Hong Kong, a seething hotchpotch of races and ambitions, was battling for its essential right to be free. It seemed to me, that despite its many shortcomings, life in Hong Kong was preferable to the conditions they would be submitted to if they were to break and be shackled by Chinese forces. If they were ever chained in Chairman Mao's foundering China, it would surely mean incorporation in the anonymous people pit of a vast land with its millions of security files; in its endless party and government instructions; its neighbourhood committees in factories in schools and homes; where setting the old to watch the young, the young to watch the old, was an accepted routine of life. In China now, all men were not brothers, with crazed Red Guards said to be fighting each other, brothers informing on each other, fighting each other, one killing the other. No, it was a fear of incorporation into the deadly crucible China had become which made the police force so determined to hold.

Unable to break or seriously threaten their courage, the mobs turned to acts of arson and industrial sabotage, culminating in attacks on firemen and engineers called in to put out the flames or repair damaged machinery. Bus and tram drivers were beaten senseless and then burned with acid, so that ultimately they had to drive behind thick meshes of protective steel. In orgies of violence, probably triggered by the knowledge that they were failing in their attempts to subdue the police and crush the government, crowds from the left-wing unions, and even children from communist schools, roamed in packs like wild animals, attacking anything confronting them. Finally on 16 May thousands of them shouting marched in the rain up Garden Road to Government House where they demanded the Governor come out and see them. He refused but he sent an immaculately uniformed aide to tell them that he would discuss any problems, but only with groups of not more than twenty people and only inside Government House. This proved unacceptable to the mob who howled and raged their displeasure, but the Governor would not budge. By midday when the rain had stopped and the sun blazed through a sweltering humidity, scores of protesters dropped in fainting fits and bouts of hysteria, while many more defected to any available shade in the Botanical Gardens behind them. But the vocal majority grew increasingly insistent as more and more thousands packed up behind them. Standing between them and Government House were rank upon rank of police, women as well as men, a physical wall placed there to bar unauthorised entry to the centre of final authority in Hong Kong. Government House appeared white and lovely, with its dignified palms and many broad-leafed trees. The driveway was swept clean of any intrusive twig and the Governor's Rolls Royce, newly polished, let its glittering body work heighten the appearance of regal order and propriety. The royal crest, set in gold, red and black, blazed high on the heavy iron bars of the front gate and was both an unendurable challenge and a magnet to the steaming mobs before it. The police stood firm, the only bar that stood between the mob and that gate, and on them finally the frenzied crowd rolled in, wave upon human wave.

One tactical advantage for the hugely outnumbered police was that at the point of final contact, the rioters had drastically to narrow their attacking front between the stone pillars supporting the heavy gates, and they never made it through. One disadvantage, and it was political as well as tactical in overtone, was the arrival among the attackers of the leading Hong Kong communist, who drew up in his chauffer-driven Mercedes. He moved from his car brandishing Chairman Mao's now famous Little Red Book of quotations. He walked about ineffectually, perspired profusely, spoke a few meaningless Mao sayings and slid back into the air-conditioned comfort of his Mercedes before being driven away from the scene after a humiliating push-start, his car's ignition having failed.

The Governor, after highly praising the courage of the police, and to show that he would not be intimidated by any more mobs, ordered that Garden Road be closed to all traffic and pedestrians. All bloodstains outside Government House, mostly from wounded policemen and women, were mopped up and covered with sand as the clamour and defiance of the conflict drained from the air. At Government House, in the trees shading that triumphant red, black and gold crest, the only contention came from the many sparrows traditionally disputing their territorial rights in the lofty palm trees.

Things were manifestly bad in Hong Kong but information coming from China indicated that Mao's Cultural Revolution, as he called it, was causing great hardship and in some cases death for many thousands of his people. It was also providing some with the opportunity to pursue long-standing feuds and family vendettas. Corroboration of this madness and more was now being ferried out of China by the gritty, yellow flood waters of the Pearl River. While no one could tell exactly what was happening in China, some of the dead showed outsiders what was occurring and which, given a similar descent into anarchy in the Colony, could encompass all the people of Hong Kong, Chinese and Europeans alike. After abnormally heavy rains in June, grisly flotillas of corpses had sailed down the swollen rivers to Macao, now firmly under Chinese dominion, and on to the waters about Hong Kong. I had gone with a number of old intelligence friends, including Philip Murray of the CIA, to inspect some of the decomposing bodies being washed ashore; most had died with their hands tied behind their backs in a manner typical of Chinese gang-style executions. Many others carried numerous gun-shot wounds. Several were cruelly mutilated: women with their breasts hacked off; men headless, some emasculated.

"Long fish," Philip told me. "That's what the Chinese call poor buggers who finish up like this. And the Pearl River flows only through a few provinces in Southern China. I wonder what the hell's happening in the larger provinces?"

"God knows." That was all I could think to say.

"I doubt God's got much place in there," Philip growled. "But you know, even before Christ got nailed to that bit of wood, Peking was not able to control these people in the south, and particularly at Guangzhou. They are excitable buggers, telling Peking to go and spit in its own dust, not to bother them. Just to annoy Peking I reckon they might come screaming over the border at us at some time."

"Could be. But I reckon the police and the auxiliaries could handle them. I have absolute faith in them."

Philip was right and so was I. On 8 July 1967 the Sha Tau Kok police post, set on a hillside in the New Territories bordering with China, had an early morning line-up of police officers attacked with unexpected and accurate machinegun fire. With two of his policemen dead in that first burst, the European superintendent in charge got the remainder of his group, including some wounded, back into the shelter of his command post. Throughout the day the enemy gunners poured in short and accurate bursts, most of which bored through the steel-meshed concrete walls to ricochet inside the command post, often hitting men huddled on the floor behind whatever barricades they had been able to devise. Five policemen were now dead and some of the fifteen wounded had been hit several times. Towards the end of the day, while the one-sided action continued, the superintendent was told he was to be relieved by two companies of Gurkha riflemen. Throwing his telephone to the floor he shouted to his men:

Gurkhas! Holy Mary! Bloody Gurkhas! If anyone can get us out of this, it will be those marvellous buggers! My dad once served with them! Bugger me!" Risking a shot through the head he stood and staring out through a weapon slit and he saw a number of small brown-faced men dressed in battle kit, their famous kukri knives in full view, making their way up to him and he exulted. *"Come on! I'll buy you a gallon of beer each. What a welcome sight you blokes are!* Even as he spoke, and with the Gurkhas apparently under orders to attack across the border, the Chinese gunners stopped firing. The superintendent was able to evacuate his wrecked and bloodied command post and get his dead and wounded out.

The following day among other news it was reported that Elsie Elliot had approached the Jockey Club, the first on her list, and they had already subscribed close to a million Hong Kong dollars which would go to a fund to care for the families of the dead policemen. Stars in the East, I thought, as I read the news. Although Elsie may have considered the police force to be *bete-noire*, her black beast, she could not help now but applaud their bravery.

At this time many of those people the communists claimed to have been fighting for had started to turn against them, enraged by the indiscriminate fury of their cause. There had been a great deal of bombing, much of it senseless, and in one case a seven-year-old girl and her two-year-old brother were killed when they picked up a bomb, that had been wrapped like a gift and left outside their home. It was also known that some rioters were stacking up huge supplies of bombs about the Colony. The public outcry against violence was widely reported, as was the murder on 24 August of Lam Bun, a popular anti-leftist radio commentator. He was killed by a death squad posing as road maintenance workers who barred him from getting out of his car; he was burned to death. As a consequence, belief in the colony's future declined among much of Hong Kong's populace and many residents sold their property and relocated overseas. Many businessmen were also getting out and relocating in Taiwan where they had been promised a lucrative tax break. Property prices were at a low but for some reason Pier Mardulyn, a director of the Belgian Bank and the owner of the lovely brick home I was renting at Tai Po Kau, came to see me one evening offering to sell me the place for fifty thousand US dollars. It was an offer I had to accept so I immediately rang Ken Myer, the chairman of Myer, and told him about it. I asked if his company could lend me the money to buy. Ken, who was a man I can only describe as a princely gentlemen, who had visited me and walked several times with me and Copper over the rugged but lovely Patsin Range, asked only if I was confident Hong Kong would get over its present crisis. I assured him it would. I got the money.

Tom Hungerford visited me at this time and he stayed for a couple of months. A great gardener, he improved my place with brick walls and walk ways all cleverly created. He agreed with my thinking about the book I was hoping to write and when I spoke of a sequel, set in Hong Kong during the riots, he suggested I should write a trilogy: one starting with my early life in Buronga, then one set in Hong Kong, with the third to be located in China. Tom himself was interested in creating a work on the riots and he worked on a book he was to call *Code Word Macao*. Ultimately to his chagrin, it was rejected by Angus and Robertson but he hoped to find an alternative publisher.

The Hong Kong Government now imposed a number of

emergency regulations and granted the police special powers in an attempt to quell the dangerous unrest. Leftist newspapers were banned from publishing, leftist schools were shut down, many leftist leaders were arrested and detained while some were deported to China. The Colonial Secretary introduced an emergency regulation which made it possible for suspect people to be detained without trial for one year. It was a law that lasted for three years but was considered necessary, for during the riots 51 people had been killed, including 5 policemen, with 15 others wounded. An army explosives expert and a fire-fighter were also killed. The bombings killed 15 people and 340 were injured. The waves of intimidation did not cease until October 1967 under orders of Premier Zhou Enlai. It became known that a general, one in command of the Canton Military Region from where the machine gun fire had come that day, secretly suggested invading and occupying Hong Kong but his plan was vetoed by Chou.

Sitting in my garden one evening with a faithful Copper snoozing at my side and a few lights showing across Tolo Harbour, I wondered tiredly how a new start could be made in Hong Kong, a place that might well be one of the world's most expertly organised and deeply entrenched centres for corruption and subversion, in a community balanced on a razor's edge both financially and politically, where outrageous extremes of poverty provided a thrusting incentive to go after the flamboyant wealth of the few. The mansions on the Peak were everyone's target and people got to live in them by curious routes and strategies. And yet, if no new start, what? The gradual subsidence of this beautiful, vital place into the dark mine of its own corruption? Or perhaps simply to be taken back and absorbed into a China which I knew would not always be the struggling bemused giant-in-chains it was at this very moment.

Of course, I thought, despite the Red Guards and their Cultural Revolution which had caused so much damage and had taken so many lives in China, they would ultimately be defeated despite the manic urgings of Madame Mao. The signs and the winds of change were altering what had taken place in China, with Chairman Mao hopefully stirring and thinking of using his army to smash his Red Guards and end his Cultural Revolution, yet another of his crazed social experiments. But how and when? I could only hope that the new crop of leaders trying to fight their way past Chairman Mao would ultimately find the key to China's future. I also hoped that once Hong Kong's windows were clean-washed the colony would shine out to Asia and inwardly to that sprawling mass of land, China, which lay just across the Pat Sin Range ahead of me.

My thinking on that night with its happy conclusion took a jolt in January 1968 when Stephen FitzGerald, known to all as Steve because he insisted that only strangers and his class enemies called him Stephen, entered China. Formerly a Third Secretary language student attached to Foreign Affairs in Hong Kong, and then a student at the Australian National University where he was studying for his Ph.D., entered China. He said anyone he knew in the China field was anxious to get into what he called the Middle Kingdom. He wrote: 'So it was on 20 January with 56 other, mostly undergraduate, Australian and New Zealand students, from the old colonial railway station in Kowloon we took the train to the Chinese border'. Foreigners in China, Steve was to find, were ready targets for political fanatics and a living example of the hundreds of years of foreign imposition and occupation of their land. For others they were simply a diversionary scapegoat for attacks. Many had been assaulted, detained and publicly humiliated. Some had been under room arrest in hotels for months. The British Embassy staff following the sacking of their Embassy, had not been allowed to leave China and were confined in Peking. Anthony Grey, the Reuters correspondent, was under house arrest where an official of the Foreign Ministry had personally strangled his pet cat before his eyes. However it was not until Steve and his group arrived in Changsha, the capital of Chairman Mao's home province Hunan that he personally met some of the Red Guards and experienced what their revolution meant to them and could mean to him.

In the hotel where he and some of the others had been billeted, a New Zealand student, Geoff Woods, had been cleaning out his suitcase, and had thrown some Chairman Mao memorabilia into a waste basket. The Red Guards discovered this devotional material about their Great Leader and Woods was denounced as sacrilegious, being anti-Mao, and some form of self-criticism and penance was demanded. Steve suggested that Woods go along with what was required; he apologised but what he said was considered to be inadequate. To the Red Guards this was devotional material of their Great leader. When discovered Woods was was being compelled to answer. Meanwhile more Red Guards were gathering and pressing into the room. Among their numbers were members of the Revolutionary Committee whose chief speaker was a woman about eighteen years old. She and others declared that Woods was China's enemy and he must be adequately and severely punished. Steve responded by saying that there was no proof that Woods was China's enemy, and taking from his pocket the Little Red Book of Chairman Mao's sayings, he read a passage in the work which said that without investigation and study one does not have the right to speak. This comment merely inflamed the young woman and others in her committee, and they all turned on Steve. By now the room was crammed with Red Guards, some standing on a chest of drawers, others on a reading desk, one on a bedside table, while a few were clambering onto the beds with cries of accusation against Steve filling the room. The original charges against Woods seemed to have been irrelevant or forgotten, as the Red Guards now had in their possession two living enemies of their beloved Chairman, his Party and all of China, and both identifiable by their unpleasant ethnic characteristics. The young woman in front of her victims was now in a state, with flecks of foam creaming about her mouth. She was, according to Steve, screaming wildly, her eyes burning with hatred. She turned to the room and yelled for a verdict: many voices demanded that the two criminals be taken before a mass rally then being held at the city stadium at Changsha, where they would be tried and sentenced to death. Many Red Guards were crying that the two had to bow and confess to their crimes. They had to be given the aeroplane treatment!

Steve recorded: 'I am terrified. I know from graphic reports and photographs that the aeroplane treatment is a torture where the victim is made to stand for hours with the head pushed down towards the ground with hands bound behind. I also know that the mass trial proposed will have an already determined outcome and that a trial conducted by extreme leftists will not be a trial but a sadistic overture to an execution. As hands reach out to take us there is a sudden still. Someone seems to have called out, above even the shouting in the room. I have no idea of what has happened. I am shaking. The room begins to empty, and moments later soldiers appear at the door with rifles and fixed bayonets. Our guides appear and within minutes they have our whole group packing our bags.'

A few days later Steve crossed the border into British territory, 'When I finally arrive and have a drink with Jack Harris and my wife Gay at the Peninsula Hotel we drink a toast at their relief at seeing me finally appear out of China and my relief at being able to'. Steve went on to say over that drink and others, that in some of the larger Chinese provinces some Red Guard units were fighting each other in bloody encounters and industrial destruction was widespread. It was only in the far south of China that the army seemed unexpectedly to take a stance and it held thousands of rabid young Red Guards at bay, preventing them from storming into Hong Kong with the intention of conducting the sort of public trials which had killed so many distinguished elderly people while at the same time causing the kind of industrial and economic chaos which was wrecking much of China.

Steve had a dramatic encounter with the dangerous Red Guards in China where he observed that foreigners were targets and scapegoats for attack because of the many years of foreign attack, abuse and occupation by foreign powers. There was also racial conflict in Hong Kong because that small island had been occupied by the English following their victory in the Opium War of 1842 and now, over one hundred years later, foreigners were generally seen as human evidence of foreign imposition on China, once regarded by their many Emperors as the Centre of the Universe. My understanding of a racial split and the reason why made me believe I was walking into a problem during the riots of the previous summer was when I was going down a street on Kowloon side and I saw three Chinese coming towards me, all closely linked together. The centre man, large and corpulent, was dressed in shorts and a singlet and as he and his companions neared me, I thought he looked threatening. Thinking perhaps of that American colonel who had been hauled out onto the street in North Korea and beaten to death, and that it might be considered cowardly if I now turned aside or withdrew, and believing I had no alternative, I walked directly into the big man. With my nose at about level with his navel, we all came to an abrupt halt. Of a sudden the big man stepped backwards, yelled something and started jumping about on one foot. The pavement must have been very hot in the middle of that day, because looking down, I saw that when we had come so close together I must have trodden on one of his flip-flops and stepping backwards, he had torn it off. I stooped down, picked up the sundered flip-flop and laughing, handed it back to him. His large face broke into a happy grin, his companions laughed and our coming together so abruptly, ended happily.

In 1969 the Queen honoured the Hong Kong Police Force for its courage during the riots, by granting the force the privilege of the 'Royal title'. Most applauded that recognition, but the odium of their alleged corrupt activities remained. However, when Sir Murray MacLehose was appointed Governor of Hong Kong in 1971, he set about expanding welfare, began a massive public housing program, and greatly improved life for the impoverished masses. He also set about looking into the allegations of corruption in many sectors of government and the business community.

It was in July of that same year that I met up with Steve again. He had been selected as Gough Whitlam's Chinese adviser when Whitlam, Leader of the Opposition, led a Labor delegation to visit China in July 1971. Henry Litton, an old friend and like Whitlam, a QC, invited him and his party to a barbeque evening at his home at Stanley. It was a fun evening, with Mick Young in great form with bursts of his rhyming slang. A former shearer with the build of one and a face like some of the battered old fighters I had known in my youth, Mick was at heart a gentle, decent and thoughtful man. Indeed, they were all good men, drinking and talking together, with the most significant comment of the evening coming from Whitlam who, in that senatorial voice of his, confided to me and Henry as we walked down a long flight of steps to the beach below his home, that if he became Prime Minister he would appoint Steve as his Ambassador to China. It was a suggestion we both applauded.

Meanwhile, Prime Minister McMahon seized on this visit, accusing Whitlam of being a pawn of a communist power and a spokesman for the enemy then being fought in Vietnam. But when on 15 July 1971 the United States President, Richard Nixon, announced his proposed visit to China, Whitlam's invitation from Zhou Enlai to visit China became an opposition coup and McMahon's attempt to gain political capital was an embarrassment for the Coalition. William McMahon had become Prime Minister in 1971 and he lost his government office at the federal elections in 1972. On the 5 December 1972 Gough Whitlam was sworn in as Prime Minister.

Early in 1973 Steve was back in Hong Kong. He came to me, said he had been appointed to be Australia's first ambassador to China, and he wanted to thank me for all the times I had bailed him out when he had been an impecunious student. We had a joke in those days when I called him my sizar, or student of limited means. He was then living in mean quarters in Kowloon directly under the flight path where planes banked before landing. But now he had cash in his pocket, and his first task on assuming command of the Embassy in Peking was to establish a bar he was to call 'The Down Under'. As soon as possible he would invite me up for a drink. With that, a brilliant Doctor of Philosophy who had resigned from External Affairs as a Second Secretary and was now an Ambassador Plenipotentiary on his way to head what was possibly the most important diplomatic posting in the world, departed for China, along with Gay and their children.

At this time I was living at Mount Davis Road with Henry Litton following a tragic event in his life. Earlier I had left my wife at our home in Tai Po Kau and moved to Shatin, and I was seeking a divorce on the grounds of incompatibility. Henry was staying in Kotewall Road with the lovely Anna-Marie and her two young sons Jules and Caspar from a previous marriage. I had come to know her well; she was a full-bosomed, blonde and bright-eyed lady. A most attractive woman with an earthy loveliness and exuberance, she had a kind of irresistible vitality about her and I invited her and Henry in late June 1972 for a visit to Taiwan. The trip was my wedding-to-be gift to them and we hiked over all the great mountain tracks I knew, ate in many small village places, laughed and drank and enjoyed to the full those sunny days of friendship, which ended for Anna-Marie on the 18 June 1972.

Henry and the others had been having a late dinner in a nearby restaurant and coffee was suggested but it was decided they would not drink where they had eaten, but at home. They had just returned to their apartment on the second floor of the twelve-storey building with torrential rain cascading down. Henry noticed that the tall trees beyond were bending in a way he associated with avalanches he had seen in the mountains of Europe, and he knew they were in trouble. Jules ran for the front balcony and it saved his life, for the building was wrenched forty-five degrees to the right-hand side and he was thrown to safety. Anna-Marie and Henry, were buried up to their shoulders, standing close together; Casper was nearby, crying.

The rain belted down and Henry, who stood taller than Anna-Marie, had one hand free and was able to keep descending rubble and rising water out of his mouth, but Anna-Marie, whose hands were trapped, could neither keep water out or rubbish away and after some time, with a final cry after having spoken to Henry, she died. Casper had stopped crying and Henry knew he was also dead. He lost count of time, but he was at peace, expecting to die, when he heard a radio, which must have been battery-controlled and somehow pressed by the rubble, began to play music. Fully awake and with a surge of hope, Henry began calling out. His voice was heard, people appeared and a brave English soldier, risking his life, dug Henry out. That soldier was later decorated for his bravery. In that apartment collapse sixty-seven people died and twenty were injured, many seriously.

Taken to upper-road level Henry discovered that his cousin and fellow lawyer T.S. Lo, having heard of the disaster, was looking for him at the site. Later, when the tired rescuers wanted to leave the area, saying they could do no more, T.S. strongly protested, saying that if they would not keep looking for survivors he would go ahead and do it alone. It was probably because of his reputation as a lawyer, known for his family connections, that T.S. was listened to, and the search continued. Henry was finally located when his voice was heard and he was dug from the mess. He was delivered first to the mortuary presumed dead but when his body stirred there was panic getting him into the hands of top medics upstairs who saved his life.

I visited Henry almost every day. He was badly injured and would need dialysis treatment over many days for his damaged kidneys. His left arm was partly paralysed because of a nerve injury and the doctors struggled to help him. Despite being very weak he insisted on attending Anna-Marie's funeral held in the Happy Valley cemetery ten days after her death. After moving slowly along the queue of Anna-Marie and Henry's many friends all I could say was for him to remember Anna-Marie as the sound of laughter. Henry gripped me so hard with his good right hand that I thought a rib would crack. He wept, and I let my own tears fall.

At the hospital, when Henry had been wheeled away for treatment, I sometimes talked with Enid, Henry's mother, expressing the friendship I had known with him. He must also have chatted about me in a similar vein for one day Enid told me she knew I was living at Shatin and she wondered if I could move out and live in a three-storied house she had just bought for Henry, as thanks for his survival. She asked if I would get the house ready for his occupation and that I could stay there and be company for him. I moved in and stayed there with Henry for four years. We became as close as brothers. I only moved out when he re-married.

Henry had been born into a multiracial family in 1934. Enid, his mother, came from the Lo family, one of the distinguished early settlers in Hong Kong. Her brother, known as M.K. was knighted for his services to law and with his younger brother he established one of the largest law firms in Hong Kong. Henry's English father John, a lieutenant in the Volunteers, was killed in the Lai Yu Mun fortress when the Japanese crossed over from Kowloon in the opening days of the Second World War. Henry later graduated with Honours in jurisprudence from Oxford and after passing the Bar Examination in 1959. He entered into private practice in Hong Kong where he was eminently successful. He was appointed a Queen's Counsel in 1970, one of the youngest ever to take silk. We were both good friends with Steve Fitzgerald, hence the barbeque party at Henry's place in 1971. We entertained Steve again in 1973, this time at Mount Davis when he was on his way to China, that historical posting.

During those get-fit-Henry days we sailed his boat, walked over every hill in Hong Kong and the New Territories, swam frequently and he recovered his fitness quickly. In the mid-autumn of 1973 we went on the Community Chest walk which Henry had agreed to take part in because Patricia Nye, a director of the UNHCR office in Hong Kong, had asked him to contribute and participate. Henry asked me to join him, and when he told me that Patricia was doing all sorts of wonderful things to help many of the demoralised refugees arriving from Vietnam and other places, I was keen to meet her.

On arrival at the government stadium where the walk was to start, we made our way towards a white tent to register. Fifty or so yards from it, Henry halted by a cluster of camphor laurel trees and laid his hand on my arm. "There she is," he announced. "That's Patricia."

He was pointing discreetly at a tall Chinese woman in slim-fitting jeans and matching denim shirt. She had class and poise written all over, a style and elegance which immediately jumps the barriers of class and country. When we moved up to her, Henry announced, "Patricia, may I introduce my room mate, Jack Harris?"

"Henry!" She flashed him a lovely smile which she then turned on me. "Jack! I've heard so much about you! That war in Korea, your success in business here. Henry says you've done all measure of other things, too!" Closer up she was more beautiful than I had expected.

"Anyone who gets to even half my age should have done something," I responded and, as Patricia's face crinkled with laughter, I knew I had met a reliable partner to get Henry back in reasonable shape after a twenty mile-walk.

It was dusk by the time we made it home from the stadium and it was almost eight o'clock before Patricia and I sat down to the steak and salad white wine French bread dinner that I was good at preparing. First, though, we had a couple of long gin and tonics, something else I was good at fixing. By this time Henry had gone to his room, exhausted from the walk. The big house was so quiet, the room in which I sat with Patricia could have been a pasture in the fields, and the food on the table might have been set for a picnic. As we sipped our wine and started to eat, a silence fell between us. To bridge the gap I noted, "Henry mentioned this morning that you are working hard to help the refugees flooding into Hong Kong?"

"Yes. So many are coming in from Vietnam, many with harrowing stories. Many of the boats are boarded by pirates who take everything the men might possess before throwing them overboard. Women and young girls are raped then tossed into the sea. Some of the boats might try and make a landing in Malaysia but those on board are beaten and forced away, sometimes to perish. It is tragic and when some do arrive, and the numbers are mounting, they are herded into canvas tents and have to live in basic conditions sometimes for years, before they are accepted overseas." She talked on for some time, outlining many of the problems confronting her organisation before concluding. "Apart from what I've detailed, we handle family reunion and adoptions. Did Henry tell you anything else about me?"

"No. Should he have?"

"Not really, but the thought just registered because he told me so much about you. It's a strange thing, but I feel now that I've known you for years." She smiled, her lips wet with wine which glistened on her small, perfect teeth. But then she snapped in a sudden, spiteful fashion, "You have known Henry much longer, of course. Did he happen to inform you that my husband has left me for a whore?" She stared hard at me as she spoke and I knew that the long walk along with the drinks of gin and wine were having more of an effect than I could have anticipated.

"No. Henry mentioned nothing like that. He only told me that you are committed to your work, to helping people."

"What a fine reference!" Her voice held that impatience women use when they scold a child or an adult fool and I was wondering what I could say to pacify her when she continued in an angry fashion, making me understand that she could become bitterly, almost vulgarly, angry. "You say that I am supposed to be committed to my work, that of helping people, which I suppose is a compliment, but this woman I speak about has nothing, is a nothing. What would my husband see in a woman like that?"

"I can't say. But I was always under the impression that Chinese women expected their husbands to play about?"

"Chinese women? I am only part-Chinese!" Her voice was cold and hard. "From my great-grandfather on, the men in our family looked like what they were, Americans of Danish descent, which is what I am. You understand?"

"Sort of, yes." I answered, being in no way prepared for the outburst my remark about Chinese husbands had produced. It seemed to me that her part-Chinese heritage was a sore point with her when compared with her Anglo-Saxon background.

"I married into a Chinese family because my mother wanted it that way." Patricia's voice broke abruptly into my thoughts. "It was one of the richest here, which was good for my mother's ego. Only marriage to my father, a doctor of medicine, gave her any status. My father, you see, was trained in America. His father had a distinguished background as a merchant. And I have a great-grandfather who found his way into the history books when the factories were under siege in Canton. But you would know about that part of our history?"

I found it fascinating then to learn more details of that history with which she was so closely associated. When she was done and I was looking into her luminous black eyes she told me she was sorry she had become so angry about her husband and his playing about. But sitting there talking, she had felt compelled to express herself openly to me.

"Forget it," I told her. "We are all inclined to blow a cork sometime. While on the subject of corks, what about another glass of wine? Would you like one more with cheese, and a glass of red?"

"No cheese. But a glass of red, yes. I don't have to drive. Someone will be along soon to pick me up." She got from her chair and stood back, staring down at me. Her bare feet, I noticed, were nicely shaped and narrowly spread on the brown parquetry floor boards. Her small bunched fists were buried, like holstered pistols, deep into the front pockets of her denims. "I don't think I've ever talked so much and so frankly to a man, just as I have done to you this evening," she said. "I guess it was something I wanted to get out of my system and I thank you for listening to me. I'd like now to say thanks properly and over that glass of wine you mentioned. I noticed a good bottle of red up there on the shelf when I was helping you fix our salad. You just sit where you are and I'll wait on you in the appropriate fashion."

I watched her pad her way to the kitchen and when she reached the shelves set high above a cutting table, her denim shirt stretched tight across her shapely breasts. Just then I wondered what had caused her husband to go looking for a prostitute at all. To me, Patricia was honed and shaped, with honey coloured skin in that kind of perfection which I had always found to be the prime ingredient of Oriental loveliness.

She came to stand by the dining table, passing the wine bottle and a corkscrew to me. I opened the bottle, tasted the wine, pronounced it good and we sat together, drinking and chatting. But I was thinking, as a healthy male, what a woman like this, with a bloom of fitness about her, would be like in bed. Probably magic, given her shape and energy. But then I had the uncomfortable feeling that I was wrong, for despite her beauty and the way her body was moulded and also because her mood seemed to have harmonised with mine so easily, there was something about this very desirable woman that said '*No!*'. Yet at the same time I understood that if that negative response could be turned around, it would say, *'Yes, take me! Love me!'* One day, I thought some lucky bloke might get the opportunity to work on that rebuttal and reverse it.

"Well," I remarked as I finished my wine. "I'm falling asleep. It's time for my pillow."

"Me too," Patricia laughed. "I must be away."

We chatted about nothing in particular for a few moments. Patricia then slipped on her shoes, I escorted her through the front door and to her Mercedes parked outside. Patricia did not attempt to touch me or kiss me goodnight. Neither of us made any mention at all of ever seeing each other again.

Chapter Fourteen

In 1974 Governor MacLehose established the Independent Commission Against Corruption (ICAC) whose aim was to combat the then-prevalent corruption which existed in all spheres of life in Hong Kong, especially in government departments. ICAC was under the command of John Prendergast, soon to be knighted for his services, but the creation of such a body, and then their methods, sparked off disgruntlement in many departments, especially among the police, the most high profiled target. Faced with a potential police rebellion and the severe disruption this would have caused to everyday life, MacLehose extended a general amnesty to the police force in order to defuse the situation. Some officers, especially the station sergeants, were however excluded and many of them fled Hong Kong, finding a sort of life in places like Taiwan and the Philippines. Two senior European officers were arrested and imprisoned and while the amnesty was effective it caused misgivings, especially among a group of honest officers who had resisted the temptation to engage and benefit from corrupt practices, but who as a result suffered career consequences. Eventually, however, the ICAC helped Hong Kong become one of the least corrupt societies in Asia.

My Buying Office in Hong Kong was doing well with a staff of forty. Apart from looking after buyers from Myer and Target, we still had those two outside accounts to help pay the costs of the operation. Our Taiwan office had a staff of ten and it was operating profitably. In total, we were shipping over one hundred million dollars worth of merchandise to Myer alone. Shipments to the outside accounts were also considerable. But I knew the trade bonanza would ultimately be China and, anxious to get in there, I asked Steve if he would invite me in to talk with their trade officials. I had also heard that Kim Il-Sung would be visiting China in early 1975 and I wondered if I could be there at that time. I was curious about this Korean, considered evil by many, and I wondered if I might get a look at him. But my main purpose was to see if and how trade would blossom out of China. When Henry Litton heard I was thinking of going to China he wondered whether I could ask Steve if he and Linda Sidall, his wife-to-be, could be invited in to accompany me.

As a three-some we arrived in Peking in the early part of the year. Steve met us at the airport. Later I met up with an old friend, David Bonavia, *The Times* and The *Far Eastern Economic Review* correspondent in Peking. During a period of ideological, political and cultural upheaval in China David had been uniquely placed to observe and report on the many changes over all levels of Chinese society. He wrote colourful prose, muscular and ringing with authority. Able to both read and speak Chinese at a high level, and with a vast range of contacts, he was a widely experienced journalist with sound observations. He was assisted by his wife Judy who, while regarded by many as his amanuensis, was in fact also a burgeoning author and working on a book about the Yangtze River which, when later published, was a bestseller.

At dusk I took off with David and Judy to wander through the ancient capital. We went through many of the streets I had read about and whose beautifully evocative names still remained, etched in classic and lovely Chinese ideographs: *The Hill of The Prince's Mansion, The Pond of Jade Depths, The Prince's Well*. I was saddened to find that so little remained of the once-splendid old Tartar capital, but thankful that the Forbidden City and the Summer Palace, where the rulers had once lived, had been protected by the army during the destructive violence of the Cultural Revolution although the ancient and majestic city walls once surrounding the city had been destroyed some time after Mao had arrived in Peking with his ragged army. Of the once massive inner walls, not a brick remained and of the nine gates which had been closed and barred at sunset each day for more than seven hundred years only the Chien Men, or Front Gate and Tienanmen, or the Gate of Heavenly Peace, were still standing.

As I paused with David and Judy in the darkening evening I could just discern that where those historical walls had once been, there was now a waste land, bulldozed flat. Asked why it had been done, why such a wall with its many gates, had been wilfully destroyed, no one seemed to know. But the three of us could see, looking about where the walled city had once been, a huge and ugly square had been created. Beyond it the land was covered with a scab of grey Russian-type model settlements stretching in every direction, waiting, I thought, for the lash of the gritty wind that would come blowing off the desert far beyond the Great Wall of China, something Mao with his army of destructive workers had not destroyed.

Later after Judy had bade us good night David and I went to the bar in my hotel. As we were sitting down I told David that Derek Davis, his editor in Hong Kong, had sent his best regards and David, who seldom swore, snapped "Fuck him!" I laughed, but I understood David's anger. One evening at a dinner party at the Davis home, Derek, slightly drunk, looked over the table to his wife Midori and commented in crude and offensive barrack-room language about her ignorance of sex. It was a conversation stopper because we all knew Midori to be a woman of class;

recently she had given a well received piano recital in the City Hall with the Governor in attendance. But then, following Derek's salacious remark, the dinner party broke up. I telephoned Derek the following day to tell him that I found his remarks hurtful to his wife and her friends. Derek laughed and said that Midori, being Japanese, would not have understood what he had meant. If that was so, I reasoned, why say those ugly words? Derek muttered something and hung up, and our close relationship was over. I could not but wonder what had happened to Derek and Midori. Once a member of the Foreign Office, Derek had resigned from a good job with career prospects because of the attitude of the Foreign Office over his marriage to a Japanese woman soon after the war with Japan. So deep was his love at this time, that Derek battled to make a living, at least until he had found success in Hong Kong.

Derek, a rambunctious foul-mouthed Welshman, was a clever but complex man who had lifted the *Economic Review* from not much more than a news sheet to an internationally accepted magazine, with contributions from some of the best journalists in the world, notably David Bonavia, Russell Spurr and Leo Goodstat. Yet he was a man of extremes. One evening again at dinner at his home, Dick Hughes the Australian journalist employed by the *Sunday Times* and the revered Dean of the Hong Kong journalistic world and the character old Craw in Le Carre's novel, *The Honourable Schoolboy*, set in Hong Kong, told a joke concerning the sexual endeavours of Chairman Mao and his skinny, bald-headed wife. Mao had once been close to death after a bout of oral sex, which Hughes referred to as a blow job. We laughed at the conclusion of the story but in the silence that fell after the hilarity, a quavering old voice asked a question, "What is a blow job?" It was Derek's mother on a visit to the Colony and Derek, furious to think that Dick might answer her, and no doubt defending what he took to be his mother's honour, demanded that Dick and his Chinese wife leave the table and his home. At the doorway Dick turned to Derek and said, "My apologies, Your Grace, but I seem to have blundered." Everybody was 'Your Grace' to Dick. Le Carre referred to him in a preface as a man of much more affectionate nature than the character in his novel.

That evening in Peking I settled David down in the lounge of my hotel and we chatted about China's past and probed towards what David saw as its future. I asked David how much longer he thought Chairman Mao would be in control, and of the rumours about him that were common in Hong Kong. It was said, among other things, that his physician constantly gave him all manner of drugs just to keep him mobile. I also noted how frail and weak he appeared to be in some of the news shots I had seen of him; that when people went to shake his hand it dangled like a stunned fish on a hook.

"What you say is true enough," David conceded. "Mao is a very old man. He did wonders bringing his army here to the capital in 49 and it was then that he should have stepped down from office. It is a pity now, that he refused to take that step, but he must have known that he should have handed the job of running this huge country with an enormous population to younger, more competent men. Mao was a soldier but politicians were needed once that last great battle was won and that peanut, Chiang Kai-shek, had been kicked out of China and fled to Taiwan, even if the Americans incredibly thought he would return here. Christ! But Mao was here, he settled in, was deified by the masses and ultimately be came to believe he deserved all that veneration. The whole deal was whipped up by Mao's propaganda machinery and enforced by his instruments of control.

The people generally were brain-washed and it would have been a mark of stupid eccentricity not to believe in what you were told to believe. So Mao moved on, all unchallenged, with his mad schemes. He caused enormous suffering, a huge loss of life, with social and economic despair even worse than when China was ruled by warlords. You know, millions of people starved because at one stage Mao insisted that rice and other foods be sent to Russia in exchange for help in building a nuclear arsenal in China. He got the help but the arsenal was never a success. Some people had almost no food, and that in provinces that were the recognised food bowls of China, but where people were reduced to eating bark and grass. There was some cannibalism, or so it was reported. And look at Mao's mad Cultural Revolution, will you? President Liu, Chairman of the People's Republic, lost his life by freezing to death while he lay naked on the concrete floor of his prison cell. He was badly beaten when in custody and he was a gentle, intelligent man. His only crime was to criticise Mao over the many deaths from hunger and to say that Mao's plans were failing. Hence the Cultural Revolution, Mao's very successful experiment in getting rid of his political enemies. It was awful, and talking about it is thirsty work!"

With his passion for drinking and his desire to talk, David went on to review some of the background to the Cultural Revolution, a lot of which was familiar to me but if David wanted to talk, I was willing to listen. He reviewed the countless suicides and how some of the most beautiful homes shrines and temples in Suchou and Hangchou had been wrecked. Young people had run crazy, copying Madame Mao's cry of destroying all that was old, creating everything new. I wondered where David was heading but knowing he wished to make a point I waited and when he asked me if I knew of the historian Wu Han, I said I did. I knew he had represented China abroad on cultural matters and that he had written a successful opera. Did I know when and where Wu Han had died? No, I did not. According to David, he had been brutally beaten and had committed suicide in October 1969.

David now came to the point he wanted to make. He said that in November 1965, Yao Wen-yuan, a close confidante of Madame Mao, had fired what David described as the opening shot of the Cultural Revolution when he attacked Wu Han on the grounds that the upright Ming official he described in his play was metaphorically equated with Peng Dehuai, the army general who had so successfully led the Chinese soldiers in the Korean War. However Peng had, like President Liu, attacked Mao and said his policies were failing. Although promoted to Field Marshal, Peng was stripped of all his commands and was later beaten to death while in prison. David then noted that, apart from Yao Wen-yuan, Madame Mao now had Wang Hung-wen and Ch'ang Ch'un-chiao as part of her group. During the Cultural Revolution these four had advanced to high positions in the government and the communist party. The backgrounds of the three men were all similar, in that prior to 1966 they were low ranking officials in Shanghai. After the turmoil of the Cultural Revolution had subsided in 1969 they maintained their power, along with Madame Mao, through control of the media and propaganda outlets and their seeming adherence to Chairman Mao's policies and wishes. It was these people, David concluded, now all members of the Politburo, who were manipulating Mao and they could ruin all of China in his name. "Who exactly is in charge?" I asked.

"That obnoxious woman, Madame Mao. She is a dangerous person with a malignant threesome beside her. They make up four buggers as far as I am concerned. Everyone is watching her, waiting and listening but with some trepidation, I should think!

There is a rumour, which I cannot write about, that Madame Mao and those three important men are establishing a power base in Shanghai. But why, the purpose is not clear."

David then talked briefly about a man named Kang Sheng. He was head of the secret police, a member of the Politburo and friendly with Chairman Mao; it was said he supplied many young ladies for the chairman's attention. It was also rumoured that he was Madame Mao's lover. He lived in a palace formerly occupied by a Manchu prince and there was said to be a cave there where he personally tortured his victims. He had lived in Russia during the 1930s and he became acquainted with Lavrenti Beria, the security man who came to our attention during the Vladimir Petrov defection. As well as Chinese, David spoke excellent Russian. Formerly a *Times* correspondent in Moscow, he had been expelled in 1969 after working there for three years, allegedly for contacting Russian dissidents. David was a sagacious man with a capacity to gather information and report on it truthfully, a special achievement.

The following day, accompanied by the Trade Officer from our Embassy we had a number of interviews and discussions with a number of senior corporate officials. All exports were handled by such corporations, of which there were seven. The men concerned with my inquiries invariably sat us in deep chairs, offered cigarettes and tea in delicate, beautifully crafted cups. The chairs generally had sundered springs and backs draped with antimacassars, curious hang-overs from the Victorian era when Europeans put Macassar oil on their hair. But the people we were spending our time with seemed to be men of modern ideas and I was able to make some hopefully good contacts which I knew would be invaluable to me when China opened properly for external trade. When that happened, I was thinking, I might first try and open a Myer office in Shanghai, once the centre of the Chinese textile industry.

After a long day I later improved my knowledge of things Chinese by visiting the peerless Temple of Heaven, untouched in its ancient perfection on the one high piece of land in the city. I was also able to enter the Forbidden City and spend time among the treasures of porcelains, bronzes, of scrolls and books housed in that remarkable place.

Prime Minister Whitlam and Ambassador Steve FitzGerald meet Chairman Mao, October 1973. At this meeting the chairman said he did not know the answer to an important question, causing Whitlam and FitzGerald to question Mao's state of mind. FitzGerald collection.

I had already asked Steve if I might go to the Peking railway station for the arrival of Kim Il-Sung. As well as being Ambassador Plenipotentiary to China, Steve also had diplomatic responsibility for North Korea so he was automatically on Kim's reception list. Steve knew that as a soldier I had fought Kim's regime during the war there and he understood why I would like to have a close-up look at the man responsible for the estimated deaths of over four million people all because of his idiotic plan to dominate South Korea, a concept which had failed so dismally.

Ambassador FitzGerald delighted to meet Premier Zhou Enlai. May 1973. FitzGerald collection.

Steve secured permission for me along with Henry and Linda to be members of his official party. On the way to the station Steve had to enter the British Embassy for a chat with the ambassador and he was absent for some time, during which Linda discovered she had left her camera behind. I tried to persuade the Chinese driver to return to our hotel, but without permission from Steve, he refused. By the time Steve returned to us it was too late for us to do anything but to proceed direct to the station. When I finally stood on that railway station I stared hard at Kim as he passed by me, remembering how Lim had once described him as a zero person with a fictitious war record. Now he had a smile on his flat, pock-marked face, but I instantly let him go as I concentrated on the elfish figure of Deng Xiaoping walking behind the Korean. Close on Deng's heels, striding along with a theatrical gait, her eyes fixed on the ground before her, was Madame Mao, the woman held most responsible for the previous humiliation and incarceration of Deng.

Standing there in all that diplomatic huddle, supplemented with many senior Chinese military officers I was suddenly aware of the significant photographic scoop that Linda had missed. As a journalist with the *South China Morning Post* with a column of her own called "Things I Hear", she was a highly regarded writer. Before leaving Hong Kong a leading newspaper group in America had appointed her as their stringer, a term for a purveyor of good or bad news, and she now stood close to me observing, but unable to record, what would have been a photographic coup, well ahead of any journalist rivals. One possibly worth a Pulitzer Prize nomination.

Both Deng and Madame Mao were world news. He had been stripped of his high party posts sometime in the years 1967-69, after which he disappeared from public view. In 1973, however, Deng was reinstated under the sponsorship of Premier Zhou Enlai and made Deputy Premier, and in 1975 he became vice-chairman of the party's Central Committee, a member of its Politburo and chief of the general staff. As effective head of the government, he was widely considered the likely successor of Zhou Enlai. All the more reason, many believed, why Madame Mao was aiming for the power that would enable her to get rid of Deng yet again, but permanently. As she approached me the glint of the sun on her steel-rimmed spectacles made her look sourly asexual; as if to heighten her thin ugliness, a blue cloth cap was pulled low down on her head. Her frame was bundled into baggy denim pants and an ill-fitting jacket. Then she and the others were gone, the reception was over, everyone left the station.

Later when we were having a drink and flinging darts at a board, I asked Steve what it was like meeting Chairman Mao for the first time. He told me that Whitlam's party had not been told they were going to have a meeting with Mao. They only found out during talks with Zhou Enlai that they were to go straight from discussions with Zhou to see Mao. When Whitlam asked Mao where he had found Wang Hung-wen, a man Steve described as a creepy bugger from Shanghai, all Mao said was, *"Bu chih tao"*. He mumbled it in that thick Hunanese accent of his: *"I don't know."* Nancy Tang the interpreter, relayed his words to Whitlam and as they left that brief meeting Steve had wondered if Mao was losing his grip on sanity. How could he not know about Wang, a member of the Politburo, and an active part of Madame Mao's clique?

As we sat at a small table with beer and peanuts I asked Steve, "Is Mao senile, do you think? All sorts of rumours are floating about Hong Kong. And the way you describe that meeting with him makes it appear he has a doubtful grip on life? If he goes, who then?"

"Who indeed? I believe Deng Xiaoping is central to China's future, but he is under threat, as you would have noticed today. However, Madame Mao is not only stalking Deng. She has many enemies and she would like to clean the slate. That is something commonly believed by journalists as good as David Bonavia.

He and others are worried about her growing strength and the power of those men from Shanghai whom she has gathered about herself."

Whitlam group visit to China, 1971.
Steve FitzGerald, Tom Burns (behind) Margaret Whitlam, PM Gough Whitlam, Interpreter, Paul Raffael (ABC), Rex Patterson, Deng Xiaoping, Summer Palace, Nov. FitzGerald collection.

We went to sit in a couple of comfortable armchairs and the muted sounds of people talking, of glasses clinking, of the feeling of companionship all about in the glow of the lights set about the room led me to ask Steve what he thought about Gough Whitlam, the man who had lifted him from a diligent student to a man of international significance in diplomacy. Steve laughed at my fulsome description of himself, and he went on to relate that he had first met Whitlam when, as he put it, the Vietnam War was running hot, and Whitlam had recently become Leader of the

Opposition. Steve had resigned from the Department of External Affairs the year before in a personal protest about our China and Vietnam policy. Whitlam had asked him to write a paper for him reflecting his views and the ideas they had discussed and found in common. Whitlam had strong views about China and he believed that Australia should have relations which were rational and logical at a time when the Australian government view of China was ideological, emotional and fear-based. For Whitlam, recognition of China was logical and good policy; it was useless to pretend that Chiang Kai-shek's government ruled China and to have it represent China in the UN National Assembly, and to sit as a permanent member of the UN Security Council was irrational and poor international policy.

In 1971 no one dreamed that going to China could be a path to anything than electoral disaster, but onto that path stepped Gough Whitlam and Mick Young. Whitlam had it all: a QC, voracious reader, seeker of knowledge, international traveller, advocate of recognition of China since 1954. And Mick Young: just a few years of formal education, sheep shearer, union organiser, features of an old pugilist and a man who peppered his conversation with that rhyming slang in which he took a boyish delight. Germaine Greer was a beer, the Chairman's Thoughts were shorts, Ted Hill was the bill, and so on. Mick also liked to sing about Joe Hill, the Swedish-born American songwriter and organiser for the Industrial Workers of the World. His execution for an alleged robbery-murder made him a martyr and folk hero in the radical American labour movement. The song about his life and death was made famous by Paul Robeson.

It was at an ALP Federal Executive Meeting in Adelaide on 13 April 1971 that Young moved they cable the Chinese Premier Zhou Enlai, seeking an invitation for an ALP delegation to visit China. The cable was simple, saying only that the delegation would like to discuss the terms on which China would be interested in having diplomatic and trade relations with Australia. After an anxious month of waiting for a reply an invitation to visit China arrived on 11 May.

The delegation was of six people, including Steve, who went on to say that nothing in Australian history could compare with that China visit: it was Whitlam's greatest achievement. It was his commitment to the struggle from opposition, not from government, an expedition of great bravado and exposure, a journey of personal diplomacy and success. Steve and I drank happily to that and to his part in the great invitation.

Steve went on quietly to explain that the images most Australians had of Asians were of poverty, instability, revolution and, most significantly, of inferiority. The White Australia Policy was largely in place when Whitlam came to power and it was an inescapable statement of what Australia thought about Asians. Since 1950 we had been fighting them: in Korea where we fought a bloody draw, in Vietnam where we got the bloody nose. But there we were, fighting communism in someone else's wars, battling with Asians. It was a fear of Asia that underlay the White Australia Policy, and Whitlam's final elimination or abrogation of it put that fear to rest. Asians and Australians could begin to understand and reach out to each other, just as Whitlam had hoped.

I took my last stroll that evening, filling in the time waiting for the evening flight out of Peking. I went again to Tienanmen and stood near its centre looking towards Chien Men, the southern gate of the ancient city wall, solid and vermillion under its remaining blue-glazed tiles. It was a reminder to me of the durability of this land and its many warring states and dynasties of the past. At one end of the square a huge portrait of Chairman Mao hung under the outer wall by the entrance to the Forbidden City, that epitome of exquisite Imperial vice, corruption and lunacy. But even as I looked at the city, its character seemed to change, and I thought of it as a tower of human resilience and aspiration. Somehow its very survival seemed proof to me that this troubled country would transcend everything the turbulent times might throw at it. For time, it seemed to me, was no more than a blink in the eye of the everlasting history of this vast country.

Some time after our return to Hong Kong, Henry and Linda were married. I was best man and, remembering a passage that John Fowles had once written, I borrowed from it. I stated that humanity can be likened to seven men trapped on a raft in a storm-tossed sea. On the raft there is the optimist who is certain he will survive, the pessimist who knows he will die, the altruist who is willing to give up his good spot on the raft, and the hedonist who will take it. There is the stoic who believes in nothing but his refusal to jump overboard and end an impossible ordeal, there is the man with the log in which he describes how his fellows are responding. Finally, we are told of the young man who is positive that ultimately the green shores will arise and he will be saved. Henry, I told the distinguished gathering, was that young man, and having survived his loss and recovered from his injuries after that dreadful Kotewall Road disaster, he was once more a leading jurist in Hong Kong. Later, following an invitation from the Governor of Hong Kong, Henry joined his administration and became Vice President of the Court of Final Appeal and a Permanent Judge. Honours and awards followed in his legal career.

I spoke of Linda too, telling how a forgotten camera, which caused a ragged cheer, had made her give up a career in journalism, and that she was now occupied in making the world look greener for everyone. With the help and encouragement of Henry she had established a Friends of the Earth foundation in Hong Kong, and one of her first and significant victories was mounting an appeal to save a number of centuries-old Banyan trees in Stanley Village from developer destruction. But it took the presentation of an appeal to the Governor of Hong Kong, one couched in the esoteric terminology of a cry from a humble supplicant to a Chinese Emperor, to finally win the day and save the trees, which will long be green and noble.

It was only a matter of a few months before chance brought Patricia and me together again. The mechanism was Philip Murray, the former CIA officer who had been forced into early retirement by breaching his contract over his affair with a Vietnamese woman. After one tour in Hong Kong he was given a senior posting in Saigon and it was there his marriage foundered when he fell in love with a Vietnamese woman who had three small children. I had lost contact with Philip but one day he came to my office, told me he was ill of suspected liver cancer, and he asked me to help him, his Vietnamese wife and her children get into Australia. I was assisted through old friends in immigration, while Patricia and her organisation helped. Philip's Vietnamese family entered as refugees while Philip paid to enter under a business category. A few months later Patricia called me to say Philip had died peacefully in the home he had purchased in Sydney.

I later called her as a courtesy, to ask if she would go to a musical recital at the Hong Kong Club with me. She agreed and it was over dinner that she told me she was divorcing her husband. The papers had been filed, her decision was irrevocable. A couple of weeks after that Patricia invited me to dinner at her home in Stanley. It had a spacious garden at the front while the home itself showed an abundance of wealth and good taste. When eating we were waited on by an old and pleasant amah and the food was excellent, the wine equally as good. After dinner Patricia showed me into a library where she took out some papers left by the first Nye, her great-great grandfather. "Look at this," she said, handing me a set of papers headed "The Opium Question". It had been printed in Canton and was dated 1875. "It shows exactly what that ancestor of mine thought of the opium trade."

"Listen," I read aloud after I had scanned the papers for a few minutes. "One of the greatest weaknesses of the Imperial administration is its nepotism and corruption. Mandarins along the coast, and especially at Canton, are enriching themselves by open patronage of the drug trade. So you have deep, involved and useless discussions at Peking on how to suppress the drug trade, even while the Emperor is receiving his commission on all the bribes, and his Viceroy at Canton is becoming a Sterling millionaire." As I read on I began to think it was a strange, even ludicrous situation. Here was Patricia, one of the most poised and intelligent women I had met in years. When we had been together at Henry's place after that long walk, the sign she wore said *"No!"* and that sign was still there. It really was fanciful, I thought, returning to what I was reading. Patricia and I were together in what was a luxurious home and which could have been a seducer's lush green pasture but here we were in a library, reading from an old book about a very small war which most would have forgotten. I left at a decently early hour but as I drove home the perfume of Patricia and the glossy sheen of her black hair haunted me.

It was inevitably only a matter of time that later I asked Patricia out to dinner and, just as guaranteed, after dinner I invited her to my apartment at Pokfulam. It was on the top floor. We sat on the patio drinking wine, watching the nearby lights on Lamma Island and beyond it, the bobbing yellow lights of the fishing boats heading out to sea. Verdi's *Othello* was playing softly in the lounge room behind us and, because it seemed appropriate to the moment, I leaned across and kissed some of my wine into Patricia's mouth.

She laughed happily "What a novel way to drink wine. A fitting approach to the 21st century, too."

I drew back from her. "21st century?"

"Yes. I like to think we should race ahead of our time," she explained quietly. "I want to believe that, in the next century, things will not be so restrictive, particularly for Chinese women, with their lives so much directed and controlled, feudal in many ways. It was of course so much worse previously with our ancestors and the cruelty of bound feet and utter subservience to men. So I just want to be free and easy. I want my divorce to go through simply and quickly. I'm asking nothing from my husband, and besides, the place I live in at Stanley is under a family trust, as is an apartment I have in London. I have an agreement with my husband that those properties will go to my two sons of that marriage after our divorce is finalised. But he is such a cheat that I fear he will not pass those properties to the boys. He will try and talk them out of the deal. I will fight him if I am able. I get nothing from the divorce, which suits me. I have a good job and I just want to be left alone, to live and love just as I wish." She paused before going on, "If I am to have a relationship with any man it has to be strictly on a come-and-go affair. Do you understand?"

"Sure." I told her and pressing my advantage, I noted, "This patio floor might be a bit hard, though. Somewhat unforgiving place to begin a warm friendship. Shall we try my bed?"

"We shall, indeed!"

As easy as that. After all my puzzling and wondering, that

"*No Trespassing*" sign came down, leaving me in momentary doubt that it had ever existed.

After being with Patricia for a couple of months and observing the long hours of office work, along with the dreadful burden of the tragic boat people's stories, it was no wonder, I concluded, that she became stressed. She had many other frustrations to face, the toughest of them all being bureaucracy, from within the social service structure, from government, and from Geneva itself. It was obvious that she needed a holiday and, remembering the great time I'd had with Henry and Anna-Marie walking in Taiwan, I prevailed on Patricia to go there with me for a couple of weeks.

The manager of the Taiwan office told us there was a wonderful old Buddhist temple set deep in the mountain range called *Kwan Ying,* the Goddess of Mercy. He provided us with maps, told us it was a rugged climb and, after he had driven us to the site and left, we found he had advised us well for we had to walk in high, sparsely-tracked country. We pushed on for a couple of hours until we came upon a rough hewn piece of granite which had been planted in the ground, with Chinese characters carved into it: *'The difficult path leads to what you seek'*, and believed we were surely on the way to the temple we had been told about.

I went ahead up the track, crashing a path through the tangled undergrowth, making an opening wide enough for Patricia to follow as I headed for some far-off trees whose lush green tops seemed to hang suspended on the heights above. I noticed a couple of large white birds circling above, heard the shrill cry of disturbed crickets and from the surface of a sun-baked rock observed a lizard with eyes like splintered diamonds staring at me. I had to go back several times to help Patricia whose legs had been cut by branches and sliced by other growth.

She never complained though but thanked me for wiping the sweat and blood away, while expressing the hope that the bloody cuts would heal cleanly. We were now in our third hour and I was contemplating abandoning the climb because I knew Patricia was finding the going harder than she could have anticipated, when suddenly, there was the temple ahead of us, its yellow roof stretching high above a faded pink wall. It possessed such an air of serenity that I almost expected it to stir as if in sleep.

We stood there enraptured, for the temple was perched like some exquisitely made bird's nest at the base of a dark rock I had earlier sighted. As we watched, the sun came from behind a cloud and hit the place, burnishing its yellow tiles, its red ceramic guttering, the purpled roof ridge. I thought everything about it had that calm look which only time wears. Then a bell pealed and it was answered by others from several points. Patricia slipped her hand in mine and we stood very close together, marvelling at the beauty. Neither of us spoke. It seemed we were both afraid to waken the old building which was surrounded by groves of wind-twisted and storm-bent trees, some so large and bent they were manifestly centuries old. I wondered if those trees might have stood there as long as the temple itself. Like them, the temple had suffered from wind and rain which was why its original colours of red and yellow and green had been seared and washed to the faintest, but most beautiful, ghosts of their old glory. In the pink-washed wall I had observed, I could see the large bare patches which revealed the crumbling masonry beneath, and there was an air of poverty or neglect about it. It also seemed, as I had first thought, to be simply and comfortably resting.

We had come out of the heavy undergrowth to find ourselves at the head of a flight of stairs. Then, hand in hand we went down the steps to a cave cut deep into the solid rock of the mountain. Inside, on a small stone altar draped with a red cloth, two large candles burned in the darkness, their light illuminating the finely carved face of a jade statue of *Kwan Ying*. Tendrils of smoke from nearby incense burners had a fragrance which invaded the place, deepening the sense of peace already given by the extraordinary beauty of the jade figure. When we had crept quietly out into the sunshine, I noticed something I had not seen on my way into the cave. It was a square cut piece of stone with the Chinese characters meaning '*The Final Meditation*', beautifully cut in place. Patricia read and deciphered the meaning with me, and now she spoke for the first time since arriving at the temple.

"What a beautiful place to spend the last moment's of one's life."

"A good spot to step into what we call eternity," I remarked. "No noise, no bad things to happen. Just the long sleep."

"I'd love that. Only the two of us, here, forever."

"Oh, come on! We've got so many things to do together, before we start thinking of our last moments. But hey, look. Someone has just come out of the main temple up there. I reckon, from the way he's dressed, he's the abbot. He's watching us. Do you see him?" I pointed to where a man stood alone in the courtyard, dressed in long, grey robes.

"Yes. Let's go up and talk to him. See if we can find out about this wonderful spot."

When hand in hand again we stood in front of a very old man I addressed him in Chinese. "Good morning, sir. We seem to have found your temple by chance."

"Perhaps not." His voice was soft and deep but perfectly tonal and I felt that it was just another part of the peace and quiet formed by the temple and its surroundings. It was difficult for me to guess the age the abbot. His skin was weathered, his eyes hooded, his mouth full and kind. "Your journey began to this temple with the first step you took on the path below. It is a steep, hard and narrow way, but you both persevered."

"My wife has cut herself badly about the legs but she never complained or thought of turning back."

"Beautiful women know the most grief. They have so much beauty that can be bruised, and which must fade. But *Kwan Ying* is always a solace to them. Those who come to pray here or in any of her temples, know that their karma and their shadow will always be at peace with her."

Patricia, who had been listening closely, spoke to the abbot and told him she had never been inside a Buddhist temple and she asked if he would show her how to pray. She hoped the abbot understood her need to use his temple. The abbot told her gently that it was not his temple and that to Buddha, a great person's many candles burn no more brightly than the poor one's single candle. He said that if one comes to Buddha with love in one's heart, then Buddha would instantly return that love. He then took Patricia to pray before *Kwan Ying*. She had been cast in bronze and her face was finely fashioned, so calm and composed that she seemed at once removed and remote from human suffering, yet also acutely aware of it. Her thousand slender gold-covered hands stretched out in benediction to all. I understood that Patricia was deeply moved by the ceremony and, when it was done, her hands trembled as she stooped to touch the lotus flower carried in *Kwan Ying's* lap as a receptacle for the troubles any might wish to bring to her.

Later as we stood outside on the steps of the temple, Patricia took my hand again and asked me: "Did you pray too? I prayed for you because you told the abbot I was your wife. I felt so proud. Say you will marry me, when you are free."

"We will marry, that I promise you. In front of this temple if you wish."

"Wonderful. When I prayed, I asked that you live to be a

hundred. I asked to live until I am ninety-nine which will give you time to bring me here, finally when I die."

Some time later Patricia decided she wanted to get away from Hong Kong: from her work, her husband and his family, her mother and the problems she was creating. She decided to study law and enrolled in the London School of Economics. She pleaded with me to understand her wish to get away, said we would be often in touch with her visiting Hong Kong on a regular basis, while I could sometimes go to London. She asked for a promise from me to wait for her until she had completed the course, and I agreed. She flew off to London and shortly thereafter Myer executives thought I should visit London and see how that buying office operated, along with their establishment in Paris. I went to London and while I worked as Myer requested, I lived with Patricia in a fine old home in Kensington, exploring the area with her. One day we went to Gloucester Cathedral because I had heard that the small wooden cross which Colonel Carne had used for holding church services while he was a prisoner-of-war had been placed in the cathedral. I discovered the cross was in a niche in the cathedral which originated in the founding of an abbey to Saint Peter in 681. The cathedral is described as consisting of a Norman nucleus, with additions of every style of Gothic architecture. The finest monument we were to find was the canopied shrine of Edward 11, while in a side chapel there is a monument in coloured oak to the eldest son of William the Conqueror. In St Mary's square outside the Abbey gate it is recorded that Bishop Hooper suffered a fiery martyrdom under Queen Mary in 1555. I found this historical record and the cathedral fascinating, although the thing that most arrested my attention was that tiny cross which brought back to me the memory of Pak, his breath choking as he died, and of

Carne living, when he most probably would have died just like Pak, if his escape had been fully mounted. Now there is that small wooden cross in memory of Carne and the many Gloucestershire men who served so bravely with him.

Chapter Fifteen

In melodramatic circumstances Gough Whitlam was dismissed from office as the Prime Minister of Australia in the morning of 11 October 1975. By the summer of the previous year Whitlam's government had lost the parliamentary support needed to pass government expenditure bills. When Whitlam refused to call new elections to resolve the parliamentary deadlock, Australia's British-appointed Governor-General Kerr, acting on the advice of the High Court Chief Justice, Sir Garfield Barwick, who years previously had acted on ASIO's behalf during the Petrov defection, agreed that Kerr had the constitutional legality and the right to dismiss Whitlam, and he did so. For the first time in 200 years the British crown had exercised its right to remove an elected Prime Minister. Kerr then commissioned Malcolm Fraser as caretaker Prime Minister on the assurance that he could obtain supply and he would then tell Kerr to dissolve both houses for election.

In the confusion Whitlam and his advisers did not immediately tell any Senate members of the dismissal with the result that when the Senate convened in the afternoon of that day, the appropriation bills were rapidly passed, and the bills were sent to Kerr to receive Royal assent. Shortly thereafter when supply had been secured Malcolm Fraser rose in the House and announced that he was Prime Minister. Labor fought back trying to reinstate Whitlam; the Speaker advised Kerr that it should be done, but Parliament had already been dissolved by proclamation, which was declared from the front steps of Parliament House.

In the general election that followed, the Liberal-National Country Party coalition won a record majority of seats in parliament. Whitlam subsequently resigned his party's leadership and Fraser was appointed Prime Minister. Following that election he visited Peking and requested Steve FitzGerald to remain there as ambassador. One year later however he resigned. On his way back to Australia he saw me and Henry Litton. He later established a consulting business and some years later he was instrumental in helping to set up a Myer buying presence in Shanghai.

The Chinese Year of the Dragon which saw the dismissal of Whitlam was also the time Zhou Enlai, the Chinese premier, died. Chairman Mao, who was described as being in poor health, was the only person beside Zhou's bedside when he passed on quietly. Later Mao declared that Zhou had been the greatest statesman China had ever produced, and a man who had played a leading role in what he called China's significant and present revolution.

Madame Mao, however, thought otherwise. She denigrated Zhou's lifetime of service to his country and she was determined that his death would go largely unremarked. Now a woman of tremendous political power, she, along with the three Shanghai men David Bonavia had once described to me as buggers, were now called the Gang of Four. They had immense power and using it, Madame Mao ordered all foreign embassies to lower their flags, but to half-mast and only for one hour. She wanted no funeral services to be held but when Chairman Mao voiced his objections she allowed a small ceremony to take place. To her rancour thousands of mourners attended, many armed with paper roses which they had cut and pasted together and, weeping openly, they congregated around the Monument to the Martyrs of the Revolution where Zhou's cremated ashes were said to have been placed. Madame Mao may have thought the matter would end there but she had overlooked the festival known as the Sweeping of the Graves, the day when bones are taken from their jars to be washed and polished. When it became known to her that Zhou's jar with its cremated remains would be of interest, she stirred herself and declared that she would be positioned in the Great Hall of the People, where she would monitor and crush any gatherings of which she disapproved.

Foreign Minister Ji Pengfei (partly hidden), Deng Xiaoping, Zhou Enlai, Stephen FitzGerald, waiting to greet PM Whitlam, Oct 1973.
FitzGerald collection.

So great was her hubris at this time that she seemed to believe that most of the population would support her should she give orders to disperse any wild or disobedient people. But rumours were spreading about how Madame Mao had helped beat the former President Liu Shaoqi and his beautiful wife during the madness of the Cultural Revolution. Liu, it was now known, had died naked on the freezing floor of his concrete cell and his wife was still being held in prison under the orders of Madame Mao. A once beautiful woman, she was described now as being a dazed, skeletal figure. When masses of people turned up to throng about and became boisterous, loudspeakers ordered them to disperse. When they refused, Madame Mao's security police swept into action. With truncheons and bayonets fixed, they bundled up hundreds of bloodied protestors, shoved them brutally into their many waiting vehicles which were driven from the square. Cleaners then gathered up and burned thousands of paper wreaths and flowers that had been placed about Zhou's urn.

When Chairman Mao was told about this he was angry. Later when he was informed that his wife's senior officers had ordered their men to open fire and killed some of the protestors, he was furious. It was also mentioned to Mao that his wife and her Gang had established a force at Shanghai which could apparently be called to support her, but he took no action against her. It was assumed that as a Taoist he was embracing the part of their philosophy that said that by doing nothing, something is done.

Something was certainly done a few days later when Chairman Mao died and Madame Mao and the members of her Gang were arrested on the orders of the Politburo. At her subsequent trial Madame Mao was proclaimed the leader of the Gang. She was vilified as a fox, a viper and a woman stuffed with her own vanity. During her trial and when sentenced to death, she spat and kicked, cursed the court officials and all those who had given evidence against her. The three men of her Gang proved to be shallow cowards who wept in court, pleading for forgiveness, which was not given. Madame Mao's sentence on appeal was reduced to life imprisonment.

Deng Xiaoping, Zhou Enlai, Gay & Steve FitzGerald, Beijing Mayor Wu De. Farwelling Gough Whitlam. October 1973. FitzGerald collection.

After the fall of the Gang, Deng Xiaoping, that small man Henry, Linda and I had seen being followed by Madame Mao when I had visited Peking in 1974, was rehabilitated and by July 1977 he had returned to his high posts. Soon Deng's superior political dexterity and broad base of skills allowed him to proceed and carry out his own policies for the economic development of China. Operating through a clever mix of compromise and consensus Deng instituted long-term planning to achieve efficient and controlled growth in China's political and business future. China's peasant farmers were given individual control and responsibility for their production and profits. Deng also stressed individual responsibility and he allowed managers in industry to determine production levels and they could pursue profits for themselves from their enterprise. In foreign affairs Deng strengthened China's trade and cultural ties with the West and opened up Chinese enterprises to foreign investment.

Beginning in the 1970s the State Council announced the introduction of Pinyin, a system of romanization of the Chinese written language, based on the pronunciation of the Peking dialect of Mandarin Chinese. Pinyin was not intended to replace the Chinese characters, but to make it possible to standardise and spell them clearly. Chinese language lessons were conducted in Pinyin, not the former Wade-Giles difficult and distorted transliteration of the Chinese vernacular. Also, it was no longer necessary for students to learn the complex Chinese characters which had once troubled me and Steve. They now also underwent the dramatic change of simplification: the character 'Yen' for salt, once 25 strokes, was reduced to 10 while Liu, a common surname, was reduced from 14 to 6. As I have been writing of a time before these changes were introduced, I have used the Wade-Giles romanization, but now Peking becomes Beijing, while Canton is Guangdong, as it should be. Names like Chou En-lai and Teng Hsiao-ping have been changed to read Zhou Enlai and Deng Xiaoping, and so on.

In January 1980 I went with Keith Rosenhain, other Myer executives and Steve to Beijing, where we had a number of conferences with senior Chinese officials in splendid surroundings. We were told we could open a Myer office in Shanghai, so we flew there to complete that procedure. The Shanghai which the communists took over in 1949 had always been a reluctant partner with Beijing, and that attitude still seemed to persist when we got there many years later. Since the beginning of the century, Shanghai had been a city where new ideas and attitudes were constantly fermenting and it was a place of revolutionary potential. A city fashioned by foreign influences and character, it was to be the vanguard of the Cultural Revolution, probably because two elements, the urban proletariat and the intellectual elite, were often ready to explode. Mao also recruited his first partisans there, but later he crushed them.

Towards the end of the Cultural Revolution in 1968 suppression of radicals sometimes took on a harsh aspect where crowds of thousands called for the deaths of those they considered to be counter-revolutionaries and murderers, all previously Red Guards. Many were killed. In Shanghai some former militants were sentenced to death, others were severely punished, many fled to safety in Hong Kong. The three men who were part of Madame Mao's Gang of Four were all from Shanghai, and although that army they had alleged to have assembled in Shanghai, should Madame Mao need it, had long ago been disbanded, the memory of them must have persisted.

Keith Rosenhain, a bon vivant and a man respectful of his fellows, received a KCMG for his efforts in establishing the office, but it was Steve, handling a difficult assignment with great charm and tact, plus his excellent spoken Chinese, who deserved most of the credit for the successful negotiations. Steve had been awarded the Order of Australia much earlier for his work in China. In February 1975 Whitlam had introduced an Australian system of Honours and Awards to replace the British Imperial System. Introduced in 1901 the British system was phased out in the 1980s, hence Rosenhain's award late in the day, having presumably been nominated by Victoria, the state in which he lived. Following the discussions, Myer was given an office in the Ching An Hotel set in what had become known as the French

Quarter, and close to the lovely home called *Hsiang Yuan* or Fragrant Garden, formerly the home of Li Hongzhang. It was set in a wide street with many beautiful trees brought in from France. Li, who died in 1901, had been a leading statesman and he made strenuous efforts to modernise China. He was responsible among other things for sending young Chinese to America to learn new skills.

I later set up office in the Ching An and I was given three executives to help me get the place in working order: the senior man was from the textile corporation, another from hardware while the third was an expert in the manufacture of shoes. All I needed was buyers from the firms I represented to get the office into operation and pay for its costs, plus the money for our three new employees.

By the end of 1980 Patricia had graduated in law from the London School of Economics and she returned to Hong Kong where she was accepted as a pupil by Martin Lee, a prominent barrister. She would work with him for one year and then be allowed to practise by herself. During the years she had studied in London, Patricia and I had seen a lot of each other, both when she visited Hong Kong during university breaks, and when I went to London either for work, or on holiday. From Hong Kong we had gone on walking holidays, going often to Taiwan or Brunei where we had climbed Kotakinabalu and looked down on Sandakan and the coastline bordered by the ruffled frills of the blue Pacific. By now my divorce had been finalised, and that lovely home Norma and I had bought during the riots for fifty thousand US dollars, now sold for two million, financial evidence of how bad things had become during the riots and how good they were now. Norma and I split the money, shook hands and we never saw each other again. I was grateful to her for some of the years we knew together, and later for the way she looked after an ageing Copper who I could no longer care for properly as I was constantly on the move, travelling with buyers or out checking our offices or some independent agents I had appointed in Malaysia and Singapore. She had called me, though, when Copper was very old and sick. I took him to the vet where he quickly died. I carried him back to Tai Po Kau, buried him in the front garden and planted a flowering shrub over his grave. May it still be blooming over him.

Patricia and I had visited what we called our Taiwan temple many times because she liked to go there to burn incense and candles, along with paper money, and place fruits and wine before *Kwan Ying* on the red-lacquered, gold-edged altar. She had prayed for success in her studies and continued happiness for both of us. We always used the rough track going to and leaving the temple and she made the climb easily enough. But this time, just after her graduation, I was aware that her progress was markedly slow and she had to stop often, saying she was short of breath, and she pleaded to go back along another, easier path down. When we got near the bus stop at the bottom, I was aware she was having difficulty with her breathing. On the bus, rocking and lurching its way back to Taipei her face flared as with a spasm of pain if it hit a particularly deep hole. I knew Patricia hated doctors despite that fact that her father was a doctor in Macao. But I realized I must urgently get her to see Peter Miles, my own medico in Hong Kong.

Against Patricia's wishes, Peter examined her the day we got back to Hong Kong. He sent her to an X-ray clinic just down the corridor from his consulting rooms and later he telephoned me. In a few quick words he picked up the whole of my world and dumped it at my feet in many pieces. After the cool impersonal voice of his receptionist had connected us he told me, friend to friend that one of Patricia's lung was badly diseased and that there was a great deal of fluid in the lung cavity. He was sure it was cancer and that the fluid would have to be tapped to be certain.

The fluid tap was done and Peter told me a few months of life was all Patricia could hope for. I remember him saying, his hard brown eyes pinned sternly on my face, that the cancer was virulent, had gone so far that nothing could be done. But she would go very quickly, without years of useless pain. He then reminded me that she was to see him in about fifteen minutes. He asked me what I wanted him to tell her. I asked what the normal message was in such circumstances. He told me remission was usually discussed, with a hopeful five years in the first case, and luckily, five after that.

"I'm not at all happy with that doctor," Patricia was saying to Peter. Her face wore a tight, fixed smile. "The one who took the fluid from my lungs hurt me. He was very sloppy."

"I don't believe you should call him sloppy," Peter remarked kindly. "He has a difficult job and he got results, all I asked for. What I'd like to do now, is to recommend that you see one of the leading oncologists here. He is a fine young man."

"No!" Patricia impatiently shook her head. "I have a sister Judy living in San Francisco. She is a laboratory technician in oncology there, said to be one of the best on that study in the world. You would know of it?"

"Yes." Peter nodded. "So?"

"So? I'll telephone her. Get an opinion." Her hand fluttered briefly as she reached out to Peter. "Please don't misunderstand me. I'm not worried about you or indeed any other doctor in Hong Kong. But if I have cancer and a sister who is involved in research on it, then I'd like to see what she suggests."

"You have my blessing," Peter rejoined, "And no matter the

treatment, you will have a long remission. Would you please tell your sister I said that? Don't forget it, please!"

"Remission?" Patricia's voice rang high while her hand flew to her throat. "What sort of remission?"

"Five years in the first instance. The way science is progressing with cancer at this time, I reckon another five after that. And so on, with luck"

"And so on!" Patricia's voice was suddenly bright and full of hope. Her dark eyes shone as she looked to me. She reached out for my hand and held it in both her own. "Will you come with me?"

Of course," I said. "Naturally. In fact, I was just talking with my best doctor friend here, chatting about you and I told him I was going to pop the question soon. Well, I'll pop it now and ask you to be my lawful wedded wife. We can exchange our vows, or whatever they do, in America. Your father and sister will be there. How about that?"

Patricia and I were married soon after our arrival in San Francisco. As the ceremony ended, a fog which had clouded the area began to lift, imperceptibly at first, but soon running away in swift wispy tatters under the impetus of the sun which suddenly shone through one ragged gap to show the sky clear and blue, welcoming us, I hoped Patricia believed, into a bright future together. She was walking slightly in front of me and I almost stumbled as she suddenly spun about.

"I saw tears in your eyes when you were putting this on my finger." She accompanied her words with a gesture of her hand on which I had placed the wedding ring a few moments earlier. "Why was that? It was when the minister said: 'Your life will be full of peace and happiness in all the years to come". Or do you know something the doctors haven't told me?'

"Oh nonsense, love," I shrugged and smiled at her. "Here we are walking into the sunshine which always makes me happy, while church ceremonies make me a bit weepy, and I'm very involved in this one. You are my wife at last!"

"Is that the truth?"

"What is this?" I laughed. "Here we are still on the steps of the church, yet you confront me with Chinese battle flags and drums?"

"I can't help worrying," Patricia remarked. "But I'm going to be all right, aren't I? Peter in Hong Kong said I will have a long remission and the doctors here, and my sister, have confirmed that?"

"You may recall from your Chinese history that there was once a man of Chi," I reminded her. "He was so pessimistic that he refused to go outside in case the sky fell onto his head." It was an old Chinese tale. "Don't tell me I have married a woman of Chi? But to answer your question, things are good but you might have a worrying time with some treatment, that's all."

That night with Patricia sleeping quietly beside me, the drifting tide of my thoughts carried me back to Hong Kong and confronted me with Peter Miles and his first diagnosis: only a few months of life were left to Patricia, and which the American specialist, a Dr Miller, had now halved.

"How sick is Patricia, doctor?" I had asked him. "Give it to me straight, will you?"

"The cancer is terminal," He responded. "Sorry to sound so brutal, but there it is."

"Exactly what have you told Patricia?"

"Only what she wanted to know, that remission is possible. I did not tell her that the cancer has metastasised and that the cancer cells have invaded her bones. Her diseased lung can be treated with radiotherapy but the malignancy in her bones will have to be treated with chemotherapy which is the introduction of toxic drugs designed to destroy the cancer cells." Miller took up a large manila envelope from his desk and passed it over to me. "I've had your wife's medical history copied for you. You may wish to read it carefully and if you have questions, come and see me."

"How long do you give Patricia? What is your expected time-frame?"

"Only a few months. But she is a strong and very fit lady despite her cancer. The inroads of the cancer make a full recovery impossible but we must give her hope. We must encourage her. Keep her happy while we do our best for her."

The following day I had hurried to see Gideon Nye who was staying at the home of his other daughter. When learning how ill Patricia was he had closed down his one-man medical practice in Macao and flown to America. I went to see him only to get another opinion because I could not fully believe what I had been told. Passing the medical report which I had been given over to him, I asked him to tell me what he thought. "What I have been told is very bad." I said.

As Gideon reached out a frail hand and took the papers he said, "Now I fear my heart will be, as the Chinese say, like a pennant waving in the wind."

I nodded but did not speak.

"As your heart must surely be," Gideon noted. "But we are in this together, my friend."

Gideon slowly and carefully read through the papers, running a forefinger under the lines. When he was done and had finally taken his finger from the last page, he rested his locked hands on what he had scanned. After a few moments he looked at me and said: "I know you did not come here to me, deliberately carrying thorns, and hoping for my forgiveness." He had paraphrased a Chinese aphorism. "You want a medical opinion from me, of course?"

"Please. The first part about the physical examination is clear enough but the summary puzzles me. I wonder if you could explain what is meant about white blood count and platelets being administered?"

"It means there is no hope because the bone scan is bad. Pelvis, ribs, skull and vertebrae, all bad. It is hard for me to say, and probably harder still for you to accept, but it is a kind cancer if I may put it that way, because Patricia will ultimately go into a deep sleep. Once the cancer invades the brain there is no hope: the water has been spilt and we cannot mop it up before it dries out."

We left America after many weeks of treatment, much of which left Patricia with bouts of vomiting, nausea, and worst of all, the falling out of some of her glossy black hair. I had been told that nothing more could be done for her, that it was time I took her home to Hong Kong. Our first trip away was to the temple in Taiwan which Patricia had often told me when under treatment that she wanted so much to visit. A road had by now been built to the temple and we were driven there. The old abbot greeted us at the gateway into the courtyard and when Patricia had moved away from him to look for a moment at a nearby flowering creeper on the wall nearby, he said softly, "Your wife has come to us for the last time. You know it, too."

His voice carried no hint of emotion, or sadness, or even pity, which I knew my own voice would have expressed if I should have had to say the same thing to someone else. It was as though the abbot was announcing the end of a short visit which of course, this life was to him. It was no more than a way-station on a journey which must end, but none might know the route, or its span.

I was shocked that the abbot could so easily have defined the situation, for during those weeks in America Patricia had been on a high protein diet and she had lost very little weight. In any case she was always slender with the fine-boned appearance expected of the great clothes-houses. Of the *haute couture* world she had known and in which she made up expertly, always dressed meticulously. I doubted, despite the abbot's remark, whether there were many among her friends who had any real notion of how close she was to death.

On our return to Hong Kong we went to live in the house I had bought on Lantao Island, the large, lovely, lonely island fringed by the pale green waters of the South China Sea. It was situated about three miles from the Star Ferry terminal at Silver Mine Bay and the land on which it had been built was part of a Chinese village abandoned ages ago. It had been well situated directly in front of a strip of coastline called San Shek Wan, or Scattered Stone Bay. It was aptly named for when the sea was wind-disturbed it roared onto the rocks in a way which made just being inside the house snug and safe and warm, a tremendous pleasure.

The house was surrounded by disused, grassed-over paddy fields cascading in high terraced stone walls which ran down the falling slope of land to the rocky foreshore. Making our way there one clear summer morning by ferry, Patricia wondered how her goldfish might be getting on in the pool I had built for them, and which should have been well looked after by the maid we employed to stay in the place. Would the pool also be covered with water hyacinth and lilies, and how did I think six cherry-blossom trees which we had shipped in from Taiwan would be doing? And the dozen miniature azaleas we had arranged under a long line of casuarinas whose falling needles would create the acid conditions so favourable to them? She was so vivacious and talkative that I simply forget she was so ill, particularly when we got to the house and she went first into the garden to check on her fish and found that the water hyacinth along with the lilies had spread. She cried with delight as the fish, their ornamental tails gleaming in the water, came up from the bottom of the pool like sunset clouds to eat on the red worms she fed them. Afterwards she dragged me by the arm to show me how already the cherry blossom trees were putting out frail green nodules. Later, standing among the azaleas, she assured me that they had found a good home under the tall casuarinas.

As Patricia spoke, a leaf from one of the trees drifted down past her face. She watched it to the ground and as it touched the grass there, she said in perfect Mandarin, a fragment from a poem we had once read together: "Luo ye bao qiu." *'The falling leaf foretells autumn,'.* I told her she had remembered it well, but she did not respond. She looked about her, at the summer garden where so much was in full flower and suddenly wrapped herself in her arms as if against the cold, so many months away. "I can hardly believe it's early autumn already," she said.

Up to that moment she had been so full of life, interested in everything, but I now understood that the long and gentle sleep her father Gideon had foretold, was close. I had been beginning to hope that the treatments she had undergone might have taken hold, that the chemotherapy she had undergone might, in fact, have suddenly reversed the tide and set her on the road to recovery. *No!* I thought, *it is nearly over for Patricia.* A few weeks later she died in hospital.

In the Buddhist temple in Taiwan I had Patricia's ashes placed in a small marble urn and the Chinese characters chosen for her name by Gideon at birth, looked lovely carved into the marble and highlighted in gold. Before placing the ashes in a vault, the abbot conducted his service in the dull glow of ranks of the tall candles set in his temple and there, in his full regalia of saffron robes and amulets and rosaries, he read in his mellow voice from an old yellowed text, shabby from years of use. It lay open on a gilt stand which had carved into its front panels the Chinese characters meaning "Buddha's Table." Between the thumb and forefinger of his right hand the abbot held a long and slender piece of lacquered wood, the shaft of a tiny metal hammer. With this, he struck a bronze bell dangling by a yellow cord from his little finger and as regular and recurrent as the beat of the sea upon the shore his voice rose and fell to the accompanying sound of the bell. He tapped constantly with the head of the metal hammer and from somewhere behind, the muted beat of a doe-skin drum wove a pulsing counterpoint through the simple embroidery of the bell sound.

To my ears, the service carried all the beauty of a symphony. It also had the curious under-water quality of sound, and the high, almost hypnotic voice of the abbot made it difficult at times for me to follow what he was saying but some of his Buddhist aphorisms did register, and a full passage of text reached me during a long pause in the drum's throbbing. The abbot was addressing a huge bronze vessel set before him wherein several tall sticks of incense were burning: "The heart of Buddha flows with the smoke of this incense so let your soul go quietly upward and blend with his. Let you go as the river which flows to the sea and ultimately becomes part of it." I watched the incense swirl above the round mouth of the bronze urn and heard the abbot calling: "Your heart is cleansed now, and free from all illusion. You are like a pure lotus which grows in water, yet allows not a drop to adhere to its lovely petals."

When the service was done, a young nun took the urn of ashes. Her head was newly shaven and dotted with scars where incense had been burned and placed on her skull, as witness of her love of Buddha. She led the way from the temple, going carefully in her rope sandals down the steps to the burial vault. I had earlier been in there, and chosen the rock ledge where I wanted the urn to rest, for once set down, it would never be moved again. Now, inside the cool dark vault, the abbot took the vessel from the young nun and placed it on the highest shelf facing the middle door; the light shafting in hit the gold-filled carvings of Patricia's name. The abbot lit one incense stick in front of the urn of ashes and prayed again. "Life is instantaneous and living is dying, but there is the re-birth of Karma. There is reincarnation and now truth is attained, and with it the source of all righteousness."

We walked out of the vault in silence and into the summer sunshine, there to meet the capricious play of the wind, the moving of trees and bamboo, the calls of so many birds. The heavy bronze door of the vault with its intricately wrought designs of flowers thudded shut somewhere behind us and, as we made our way up the steep and rugged flight of stone slabs I paused and looked back at a gracious old pine tree crouched there, I hoped, in protection over Patricia.

I bade goodbye to the abbot on the terrace facing his temple and the old man laid his hand briefly on my shoulder.

"I blessed both you and your wife here today," he told me. "I know how much you loved the life you leave here today, in ashes. But from now on, she will always be with you. Later, should you also wish, you may have your own ashes placed beside hers. That will be enough. Have no prayers said for your soul at that time. I have said them all for both of you."

As I climbed over the crest of the last hillock to start down the track where Patricia had cut her legs on that first ascent, I looked back at the temple. It was soft in the rays of the sun, half hidden in the foliage about it, as peaceful as the first day when we had come upon it. Of all the places we had known together, it had seemed somehow to have forged a particularly strong link between us, as if it were our own place, infinitely more personal now with that urn standing in the vault.

Making my way down that steep and unforgiving track where I had once gone back to wipe blood from Patricia's cut legs, I found myself going carefully as if she were beside me and I was accommodating to her pace. I felt certain as well that if I were to turn around she would be there, a little hurried and out of breath, but smiling. She would look delightful, her skin burned brown by the sun, her eyes full of pleasure at meeting mine. I had wondered how I would feel walking away from the place where I had now left her. I had expected grief, loneliness, even helplessness, with my cup of happiness very low. However, as I went from the temple she had so adored, I knew she would always be with me. What she was would always accompany me, and the temple behind would always associate us with the farewell chimes the abbot had struck on his tiny bell while praying. I knew that Patricia's essence and spirit would always be with me, even though she was gone. But gone where? Only, and I knew it well, from my immediate sight.

Chapter Sixteen

I was advised to take Patricia's former husband before the Hong Kong Supreme Court after he had declared the documents giving certain properties to his sons were not enforceable. However, on the front steps of the court before we appeared, he agreed in front of our solicitors to sign the properties over to the beneficiaries. I was satisfied, having carried out Patricia's wishes.

Had she lived I may have decided differently when I was approached by a so-called head-hunter and offered the top position in the Macy Department Store buying office in Hong Kong; it meant a large issue of bonus shares in that company, a salary that was one of the highest in the region, and other attractions as well. I presumed I was offered that position because I had worked with many of the buyers from Alexanders of New York and I understood their market. But I refused the offer because I knew my way with the Myer Company and I liked its executives, especially Ken Myer who, at that difficult period in Hong Kong, had organised the loan which enabled me the buy a house which, when sold, had left me financially secure.

At that time anxious to develop the China market, I spent many days in Shanghai, but it was difficult to get buyer interest in a new and challenging country, given the competition and marketing skills of established and trusted trading centres. And there were many of them: apart from a vibrant Hong Kong, there was Japan, the Philippines, Indonesia, Singapore, Malaysia, emerging countries like South Korea and South Vietnam. And of course, Taiwan, a booming island. When I opened a buying office in Taiwan in the early 1970s, it was under martial law. Called

Formosa or Precious Island by the Dutch many years previously, it is a verdant country with many mountains, its highest being Yu Shan, or Jade Mountain. Higher than Japan's Mount Fuji, it is always like Fuji, snow-capped and beautiful. Because of the martial law constraints, mountains like Yu Shan could not be climbed so I contented myself with smaller mountains about Taipei and I often climbed Mu Chih Shan or Thumb Mountain. It was not much more than a wooded hill, interlaced with walking tracks and many small, clear streams. Ancient Buddhist temples were dotted about the place, some of them set near to where streams flowed and when priests were in attendance, small bells were sometimes struck. The sound created a sense of peace and religious serenity.

But there had once been considerable conflict and death in the towns and villages down below where I was walking. When Taiwan was turned over to Chiang Kai-shek and his Nationalist Government in late 1945 following the defeat of Japan, many Taiwanese welcomed their liberation from Japanese control after a brutal occupation of nearly fifty years. But when the Nationalist so-called freedom appeared to be no better than the slavery known under the Japanese, many of the Taiwanese urban middle class voiced their objections in the streets early in 1947. They were massacred in their thousands.

In 1949 following the victories of the Chinese communists on the mainland of China, over a million Nationalist soldiers with their leader Chiang fled to Taiwan, with much stolen Chinese treasure. Government officials and other refugees poured in; it seemed that the final defeat of Chiang and his battered army was only a matter of time. But that general and his men were saved from total defeat when in mid-1950 North Korean soldiers invaded the south of that Korea. President Truman, convinced of Beijing's complicity in that invasion, ordered the American 7th

Fleet to be stationed between Taiwan and China. That halted any communist invasion and a division of Chinese troops stationed in the province opposite, ready to attack Taiwan in late-1950, were sent instead to fight in Korea. Clad in summer uniforms with cloth shoes suitable to a climate in the south, they died in their thousands in the freezing winter that of that year.

During that war the United States hugely increased its economic and military aid to Taiwan and Chiang Kai-shek offered to send his army to fight the Chinese in Korea. General MacArthur visited Taiwan early in 1951 but when he viewed a parade of that army he concluded they were nothing, as he put it, but a rabble. Also, they had run from Mao's army in China so how could they now fight that same, and by now improved army in Korea? Even so the strongest voices associated with Chiang, many of them from America with a dread of Communism strengthened by Joseph McCarthy's nationwide militant anti-communist crusade, and the religious bodies who had tried for so many years to get Chinese souls into their heaven, continued to persist on the inevitability of the reconquest of China by Chiang Kai-shek. That belief was part-predicated on an imagined scenario of a mass peasant uprising in China followed by a popular demand for a Nationalist return.

When walking the streets of down-town Taipei in the early 1970s I was often astonished by the numbers and the size of huge banners splashed with red-painted Chinese characters, all exhorting Chiang's infallibility and the certainty that he would return to his beloved China. Australia established a small diplomatic presence in Taiwan, America had a large Embassy, Taiwan had a seat in the Security Council with a vote, and her future as a Chinese power seemed assured. But in 1971 Taiwan was ousted from the Council and the Chinese People's Republic with its five hundred million or so inhabitants took the rightful place of Taiwan, with fewer than twenty million people.

The previously held conviction that Chiang would invade and conquer the mainland had led to the economic modernisation of Taiwan, with an increased American demand for Chinese goods transforming Taiwan from an aid country to a prosperous trading partner. A new generation of Taiwanese leaders had emerged, mass Taiwanese resentment of Chiang had largely subsided, and the country was greatly altered by the pursuit of individual economic advancement spurred first by the war in Korea and later the conflict in Vietnam, when Taiwan was used as a base for many American supplies. Its tanks were repaired there, its aeroplanes were maintained, and it became a popular centre for American soldiers on leave from the war.

My own cup of happiness was refilled in Taiwan when I met Julie Yuan there in the late seventies. She was the manager of a large factory making plastic Christmas trees which the Myer office were buying in quantity. She was beautiful with clear Oriental lines, classical in a style approved by many people. She had dark challenging eyes and a figure moulded to stir desire in any man. She laughed readily, showing good teeth, and she could be amusing in a direct and sensible fashion. She seldom talked about herself, but she could throw her views into other people's problems and listen carefully to any points which might be raised. Knowing that I had studied a Chinese poet who was a favourite of her mother, she invited me to dine at her home. I found the apartment lovely, set near the centre of Taipei city; it had thick-piled Tientsin carpets and some of the Ming Dynasty porcelains which I explored on their shelves were as good as any I had ever seen in a private collection. One piece, a bowl so fragile it seemed to consist only of shimmering glaze. I held it ever so gently as I translated the Chinese characters etched on its side, *'A fine vessel for the rich and harmonious'*. My words drew such a wild round of applause that I knew I had been instantly accepted into Julie's family. Along with the parents there were six daughters and one son, waited on along with their parents, by two servants from the Philippines, dressed in the traditional white top, black trousers, soft black slippers and white socks.

The Yuan children all now adults, had been well educated. The eldest worked in Paris in a Taiwan Government Liaison Office, whatever that term meant. The second eldest was an accountant based in Houston. The other women all had good jobs while the son was studying science at Taiwan's top university. That night, armed with a dozen carnations, I was received by Julie and introduced to her family in a room panelled in rosewood where in a far corner I could see a Han Dynasty war drum used as a pedestal for the stone-carved head of a temple god, probably vandalised from a temple in China years previously. I reflected that the room was a perfect setting for Julie, dressed in a simple white linen dress and gold-roped sandals. Her long sleek black hair was gleaming with health. We sat to eat in another room, classically dignified with impeccable samples of export and Imperial porcelains. Julie appeared to be an expert on them and while we ate, she chatted easily about the way over-glaze enamels could so effectively highlight or complete a design painted in a glazed blue, or how well fired glaze would range in colour from tan to dark chocolate. Later over tea she told me about the orchids and African violets which her mother cared for and decorated the apartment with. As Julie spoke I found myself thinking how poised she was, how lovely she looked, how much she was in command of herself.

Julie's mother and father were known to all as Ma and Pa. I was later to find that Ma possessed a robust intelligence and that she had once come from a wealthy land-owning class who had lived on vast acres situated about a one-hour drive from Shanghai.

It was all taken from them when the communists came to power in 1949. Many of her family, hunted and persecuted, had mostly died and now the Ma I came to know was obviously determined that her family must always keep together, and that she would personally ensure its smooth working in the cause of common peace and happiness. But come to think of it, all Chinese elders expect to be fully in charge and they believe that the best way to protect their children is by preparing them for their future and arming them with skill and an inner confidence to succeed in whatever task or business they might undertake. I took Ma to be essentially a good woman, always pleasant and reserved.

I came to understand that the social and family life of the Yuan family had its own special charm: manners were casual, meals were banquets, courtesy was imperative. They could be summed up as being vital and positive people and I felt very much at home in their pleasant company. I got to know Pa well, particularly when we walked together. Small in build, he had a manly handsomeness along with a careless but clean manner in dress. He was genial and sensible and, like his wife, close to his family, fostering their talents, applauding their triumphs, supporting their failures and disappointments, but all in a free and easy manner. I could see he was a man who had adjusted his psyche so as to suffer as little as possible from some of life's inevitable drawbacks. He had a good mind which ranged over an enormous variety of topics, with an interest in public affairs, history and literature. But probably because he had once been a wealthy man in China with a prominent role in life, he had evolved modes of thought and action by which he could dismiss or evade the more distressing and hurtful events of his past life in China.

Pa had entered Taiwan in 1947. He was an accountant who had been ordered to establish a government-controlled monopoly on the production and sale of sugar. It had become a successful business, earning money for the government and including, I presumed, Pa himself. He lived in a fine apartment and had a house near where I sometimes walked on Thumb Mountain.

Pa had a slow step and we walked together with me accommodating my pace to his. He often talked about Chiang Kai-shek who he believed in, and generally speaking, I initially let him make his points. But as our friendship grew I had to point out that during the war Chiang had refused to let those armies trained by the American General Stilwell fight and beat the Japanese as they had proved they could. Stilwell had a couple of remarkable victories against the Japanese in Burma, but Chiang put a halt to any of Stilwell's later battle aspirations. That was because Chiang was afraid that if any of his generals became powerful and in command of a fighting army, they might threaten his top position and indeed oust him. So he had Stilwell withdrawn just when he was winning those battles and when the Chinese soldiers had come to trust him, and the way he had taught them to fight. His replacement never did show Stilwell's combative spirit, and their fighting ability along with the morale and effectiveness of Chiang's armies quickly declined.

It was also a fact that Chiang's largely passive fighting stance against the Japanese cost him the prestige and support among the Chinese population, something the communists gained because of their fierce anti-Japanese resistance. The communists built up large battle-hardened armies on the strength of a Chinese nationalist sentiment. It seemed to me, I told Pa, that among the reasons Chiang had lost China was the fact that he had no coherent plan for halting massive increases in inflation, stopping corruption, and trying to implement the social and economic changes to bring his country into the 20th century.

As an accountant Pa had to agree with this and also what I also pointed out: that T.V. Soong, the financier and official of Chiang, and his brother-in-law, had through corruption and his theft of millions of dollars from American aid sent to China during the war, become one of the richest men in the world. He fled China when Chiang was losing his war against the communists, and set up a banking and business empire in America. Pa asked me how I knew about Soong's alleged corruption. I in turn asked him if he had ever heard of a man named Donald, an Australian who was later dubbed 'Donald of China'. Pa professed ignorance so I told him what I had learned from an ex-university friend who was doing a thesis on Donald, a man who, I was told, had a direct influence on events in China. A former managing director of a Hong Kong newspaper, he resigned in 1908 and travelled to China to write a history of the press in that country. He became editor of *The Far Eastern Review* in Shanghai where he met Charlie Soong, the wealthy father of the three lovely Soong sisters. Donald later became a close friend of Sun Yat-sen who married one of the sisters named Ching-ling, and Chiang Kai-shek who married Mei-ling, claimed as the most beautiful. The third sister Ai-ling married H.H. Kung, the richest man in the country. All three sisters attended the Wesleyan College in Georgia and in later life, along with their husbands, they became the most significant political figures of the 20th century.

In 1936 Chiang was arrested and incarcerated in the former capital city of Xian, and Donald played a leading role in his release. Donald became an important figure in Chiang's group which was based in Chungking, the Nationalist wartime headquarters. It was there that Donald told Mei-ling that her brother was the most corrupt man in China and that he had stolen millions of American dollars from a fund that should have been used to fight and beat the Japanese in China. Mei-ling, it is alleged, screamed and swore at Donald, turned her back on him and walked away.

She never again sought his company, and she never once spoke to him. Donald who for years had treated Mei-ling like a beloved daughter, was emotionally shattered by the experience, especially as T.V. Soong kept on stealing more millions of dollars, as did most of Chiang's senior officials.

A photograph of the author taken in 1985 when he was working in Taiwan with IDP, the acronym for a number of Australian universities recruiting Asian student to study in Australia.

Pa seemed to think I had a good point, but even so, his faith in Chiang was strong and when Chiang died in April 1975, he attended his funeral with thousands of others. It was conducted outside the massive memorial Chiang had ordered to be constructed in his name in the capital. He believed it was a unique building to exemplify his greatness. Chiang's death was followed by a caretaker presidency until his son Chang Ching-kuo was formally elected president in 1978. He could not, I hoped, be as shallow, corrupt and as hopelessly ambitious as his father.

Married to Julie Yuan in mid 1983 in our home at Canning Vale. The Italian fireplace from the old Hong Kong Club is in the background.

I have noted that my cup of happiness was later replenished: that took place after Julie and I were married in mid-1983. The ceremony took place not far from Tom Hungerford's place at Canning Vale. On an earlier visit to Tom I had bought fifteen acres of land which he had pointed out to me. When he knew I had bought at auction the lovely old Italian fireplace that had occupied a spot in the White Room of the Hong Kong Club before the club was demolished, he suggested I should put it in a home to be built on that land. He would oversee the construction of the building which could later be rented out until or if we decided to occupy the place.

Julie and I returned to Hong Kong and she later presented me with the most miraculous gifts of my life: first a handsome and healthy boy we christened Stephen, after Stephen FitzGerald who like him was always called Steve, then a girl we called Joanne after my favourite film star, Joanne Woodward. Then, having found a replacement I resigned from Myer in 1985 after twenty years because I wanted to do a thesis on a famous Chinese author. When I had completed that study at the University of Hong Kong, I was offered a good position in Taiwan running an Australian government-sponsored scheme which offered places at universities and colleges to selected Chinese students. It ultimately became a successful operation, with offices being opened up in all major Asian cities.

So, our world rolled along, residing comfortably in Taipei city, but thinking now and again about living near Perth where our children would have a good life and education. I often remembered the fresh beauty of the rivers I had found there in the company of Tom Hungerford. One day we walked to the confluence of the Swan and the Canning. It was springtime, and the midday air was drenched with the smell of small growth while the hard grey stones by the river made a sharp contrast with the silver grey of the giant eucalyptus guarding the banks. I had lived and worked for thirty years outside Australia and I had to wonder about our future. As a family we were happy together and in ourselves. We believed our lives had value but few people are so conceited as to wholly trust their own judgment in such matters. Julie and I were still romantically in love and so we surrendered ourselves to the perceived pleasures ahead of us, and to the inherent excitement of all living together in a vast, free, and beautiful land called Western Australia.

It was a good life with time slipping peacefully by as Steve and Joanne did well at school, later at university and afterwards in their professional pursuits. Julie was happy giving piano lessons while I wrote a lot and walked Ginger my cocker spaniel by the river, occupied by tame black swans and many other birds. But on the 14 April 2014 I received a sad letter from David Butler; in part he wrote, *'Thanks for your books and the wonderful notes in your own hand in each of them. Our friendship is truly deep and heartfelt. You helped me in overcoming the severe strokes I endured. This is my first attempt at a letter in many months. I find I am thinking more often about 9 Platoon and the men who made it. They were wonderful chaps and great at soldiering. You have achieved so much in your life- I was honoured to serve with you. Love to Julie, forgive my hopeless scrawl.'*

These are the expressed thoughts of a former major general, twice wounded in action and twice decorated for bravery. As a lieutenant colonel he was awarded a DSO for his service in Vietnam. Judged a superb battalion commander, always careful about the nine hundred men under his control, he risked his life one night when being told that a returning patrol had been in action, and that some men were wounded. Immediately he went forward, accompanied by the medical officer and they linked up with the patrol. Assistance was rendered and the group then made its way back to base but the medical officer, apparently exhausted, stumbled over the white tape marking the mine cleared area and he trod on an explosive device. The detonation seriously wounded the doctor and Butler. Both men survived but Butler was left with a bad limp and a pain that troubles him, even today.

David Butler is a gentle man, the second son of a minister of religion whom the war in Korea made into a fighter who believed in what was the good for people under threat. A gallant soldier, prudent in judgment, he was strengthened as he battled forward, accepting his wounds bravely and if one had been serious enough to kill him we would feel that his fight had been justified. David though, has a firm grip on his days, one that is lessening now, but when he lets go it will be with much more honour than he has so kindly afforded me.

Now, the writing is done: it is time for Ginger, aged like the man who loves him, to take me out for a walk. Both of us are thankfully fit and so I will go on my way, thinking with him.

Testimonials to Jack Harris

Seize the Day is an excellent book with good maps, interesting photographs and an admirable forward by David Butler, a retired Major General. Harris has written frankly and several brutal episodes are covered. Concerning his frankness, this is his story and the reader can better understand the man better for his honesty. It must be added that he was a very good soldier who was awarded a Military Medal for bravery. The brutal parts are necessary to explain the motives of several of his South Korean agents. Harris did two tours of duty in Korea, one as an infantry platoon sergeant and the second one on the intelligence side, training and deploying his agents behind the North Korean lines.

One thrust of this book concerns intelligence operations behind the enemy positions. The stress and physical effort involved show the incredible determination of Harris and his agents. He includes an account of a remarkable plan to rescue the Commanding Officer of the British Gloucester Regiment, Lieutenant-Colonel Carne, VC. DSO. a prisoner-of-war. The plan was never implemented but it gave Harris the theme for one of his books of fiction he wrote in later years and which was awarded a literary prize.

When one appreciates his courage and devotion to duty in the army one may wonder about his background. Jack tells of his life during the depression and his description is masterly. His story illustrates his compassion and loyalty and above all his ability to look after himself. He is also quite frank about is personal life during which there was much joy but also unhappiness. Jack was also placed to be involved in the Petrov defection, he was in Hong Kong during an important phase of its history, and he worked out of China shortly after the Cultural Revolution of 1967.

Reviewed by Brigadier Jim Shelton (ret) January, 2015.

Jack Harris was an officer who joined ASIO after a remarkable military career. He served with the British Commonwealth Occupation Force in Japan between 1946 and 1950, when he learnt Japanese. He then served as an infantry sergeant in the early days of the Korean War, and was wounded in action in October 1950. While recuperating in Australia he studied Chinese, completing a one year course at the RAAF School of Languages and he was then seconded to ASIO. Wanting to return to Korea he contacted the head of army intelligence volunteering for a second tour in Korea.

Back in Korea, Harris commanded a special agent detachment tasked with infiltrating intelligence agents into enemy territory. Dressed in Chinese uniforms with Chinese weapons, Harris and his South Korean agents made nine successful forays deep into enemy territory. Because Korea had previously been a Japanese colony, Harris could converse with his Korean agents in Japanese. Harris was so successful in patrolling beyond the enemy front that it was decided a rescue attempt would be made to lift Lieutenant-Colonel Carne, VC.DSO. from his prisoner-of-war camp. Early in July 1953 Harris was asked to go out for the tenth time and make sure that his route through enemy territory was safe for the Carne rescue attempt. Harris and the agent with him were ambushed, Harris was wounded, his agent was killed. Making it back to the Samichon River Harris swam to safety. The rescue attempt was abandoned, but Harris was awarded a Military Medal for bravery..

After a further period in Korea as a Chinese interpreter for the UN Command's Military Armistice Commission, Harris because of his wounds was medically downgraded and he could no longer serve with an infantry. He therefore left the army and in May 1950 formally joined ASIO and initially spent some time helping to guard the Pertovs during their appearance before a Royal Commission on Espionage in Australia. Harris also went back to school, matriculated and obtained a bachelor's degree in Oriental Studies. In 1961 he was sent to Hong Kong, initially for three years, which was extended to six. He resigned from ASIO in his fifth year to become a director in Myer Overseas, opening buying offices in Hong Kong, Taiwan and China over a twenty year period. During that time he obtained a master's degree from Sydney University and a doctorate in Chinese from the Hong Kong University. Harris is also a talented writer; he has written several novels, one of which earned him an award in the 1957 Sydney Morning Herald literary competition.

David Horner, AM,
Professor of Australian defence history in the Strategic and Defence Studies Centre at the Australian National University.

Order

Seize the Day
A. M. (Jack) Harris.

ISBN 9781922175717   Qty

RRP   AU$24.99   .....

Postage within Australia   AU$5.00   .....

TOTAL* $_____

* All prices include GST

Name:..

Address: ....

....

Phone: ....

Email: ....

Payment: ❏ Money Order ❏ Cheque ❏ MasterCard ❏ Visa

Cardholders Name:...

Credit Card Number: ....

Signature:..

Expiry Date: ....

Allow 7 days for delivery.

Payment to: Marzocco Consultancy (ABN 14 067 257 390)
PO Box 12542
A'Beckett Street, Melbourne, 8006
Victoria, Australia
admin@brolgapublishing.com.au

Be Published

Publish through a successful publisher.
Brolga Publishing is represented through:
- **National** book trade distribution, including sales, marketing & distribution through **Macmillan Australia**.
- **International** book trade distribution to
    - The United Kingdom
    - North America
    - Sales representation in South East Asia
- **Worldwide e-Book distribution**

For details and inquiries, contact:
Brolga Publishing Pty Ltd
PO Box 12544
A'Beckett St VIC 8006

Phone: 0414 608 494
markzocchi@brolgapublishing.com.au
ABN: 46 063 962 443
(Email for a catalogue request)

www.ingramcontent.com/pod-product-compliance
Lightning Source LLC
LaVergne TN
LVHW051544070426